Affective Transformations

Affective Transformations: Politics—Algorithms—Media

edited by

Bernd Bösel and Serjoscha Wiemer

μ meson press

Bibliographical Information of the German National Library
The German National Library lists this publication in the Deutsche
Nationalbibliografie (German National Bibliography); detailed
bibliographic information is available online at http://dnb.d-nb.de.

Published in 2020 by meson press, Lüneburg, Germany
Funded by

Deutsche
Forschungsgemeinschaft
German Research Foundation

in conclusion of the scientific network
"Affect- and Psychotechnology Studies" (SCHR 1505/1-1)
Additional funding was provided by

www.meson.press

Design concept: Torsten Köchlin, Silke Krieg
Cover image: Anh Tuan To | Unsplash
Copyediting: Selena Class, Joely Day

The print edition of this book is printed by Books on
Demand, Norderstedt.

ISBN (Print): 978-3-95796-165-5
ISBN (PDF):   978-3-95796-166-2
ISBN (EPUB): 978-3-95796-167-9
DOI: 10.14619/1655

The digital editions of this publication can be downloaded freely at:
www.meson.press.

Contents

Affective Transformations: An Introduction

Bernd Bösel

Even affects have their history. There is not just a history of events, or of people, or of things, but also one of affects, feelings, emotions, moods, and sentiments. The question of how to address affective states is inseperably linked to the genealogy of their conceptualizations and operationalizations (Dixon 2003; Bösel 2018). The Austrian philosopher Günther Anders understood as much in the middle of the 20th century and consequently demanded that historians should tend to these untold stories (1956, 271). He coined the term "plasticity of feelings" (Anders, in: Müller 2016, 101) to address this changeability, and being one of the foremost philosophers of media and technology of his generation, he had a sharpened awareness of how technologies modify the ways populations feel, imagine, and think. Half a century later, the history of emotions has become a burgeoning branch of historical scholarship (Plamper 2015), but due to discursive and institutional separations, these pursuits have largely ignored the contributions of media scholars who have written extensively about the psychological and sociological impacts of media innovations—and it goes without saying that these impacts include the transformations of affects, or, to use a phrase that has become persistent in the last decades, of "structures of feeling" (Williams 1977).

With the advent of the "affective turn" (Clough 2007) since the mid-1990s, purportedly psychological concepts like feelings, emotions, or affects received a renewed and broadened acknowledgment (some say *once again*) as foundational entities for questions in aesthetics, cultural studies, epistemology, and even ontology. After several decades of the humanities being preoccupied with language and structure, this new turn to affect gained so much attention and yielded such an enormous output that even the idea of giving a full account of the relevant contributions soon became obsolete. But since the 2010s, another transformation set in. The emancipatory potential of affect studies and of affects in general has been called into question. Some have argued that affect scholarship has been seriously flawed (Leys 2017), while others point out that we are now within an era of digitalization that seems much more to produce divisive affects and create sadness than the affects of joy or hope that were promised by cyberutopians (Lovink 2019). The fascination with all things affective has, in consequence, lost its former innocence and euphoria. Scholarship on affect now has to prove that it can cope with the return of the affective real that technology, economy, and politics entail.

Two seemingly contradictory developments serve as starting points for this volume. First, current technological innovations such as affective computing, mood tracking, sentiment analysis, and social robotics all share a focus on the recognition and modulation of human affectivity. Mechanisms like individual affect regulation or emotion management are being increasingly transferred onto personal digital devices. These algorithm-based technologies collect and process affective data and nudge users into normalized behavior and patterns of feeling. Affect gets measured, calculated, controlled (Angerer and Bösel 2016).

Second, recent developments in politics, social media usage and right-wing journalism have contributed to a conspicuous rise in online hate speech, cybermobbing, public shaming, "felt truths," and resentful populism. In a very specific way, politics and power have become affective. In light of the rise of neo-nationalism, religious and conspiratorial fanaticism, and presidentially decreed patriotism, the question of what a "politics of affect" (Massumi 2015) does, can or should mean attains an unparalleled urgency. Affect gets mobilized, fomented, unleashed.

We thus witness, on the one hand, the emergence of what we propose to call "affective media," understood as technologies and applications that rationalize affects by processing them algorithmically. On the other hand, we observe that social media affects become irrational and seem to have disruptive effects on the political and social orders of Western democracies and the whole globe. These two deeply divergent affective transformations deserve a more comprehensive delineation.

Transformation 1: The Becoming-Rational of Affect

In the last two decades, efforts to develop what is now variously called "artificial emotional intelligence" (Yonck 2017) or "emotional AI" (McStay 2018) have come a far way from the typical 20th century view that affects and emotions pertain to the irrational side of human beings and are thus non-computable. When Rosalind Picard (2010) recalls how her pioneering work on affective computing was ridiculed in the mid-1990s—even in such a technologically progressive milieu as the Massachusetts Institute of Technology—it is difficult not to acknowledge the immensely changed situation, even if one can still be skeptical about the potential benefits of her and her peers' project. If the "rationality of emotion" (de Sousa 1987), to allude to a book title that preceded the onset of computational work on human emotionality by a decade, needed further and more practically oriented proof, Picard and all the researchers following her lead in this now burgeoning discipline seem to have driven the point home.

With the dawning of an "age of affective computing" (Tuschling 2014), i.e., the implementation of computer-based automation of affect detection and regulation, an absolutely vital part of human life begins to be organized by something that is not just a new technology, but a disruptively new dispositive. Affects and emotions were traditionally something that humans have had to deal with on their own to a large extent. Any help they might have enjoyed in this regard was provided either: by private groups of friends and relatives; within confessionally based or philosophically inclined communities, where spiritual advisors provided some help and guidance; by the newly emerging sector of so-called psy-disciplines (Rose 1996) that consists of highly trained, secular professionals that offer help regardless of confessional questions (a new development in the 20th century); or, as a more remotely effective field, by artists who catered to emotional needs through their works and performances, which, due to the distribution of home media, could increasingly be adopted for individual "mood management" strategies (Zillmann 1988). But an automated and strictly personalized registration of affective data via digital devices is something that neither private, nor professional, nor artistic emotion regulation could ever have provided. We are therefore witnessing a major transformation in regard to how humans' emotional lives are organized.

It was only in the late 2010s that this development started to receive significant academic attention. Andrew McStay, in his noteworthy book *Emotional AI*, brings forward the proposition that "we increasingly 'live with' technologies that feel and … are sensitive to human life in ways hitherto not seen" (2018, 3), but also cautions that "emotional life is being defined in biomedical terms that suit technology, industrial categorisation, ranking systems, commercial culture, surveillance and political interests in happiness" (186). He introduces the term "empathic media" with regard to emergent media technologies that can "sense and discern what is significant for people, categorise behaviour into named emotions, act on emotional states, and make use of people's intentions and expressions" (2). Understood in this sense, empathic media encompass not only smartphones, wearables and other personal tracking devices, but also large-scale sentiment analysis as well as "empathic cities" like the Smart Dubai initiative, which in its effort to digitize all of Dubai's public services also aims to measure happiness (155–160). McStay's *Emotional AI* is notable not only for being, as far as we can see, the first monograph assessing the various fields of research pertaining to the automated computation of human affects, but also for the many interviews the author conducted with developers, CEOs and other individuals in the empathic media community, thus providing his readers with many insights into the visions and also possible nightmares that these new technologies entail.

Many of these developments have been incorporated into the big picture Shoshana Zuboff draws in her alarmist narrative concerning *The Age of Surveillance Capitalism* (2019). Over the course of her extensive retelling of how first Google, then Facebook and Microsoft, discovered that so-called data exhaust can be used to analyze and even predict individual users' behavior, she directly addresses how the capture of affects and emotions has become one of the major data supply routes that these and other companies capitalize on. "These supply operations are aimed at your personality, moods, and emotions, your lies and vulnerabilities" (Zuboff 2019, 199). And in relation to personal digital assistants like Microsoft's Cortana, she points out that

> [t]his is a new frontier of behavioral surplus where the dark data continent of your inner life—your intentions and motives, meanings and needs, preferences and desires, moods and emotions, personality and disposition, truth telling or deceit—is summoned into the light for others' profit. (254)

She also retells how the emotion analytics company Affectiva, co-founded by Rosalind Picard, shifted within just a few years from its orientation towards medical and therapeutic applications to market research and thus capitalist goals exclusively (287).

First, affects had become computable (at least to a certain extent); now, they had become calculable and valuable in strictly monetary and financial terms, contributing to the emergence of the "psycho-computational complex" (Stark 2018, 206) that threatens to seriously undermine the way democracies operate. The election of Trump and the Brexit vote proved to what extent the calculation of constituents' affects can be, and actually are, instrumentalized for the advancement of authoritarian and populist policies.

Transformation 2: The Becoming-Irrational of Affect

The global implementation of social media fell in the very same period that saw the development of what is now called "emotional AI." Social media promised participation at a low-threshold level and for a brief time were being championed for enabling political engagement beyond going to vote in elections every few years. They were even interpreted as the necessary condition for the Arab Spring uprising and thus affording especially young people with a welcome means of communicating that equaled the creation of a new public sphere, the so-called "affective publics" (Papacharissi 2015).

The narrative that social media first and foremost help suppressed groups in their emancipatory struggles against state power has, however, since been countered by the fact that the very governments that were under attack quickly incorporated social media into their counterinsurgency strategies (Howard and Hussain 2013). Since the aftermath of the Arab Spring uprisings, obtaining full control over the internet has been a primary goal for illiberal governments around the world, with the People's Republic of China being the most striking example of how effectively online traffic can be monitored by resourceful state agencies. Due to the "Great Firewall," Chinese citizens have been forced to use only governmentally controlled—and thus thoroughly censored—social media (Griffiths 2019), and other authoritarian countries are now following China's lead.

But the problem with social and online media technologies is not just one of top-down suppression versus bottom-up insurgencies. What techno-utopian approaches failed to acknowledge for quite some time is the extent to which far right movements and parties have adopted online guerilla tactics in their fight against whatever they define as hegemonic powers, be it mainstream media, progressive politicians, activists, artists, feminists, public intellectuals, refugees and migrants, or other minorities and marginalized groups. It was only after the election of Trump and the Brexit vote that mainstream commentators in Western democracies started to understand how much the surprise victories of socially regressive and misleading campaigns were supported by far-right movements that operated on a technologically and medially sophisticated level.[1] Within just a few years, web-based humanitarian causes had been

---

1　In the edited volume *Digital Cultures and the Politics of Emotion* (Karatzogianni and Kuntsman 2012), which pioneered the intersection of the hitherto largely separate discourses of affect studies and digital media studies, hardly any mention of online

swept away by the "now unstoppable force of public humiliation as viral entertainment," as Angela Nagle (2017, 5) summarized the development of the "online culture wars" of the 2010s in her controversial essay *Kill All Normies*.

Online extremism has since been increasingly investigated and understood as one of the most pressing dangers for democracy (Ebner 2020). All the extremist groups that use social media for the solicitation and radicalization of their members seem to follow a tribalist logic, regardless of whether they have an Islamist, anti-Islamic, antisemitic, fascist, masculinist, nationalist, or racist agenda (or, as is often the case, a mixture of these positions). The most pressing question from a strictly media theoretical perspective is: To what extent is this radicalization and intensification of extremist positions a side effect of the operational logic of social media? In an opinion piece for *The New York Times* in March 2018, Zeynep Tufekci called out YouTube's presumed algorithmic bias toward extremist content. In its constant quest for capturing the attention of ever more users for an ever longer amount of time, YouTube's algorithm seems to present ever more "inflammatory content" and thus, whether willingly or not, works to the effect of being "one of the most powerful radicalizing instruments of the 21st century" (Tufekci 2018). Even though this problem has yet to be understood more deeply—a task that is aggravated by (not just) Google's secrecy concerning its algorithms—this extremophile tendency of platform capitalisms' algorithmic logic certainly contributes to the ubiquitous affective intensification and the general becoming uncontrollable of affect.

Bernard Stiegler once warned of what he called "uncontrollable societies of disaffected individuals" ([2006] 2013a), but since this was before the advent of extremophile social media, Stiegler attributed this to the destructive effects of 20th century mass media. To take into account the disruptive effects the new platforms have had, one should probably rather speak of "misaffected individuals" and thus replace the term "disaffection" with its

hate, cyberbullying, or other abusive behavior is to be found—with the notable exception of an analysis of how social media were being used during the Bulgarian 2009 parliamentary election campaign by the respective candidates. In this article, Julia Rone concludes that social media "turn out to be a haven for nationalists, who otherwise do not have access to major media outlets" (2012, 220) and asks the rhetorical question: "Can we really continue proclaiming the democratizing potential of social media in such a case?" (219). It seems that her understanding of the affective dynamics of an Eastern European country enabled Rone to acknowledge much earlier than most of her Western colleagues that instead of an intrinsically democratizing tendency, social media have the potential to inflame and exacerbate already existing sentiments and affects.

connotation of no-future boredom, discontentment and a general feeling of ennui, with "misaffection," a rather unusual word that nevertheless seems capable of expressing a rather strong affect that is in some way misguided, inappropriate, or even severely destructive. As Stiegler (2013a, 7f.) intended to draw a connection between "disaffection" and the question of ethics—insofar as the disaffected individuals feel like they have lost their place, their milieu, or their ethos in the original sense of that ancient Greek term, and thus any basis for an ethics to hold on to—"misaffection" promises to convey much more clearly the affective misguidedness that informs all the anomic, resentful, and violent behavior that increased in such a frightening fashion in the past few years.

While pointing out the role social and algorithmically controlled media played in this development of affect becoming irrational and uncontrollable, a thorough analysis should of course be cautious of the pitfalls of technodeterminist reduction. Political, economic, psychological and environmental conditions and developments all have massively contributed to the acerbations of discontentedness (for the US-American context, see Hochschild 2016). Nevertheless, not to take into account media technologies and their operational logic would be historically naïve. Technologies are not just passive instruments that can be used in this or that fashion, with this or that intent; they rather have affordances of their own, and reshape and format the process of psychic and collective individuation, as Gilbert Simondon (2017) put it—and his clear view of how psychic, collective, *and* technical individuation processes are constantly entangled and influence each other makes Simondon's philosophy and psychology particularly fruitful in the early 21st century.

It has now become abundantly clear that social media platforms are driven by algorithms that favor emotionally engaging messages, images and videos, and thus contribute to the spread of what is sometimes called "affective contagion" (Sampson 2012, 55–60), the "shitstorm" being perhaps the most prominent example of this collective imitative behavior (Stegbauer 2018). But, while the logic of platform capitalism certainly operates as a positive reinforcement apparatus for these affective outbursts, the connotation of a contagion as a seemingly natural force that spreads like a virus distracts us from the fact that many, if not most, of these events are carefully planned and orchestrated by extremist online activists who are engaging in their respective "emo wars," to use an exposingly straightforward term that was coined by the Identitarian movement (Stegemann and Musyal 2020, 97). Our understanding of how the cumulative effects of vast sociological transformations and rapid technological changes have made possible a collective affective upheaval, which in its intensity seems entirely irrational, is as yet insufficient even if contemporary academic efforts do their best to make sense of these developments.

Affective Media: A Lesson in Digital Pharmacology

Both transformations, the becoming-rational of affect and its becoming-irrational, are made possible by the digitalization of the life-world. In fact, the commonality of their trajectories is so conspicuous that we can pose the question of whether, instead of being two distinct and divergent developments, they are not rather a single one with paradoxical effects. That new media technologies bring about completely divergent effects at the same time is certainly not a new thought for media theorists. This ambivalence is already deeply ingrained in the early theory of writing, as it has been established via Plato's critique of its supposedly negative effects on philosophical discourse. Being simultaneously a remedy against forgetting and a poison for memory, writing's status as a *pharmakon* in the ancient Greek double meaning of the term was brought to the fore by Jacques Derrida's ([1972] 1981) erudite reading of Plato's *Phaedrus*, which in turn inspired Bernard Stiegler four decades later to extend this fundamental "pharmacological" ambivalence to technologies in general. For Stiegler, pharmacology means "a discourse on the *pharmakon* understood in the same gesture in its curative and toxic dimensions" (2013b, 4). With digitalization being the most recent pervasive technological change, he consequently demands that "digital pharmacology" becomes a primary field of academic research and thought (Stiegler 2016, 296).

Now what can this mean exactly for the question of affective transformation(s)? Both sides of this transformation, the becoming-rational and the becoming-irrational of affect through digital media technologies, can be analyzed as manifesting their respective pharmacological ambivalence. While the developers of affective computing see their innovations as a remedy for technological alienation and as a therapeutic tool for people who purportedly lack in empathy or suffer from alexithymia, the implementation of their standard methods of affect detection and regulation will inadvertently increase the dependence on these technologies and probably even diminish unmediated "emotional granularity" (Feldman Barrett 2017, 3), i.e., the capability to distinguish between different affective states and to act correspondingly and responsibly. On the other side, the spread of online hate and resentment via social media is a serious social pathology that threatens the very basis of social cohesion—but this cohesion is now unthinkable without the proper functioning of the means of telecommunication that works as a remedy for isolation and loneliness.

Affective media—that is, media which do not just store and broadcast, but also process affects—operate both on individual and social levels. Approaching them pharmacologically means to describe their remedial as well as their toxic sides. Only by producing knowledge about all of the ambivalent effects will it be possible to develop what we might call a progressive politics of affective media. Such a politics would have to include therapeutics capable of countering the social pathologies that are already known as well as those that await their full description or will emerge in the future. Such a politics will also have to address some fundamental questions, such as: What do we really expect from affective media? What common good can we envision when we acknowledge that they will increasingly become a part of our media environment and constitute a technologically enhanced "ecology of affect" (Angerer 2017)? And how can we make sure that we would even recognize that affective media actually improve our social and psychological conditions—or, vice versa, fail to do so?

The contributions in this volume address these and further questions. By assembling scholars from different fields of research, we want to examine the apparent paradoxicality of affective media. When the ways we deal with our affectivity become unsettled in such a dramatic fashion, we obviously have to rethink our ethical, aesthetical, political and legal regimes of affect organization. This is not just a purely academic task, but rather an issue of responsibility.

Acknowledgments

Early versions of the contributions in this volume were presented at the international conference *Affective Transformations: Politics, Algorithms, Media* that took place at the University of Potsdam, Germany, in November 2017 and was hosted by Prof. Dr. Marie-Luise Angerer, who also holds the chair for media theory there. It was organized by the research group Affect- and Psychotechnology Studies, which was funded by the Deutsche Forschungs-gemeinschaft (DFG) from 2015 to 2018.

We want to thank all of the members of the research group for a most fruitful collaboration. Special credit goes to Dr. Niklas Schrape, Prof. Dr.

Claus Pias and the Leuphana University Lüneburg for coordinating and administrating the research group during the first half of its duration, as well as to the University of Potsdam for managing its second half. The publication of this volume was generously supported by the DFG as well as by ZeM—Brandenburgisches Zentrum für Medienwissenschaften.

Finally, we are very grateful for a smooth cooperation with meson press, whose hybrid publishing policy and general focus on contemporary debates in media studies made it the logical choice for this publication. Special thanks go to Andreas Kirchner for his continuous support.

The research group continues to investigate the transformative effects of the implementation of affective media and has founded the work group Affective Media Technologies within the German Society for Media Studies. The editors of this volume presently also act as speakers of this work group. Please consult the website affectivemediastudies.de for further information.

References

Anders, Günther. 1956. *Die Antiquiertheit des Menschen: Band I: Über die Seele im Zeitalter der zweiten industriellen Revolution*. München: Beck.

Angerer, Marie-Luise. 2017. *Ecology of Affect: Intensive Milieus and Contingent Encounters*. Lüneburg: meson press.

Angerer, Marie-Luise, and Bernd Bösel. 2016. "Total Affect Control. Or: Who's Afraid of a Pleasing Little Sister?" *Digital Culture & Society* 2 (1): 41–52.

Bösel, Bernd. 2018. "Affect Disposition(ing): A Genealogical Approach to the Organization and Regulation of Emotions." *Media and Communication* 6 (3): 15–21.

Clough, Patricia T., ed. 2007. *The Affective Turn: Theorizing the Social*. Durham, NC: Duke University Press.

Derrida, Jacques. (1972) 1981. *Dissemination*. Chicago: University of Chicago Press.

de Sousa, Ronald. 1987. *The Rationality of Emotion*. Boston: MIT Press.

Dixon, Thomas. 2003. *From Passions to Emotions: The Creation of a Secular Psychological Category*. Cambridge: Cambridge University Press.

Ebner, Julia. 2020. *Going Dark: The Secret Social Lives of Extremists*. London: Bloomsbury.

Feldman Barrett, Lisa. 2017. *How Emotions Are Made: The Secret Life of the Brain*. New York: Houghton Mifflin Harcourt.

Griffiths, James. 2019. *The Great Firewall of China: How to Build and Control an Alternative Version of the Internet*. London: Zed Books.

Hochschild, Arlie R. 2016. *Strangers in their Own Land: Anger and Mourning on the American Right*. New York: The New Press.

Howard, Philip N., and Muzammil M. Hussain. 2013. *Democracy's Fourth Wave: Digital Media and the Arab Spring*. Oxford: Oxford University Press.

Karatzogianni, Athina, and Adi Kuntsman, eds. 2012. *Digital Cultures and the Politics of Emotion: Feelings, Affect, and Technological Change*. London: Palgrave Macmillan.

Leys, Ruth. 2017. *The Ascent of Affect: Genealogy and Critique*. Chicago: University of Chicago Press.

Lovink, Geert. 2019. *Sad by Design: On Platform Nihilism*. London: Pluto Press.

Massumi, Brian. 2015. *Politics of Affect*. Cambridge: Polity Press.

McStay, Andrew. 2018. *Emotional AI: The Rise of Empathic Media*. London: SAGE Publications.

Müller, Christopher John. 2016. *Prometheanism: Technology, Digital Culture and Human Obsolescence*. Includes a translation of the essay "Promethean Shame" by Günther Anders. London: Rowman & Littlefield.

Nagle, Angela. 2017. *Kill All Normies: The Online Culture Wars From Tumblr and 4chan to the Alt-right and Trump*. Alresford: Zero Books.

Papacharissi, Zizi. 2015. *Affective Publics: Sentiment, Technology, and Politics*. Oxford: Oxford University Press.

Picard, Rosalind W. 2010. "Affective Computing. From Laughter to IEEE." *IEEE Transactions on Affective Computing* 1 (1): 11–17.

Plamper, Jan. 2015. *The History of Emotions: An Introduction*. Oxford: Oxford University Press.

Rone, Julia. 2012. "The Seducer's Net: Internet, Politics, and Seduction." In *Digital Cultures and the Politics of Emotion: Feelings, Affect, and Technological Change*, edited by Athina Karatzogianni and Adi Kuntsman, 214–29. London: Palgrave Macmillan.

Rose, Nikolas. 1996. *Inventing Our Selves: Psychology, Power, and Personhood*. Cambridge: Cambridge University Press.

Sampson, Tony D. 2012. *Virality: Contagion Theory in the Age of Networks*. Minneapolis: University of Minnesota Press.

Simondon, Gilbert. 2017. *On the Mode of Existence of Technical Objects*. Minneapolis: University of Minnesota Press.

Stark, Luke. 2018. "Algorithmic psychometrics and the scalable subject." *Social Studies of Science* 48 (2): 204–31.

Stegbauer, Christian. 2018. *Shitstorms: Der Zusammenprall digitaler Kulturen*. Wiesbaden: Springer.

Stegemann, Patrick, and Sören Musyal. 2020. *Die rechte Mobilmachung: Wie radikale Netzaktivisten die Demokratie angreifen*. Berlin: Econ.

Stiegler, Bernard. (2006) 2013a. *Uncontrollable Societies of Disaffected Individuals: Disbelief and Discredit*, Volume 2. Cambridge: Polity Press.

———. 2013b. *What Makes Life Worth Living: On Pharmacology*. Cambridge: Polity Press.

———. 2016. "Digital Knowledge, Obsessive Computing, Short-termism and Need for a Negentropic Web." In *Digital Humanities and Digital Media: Interviews on Politics, Culture, Aesthetics, and Literacy*, edited by Roberto Simanowski, 290–304. London: Open Humanities Press.

Tufekci, Zeynep. 2018. "Youtube, the Great Radicalizer." *The New York Times*, March 10th, 2018, https://www.nytimes.com/2018/03/10/opinion/sunday/youtube-politics-radical.html.

Tuschling, Anna. 2014. "The Age of Affective Computing." In *Timing of Affect: Epistemologies, Aesthetics, Politics*, edited by Marie-Luise Angerer, Bernd Bösel, and Michaela Ott, 179–90. Zürich: diaphanes.

Williams, Raymond. 1977. *Marxism und Literature*. Oxford: Oxford University Press.

Yonck, Richard. 2017. *Heart of the Machine: Our Future in a World of Artificial Emotional Intelligence*. Arcade Publishing: New York.

Zillmann, Dolf. 1988. "Mood Management: Using Entertainment to Full Advantage." In *Communication, Social Cognition and Affect*, edited by L. Donohew et al., 147–72. Hillsdale, NJ: Lawrence Erlbaum.

Zuboff, Shoshana. 2019. *The Age of Surveillance Capitalism: The Fight for a Human Future at the New Frontier of Power*. London: Profile Books.

LIMINALITY

AFFECT/EMOTION DISTINCTION

PROCESS THOUGHT

RITUAL

LIMINAL AFFECTIVE TECHNOLOGY

1

Affect: On the Turn

Paul Stenner

For some influential advocates of the "affective turn," the concept of affect stands for a spontaneous, collective, subjective and progressive becoming-other that promises "new possibilities" that are never quite articulated. This perspective has great potential, but risks lapsing into a naïve celebration of affect that is ill-equipped to grasp the negative aspects and uses of experiences of becoming (i.e., liminal experience). A liminal occasion is an occasion of passage between categories during which, for whatever reason, the forms of process associated with modes of being are subject to metamorphosis. A focus on liminality, it will be argued, has two chief advantages. First, it allows us to focus on the affectivity that comes into play when we, or our circumstances, are in

the process of transformation. This highlights the fact that many of the positive, exciting, desirable features attributed to "affect" are characteristics of liminal occasions, but also that these occasions can have a darker side. A second advantage is that it encourages us to recognize the long history through which different "technologies" have emerged to manage, generate and communicate the liminal affectivity typical of liminal occasions. The oldest of these "liminal affective technologies" is ritual, which dates back to prehistoric times. Without denying the distinctiveness of the present moment, in which affectivity is routinely summoned and manipulated by a host of new technological means, this argument opens up new ways of locating our present within a broader genealogy.

Introduction: Turn, Turn, Turn Again

In calling this contribution "affect on the turn" my intention is to harmonize with the title of the *Affective Transformations* conference held in Potsdam in November 2017, and also with one of its recurrent themes: that the affective turn may have turned a little sour. I originally come from Somerset in the south west of England, and there we describe foodstuffs as being "on the turn" when they are at the point of going rancid or rotten: milk, perhaps, or an apple. In this context, being "on the turn" is not necessarily a bad thing. Milk has to "turn" if it is to become a nice cheddar cheese, and apples must be on the turn if they are to become the good scrumpy cider that Somerset is also famed for.

So, in what sense might the "turn to affect" be "on the turn"? And might it turn into something rather nice? As many delegates discussed at the conference, too much literature within the affective turn takes an overly celebratory stance on affect (for critiques, see Hemmings 2005, Greco and Stenner 2008, and Leys 2011). Affect has come to signify spontaneity, collectivity, *avante-gardism*, and progress. This stance can seem a little naïve when it misses some of the very problematic and even exploitative ways in which affectivity is technically summoned and manipulated in the infotainment circuits of our digitalized epoch of global capital (Angerer, Bösel, and Ott 2014; Angerer 2017). In response to this naivety, the first part of my paper will conduct a critique of the concept of affect upon which the affective turn appears to turn. I will then propose that some of these weaknesses can be clarified and addressed by crafting a concept of liminality that enables us to attend to the ways in which liminal experience is managed, summoned and navigated by means of *liminal affective technologies*. Put crudely, the notion of liminality, at least in the anthropological sense given to it by Arnold van Gennep (1909), concerns human beings when they are "on the turn" (i.e., when they are going through the passage of becoming-other), and liminal affective technologies are the cultural means of facilitating and overseeing such sensitive occasions of becoming. In fact, even cider may serve as a component in a liminal affective technology if it contributes to the stirring of emotions associated with some sort of becoming (a drunken rite of passage into what passes as adulthood in some quarters of Somerset, for instance).

Summary Critique of the Affective Turn

I will begin the critical part of my contribution with a quick account of my research interests and background. I completed a PhD in the field of social psychology at the University of Reading, UK, focusing on the social dimensions of experiences of jealousy (Stenner 1992). Through that work I became familiar with psychological literature on the emotions, but I was also influenced by contributions to the study of emotions from sociology, anthropology and history, post-structuralists such as Michel Foucault, Gilles Deleuze, Hélène Cixous and Michel Serres, and by the recent rise of interest in social constructionism across the social sciences. The theoretical questions raised by post-structuralism and social constructionism excited me enormously, and it was perhaps this excitement that transformed me into somebody who wanted to be an academic social scientist. This was about more than just me as an individual. I was fortunate enough to have Rex Stainton Rogers and Christie Davies as supervisors, along with a group of like-minded PhD students, and Rom Harré as an external examiner. Harré had edited an influential volume called *The Social Construction of Emotions* (1986). Theoretically, this was a challenge to the so-called essentialism and positivism associated with the psychological and biological literature on emotion, which tended to reify emotions as naturalistic mechanisms to be approached solely by experiment. It seemed to me that the positivistic approach tended to ignore much of the complexity and cultural nuance at play in emotional experience, including the historical and geographical variety identified by anthropologists, historians, and sociologists. Methodologically, this interest meant a turn to text or discourse as the primary means through which the meaning of emotional experience gets constructed in real-time interactions and other forms of communication. In line with this "turn to text," I studied the various different accounts of jealousy that are constructed in everyday discourse, and in the more specialized discourses of writers, scientists, lawyers, health professionals, and others (see Stenner 1993; Curt 1994; Stenner and Stainton Rogers 1998).

I mention this "turn to text" or "discursive turn" because the affective turn that is my subject today was very much a turn against the discursive turn. The first use that I have found of the phrase "affective turn" was at a feminist conference organized in 2001 by Anu Koivunun. Koivunun used it to refer to a growth of interest in affects, emotions and embodied experiences across the social sciences and humanities. This body of work makes no clear distinction between affect and emotion, and can actually be considered part of the discursive turn. For this reason I reserve the phrase "affective turn" for a more specific intellectual movement. The phrase made its first appearance in the title of a book with Patricia Clough and Jean Halley's edited volume *The Affective Turn*, published in 2007. Here, the concept of affect at play in the phrase "affective turn" is sharply distinguished from emotion. Clough and Halley contributed to an avant-garde movement that uses a concept of affect to turn against the discursive turn. Affect, in their sense, is strictly separated from discursive practices and is defined as being in principle inaccessible to discursive articulation. It is an autonomous and pre-personal force or capacity that exists outside of any consciousness. The starting point for this affective turn is the idea that the discursive turn was a kind of discursive imperialism that neglected a vast and vital territory of affective dynamics and forces. If for advocates of the discursive turn, discourse symbolizes a principle of progressive freedom from naturalistic essentialism, then for advocates of the affective turn it symbolizes a certain entrapment within a spider's web of official meaning. The aim is still liberation from the strictures of established structure, but now progressive freedom is sought through stopping our talking heads from making their discursive sense.

By 2007, the affective turn was already a torrent of scholarly activity, but this torrent was fed by tributaries that began flowing more than ten years before. During the 1990s I was teaching an undergraduate psychology course entitled *Affect and the Social*, first at the University of East London and then at University College London. This meant that I kept quite a close eye on developments in the literature. I noticed three separate developments that would soon flow together into the affective turn. I will simplify by noting three publications that appeared in 1995, each of which challenged the constructionist focus on discourse and proposed a concept of affect that promised the hope of change and progressive freedom (for a more detailed account, see Stenner 2017a). Each works with a different concept of affect, drawn from a re-engagement with classic psychology on the part of humanities scholars.

The first was Brian Massumi's article, *The Autonomy of Affect* (1995), which drew heavily upon Deleuze's readings of Bergson and Spinoza. Massumi announces the wish to part company with the linguistic model of theory, proposing an account of affect as an autonomous pure intensity. Since in this account affect is a virtual force that by definition escapes any signifying order, it is sharply distinguished from "emotion" (for a sustained appreciative critique of Massumi's use of social psychology to draw this distinction, see Stenner 2018). All of this is argued in the name of the freedoms of novelty. Hence, in Massumi's article we have the characteristic rhetorical features of a critique of the discursive turn, a positive presentation of affect as solution, and a statement that at stake in all this is something new and progressive.

The second publication from 1995 was an article called *Shame in the Cybernetic Fold*, written by Eve Kosofsky Sedgwick and Adam Frank, prominent scholars in the field of queer theory. This article begins with a scathing attack on the limitations of critical discursive theory and proceeds to celebrate the biological theory of the affects proposed by the US psychologist Silvan Tomkins. Again, through embracing Tomkins as a psychologist who, to quote Sedgwick and Frank (1995, 23) "understands *us*," what is at stake is freedom from what they described as the "moralistic hygiene" of critical discursive theory.

Third was the awakening of interest in affect within psychoanalytical psychosocial studies. In 1995 Anthony Elliott and Stephen Frosh edited a book called *Psychoanalysis in Context*, which marked a notable resurgence of interest in applying psychoanalytic theory to sociological questions. There is obviously a long tradition of reflection on affect within psychoanalysis, but at this point a psychodynamic account of affect was presented as a challenge to the perceived hegemony of social constructionist theory. Ian Craib (1997), for example, described social constructionism as a kind of mass manic psychosis, itself explainable by the unconscious affective dynamics at play.

Of course, there is a lot more to the affective turn than these three sources from 1995 (see Gregg and Seigworth 2010). But identifying them and specifying their common ground allows us to see how and why they might flow together to: a) challenge the linguistic imperialism associated with the turn to discourse; b) find resources within psychology for an ultimately unconscious, biological and autonomous concept of affect that comes to be clearly distinguished from emotion; and c) adopt a rather celebratory stance where affect comes to stand for all things spontaneous, *avant-garde*, and progressive (i.e., that promise to break free of discursive imperialism). For me, Patricia Clough (2010, 223) sums up these features of contemporary affect theory when she aims at "toppling… semiotic chains of signification and identity and linguistic-based structures of meaning making" from their "privileged position." Today, affect theory is more or less premised upon the firm distinction between affect and emotion that follows from this stance. In the introduction to their *Affect Theory Reader*, for example, Gregg and Seigworth (2010, 1) state that affect implies "vital forces beyond emotion."

Although these developments have much to commend them, in my view this pristine concept of affect upon which the affective turn has come to turn is problematic and confused. Gregg and Seigworth (2010, 4) acknowledge this when they warn their readers that "first encounters with theories of affect might feel like a momentary (sometimes more permanent) methodological and conceptual free fall." In my view, this is because much of it simply *is* a conceptual free fall and free-for-all.

In *Liminality and Experience* (Stenner 2017a), I identify eight different concepts of affect that are mixed together in this literature, leading to all kinds of confusions. Without repeating these here, I will instead quickly examine one of the ways in which Brian Massumi distinguishes affect from emotion in his 1995 article. I focus on this way of drawing the distinction simply because it has been enormously influential. The distinction is pitched at a very abstract level and is presented with a bare minimum of empirical illustration (Massumi makes some quite idiosyncratic interpretations of a series of psychological experiments, which are discussed further in Stenner 2018). He states that his "clearest lesson… is that emotion and affect… follow different logics and pertain to different orders" (Massumi 1995, 88). Affect apparently follows a logic of *intensity* that is autonomic in nature and to do with the effect rather than the content of events. Emotion, by contrast, follows a logic of *quality* that is semantically or semiotically ordered, and hence is fixed by the binary distinctions of a conventional system of signification. So, for Massumi, we must distinguish two parallel but completely different orders. One order is about content, quality and semantics, the other about effect, intensity, and autonomic processes. For Massumi, emotion belongs to the first order because an emotion, like shame or fear, is a subjective content, with distinctive qualities that have been semantically fixed by socio-linguistic conventions. Affect, however, he defines as intensity, and insists that it is "a non-conscious, never-to-be-conscious autonomic remainder. It is outside expectation and adaptation… disconnected from meaningful sequencing, from narration…" In short, for Massumi emotion is *qualified intensity* or, to put it differently, affect that has been captured within meaningful and hence socially functional narratives and semiotic circuits. Affect, by contrast, is that which necessarily escapes this kind of capture, and so remains virtual, as a potentiality that can never be assimilated.

Now, to be clear, I am not denying the value of drawing some sort of a distinction between the actual and the virtual, or between discursive symbolism and more basic psychological processes. Such distinctions are in fact quite important to the theoretical approach to psychology that I adopt and help us to avoid a crude "mind/matter" bifurcation. But I am questioning a simple mapping of such distinctions onto the words "affect" and "emotion." Massumi (1995, 88) defends this move by invoking Spinoza, whom he describes as "a formidable philosophical precursor on many of these points: on the difference in nature between affect and emotion, on the irreducibly bodily and autonomic nature of affect…" Of the two claims outlined in this proposition, I will start by quickly discarding the second. It seems to me that Spinoza nowhere argues for the "irreducibly bodily and autonomic nature of affect," although I confess to being uncertain about what the phrase "irreducibly bodily" actually means. Spinoza (1677/1989) is most famous for his thought/extension parallelism, and this involves a resolute refusal to consider thought and extension as two separate substances, and hence to treat the universe either as "irreducibly" material/physical or, for that matter, "irreducibly" mental/subjective. As I have argued along with Steven Brown:

> The first step in analyzing encounters is to maintain the parallelism of body and mind. This involves, for Spinoza, a separate explication

> of how affects order relations between bodies and between ideas. Proximate causes are sought within each attribute. The body cannot act as the cause of changing order within ideas, nor do ideas directly bring about modifications in bodies. Since "the order and connection of ideas is the same as the order and connection of things" (E. II. prop. 7), what is sought is the dual expression of the encounter as it presents under each attribute. (Brown and Stenner 2001, 90)

Turning now to the first claim, it seems to me that Spinoza did not draw any such distinction between affect and emotion, let alone argue for a difference in nature. Spinoza wrote in Latin and used the term "affectus" (as well as variants like "afficio" and "affectio"), and he never employed the word emotion, which was barely used anywhere until the early nineteenth century. The affections of a body are the modifications that occur in the course of an encounter with another body. Spinoza discusses the affects at great length in his most famous book, the *Ethics,* and when he deals with concrete examples of affects, far from marking a difference in nature from emotion, he discusses what we would now routinely call emotions. That is to say, he discusses experiences called things like anger, fear, joy, jealousy, envy, and so forth. The important thing is his *approach* to these emotions, which always emphasizes modifications wrought by encounters. Anger, for Spinoza, is thus a particular kind of modification that occurs in particular types of encounters (for more detail, see Brown and Stenner 2001).

It is however important to grasp that Spinoza does not limit his understanding of affects to human emotions. On the contrary, as a philosopher Spinoza was looking for much broader generality. For Spinoza, *all* entities—whether animal, vegetable, or mineral—are to be understood in relation to the affects they are capable of in their encounters with other entities. His philosophy is thoroughly relational, contending that anything that exists does so as a function of its relations, and hence of the affects it is capable of going through. In this sense he proposes what Leo (2016) aptly calls an "affective physics." When it comes to human beings, those affects typically take the form we know of as emotions. Hence although Spinoza does not assert this, there is a plausible basis for a distinction in which affect would be an ontological or metaphysical concept applicable to all entities, whilst emotion would refer to affects in so far as they express themselves at a specifically anthropological level. An ontological concept of "affectus" would thus apply equally to slugs and to people, but without implying that the affects of slugs and people are the same. A slug is not capable of being affected and of affecting others in the manner that we call "jealousy," for example. And this is not to deny that there may be slug affects that in some respects exceed the capacities of human beings.

Things are no less disappointing if we try to extract a fundamental difference between affect and emotion from Tomkins's work or from psychoanalysis. Like Spinoza, when Tomkins (e.g., 1963) discusses the affects that make up the affect system, he refers to what ordinary people would call emotions: the experiences we call anger, fear, shame, disgust, joy, and so forth. In his published work, Tomkins uses the word "emotion" very rarely, and the reason that he prefers the word "affect" is that he wanted a more scientific term that would allow him and his readers to step back from routine and common-sense assumptions about emotions. In short, what ordinary so-called "lay folk" call their "emotions," the scientist—with the benefit of their objective research—recognizes as proper to an innate system of affects.

André Green (1999), who is probably the main psychoanalytic authority on affect, points out all kinds of nuances between the words used for emotion, feeling, affect, sentiment, passion and so on in French, German, and English. His ultimate position is that within psychoanalytical discourse, affect should be a metapsychological term and not a descriptive term with a specific referent. The word "affect," in other words, should be reserved for use as a categorical term which groups together "all the nuances that German (Empfindung, Gefühl) or French (émotion, sentiment, passion, etc.) bring to this category" (Green 1999, 8).

The Affective Turn as a Deeper Return of Process Thought

On the basis of these kinds of arguments, I submit that the concept of affect I have critically outlined is not capable of sustaining an entire turn or a new field of "affect studies." But this does not mean that this literature is so far on the turn that it should turn us off. On the contrary, to my mind the "affective turn" is actually part of an emerging intellectual agenda whose stakes are much bigger than is conventionally thought. To return to the metaphor I used in the introduction, I propose that we have not let the apples turn far enough to get the cider we desire. But to understand why this is the case we need to re-orient ourselves. In my view, the turn to affect is not a rejection of the discursive turn but a deepening of it. The discursive turn—in its more sophisticated forms at least—was never in fact about linguistic imperialism, but was a protest against the overly static mode of thought that had previously dominated: it was a protest on behalf of thinking in terms of processes (or, for short, *process thought*). The affective turn is, to my mind, best understood as a deepening of process thought. This deepening extends process thought in a transdisciplinary direction, applicable as much to the natural sciences as to the social and cultural disciplines (the discursive turn, by comparison, was primarily about defending the humanities and social sciences from the incursions of a positivistic strain of natural science).

Understood in this way, the distinction between affect and emotion is not our main concern. There is a more important distinction at play within it, and that is the distinction between event and structure. For example, when Massumi (1995, 87) argues that approaches are "incomplete if they operate only on the semantic or semiotic level," he states that what they "lose, precisely, is the expression event—in favour of structure." Structure, for Massumi, "is the place where nothing ever happens, that explanatory heaven in which all eventual permutations are prefigured in a self-consistent set of invariant generative rules." Event, by contrast "is the collapse of structured distinction into intensity, of rules into paradox." The real issue in Massumi's work, it seems to me, is the identification of affect or intensity with event and emotion with structure. It is this concern with events that is the source of his preoccupation with the emergence of novelty. It is this emphasis on what Massumi calls the "virtual as cresting in a liminal realm of emergence" (Massumi, 1995, 92) that needs to be rescued from the confusion that is caused by a premature distinction between affect and emotion.

To perform this rescue, we need to think processually. We need to recognize that a structure is not in fact something static but is an organized and indeed self-organizing pattern of processes. A structure, in short, is a form of process that is ultimately composed of events. An event is an occurrence (or sequence of occurrences) that either perpetuates or transforms structures or forms of process (see Sewell 1992; Greco and Stenner 2017).

Affect as Experience on the Turn: Liminality

Having completed the critical part of the paper, I will now offer a positive proposition—or at least sketch (for a more sustained presentation of the argument see Stenner 2017a)—an alternative theoretical framing for some of these issues. I propose that the preoccupation amongst affect theorists with what might be called "intensive events of becoming" can be usefully re-framed with a suitably crafted concept of liminality and liminal experience. Crafting this concept of liminality means moving well beyond its origins in the field of anthropology, where it refers to the middle phase in a rite of passage (Van Gennep 1909; Turner 1969). In my own work, I have extended the notion of a liminal occasion to include any occasion of passage during which some form of *becoming* takes place. I have called this *ontological liminality*, and from this perspective *anthropological liminality* is a specific or limited case (Stenner and Moreno 2013).

Let me link this with my theme of being "on the turn." At a specifically anthropological scale and focus, liminal occasions are significant *turning points* in the lives of individuals and collectives. Van Gennep called these turning points *transitions* or *passages*. A rite of passage is a ceremonial pattern of rites that accompanies "a passage from one situation to another or from one cosmic or social world to another" (van Gennep 1909, 10). These turning points or transitions are occasions when what I call "psychosocial forms of process" are suspended or interrupted, or collapse, or go through some sort of transformation or metamorphosis. I use the unfamiliar phrase "psychosocial forms of process" because human social and personal existence is a complex and tightly patterned unity of subjective experiences and objective expressions, bound up in flows of coordinated action mediated by discursive communication and situated within broader dynamics of power. The phrase "psychosocial form of process" is therefore designed to indicate that the routine practices of ordinary "everyday life" always presuppose a complex and fragile composition of forces that are ultimately processual in nature and composed of flows of events. For this reason, occasions during which those forms of process are interrupted, or suspended or transformed, tend to be very emotionally intense for those involved, and they tend to generate a particular quality of affect that I call *liminal affectivity.*

Philosophically speaking, I locate the approach I adopt within a tradition of process thinking that is inspired by the British philosopher and mathematician Alfred North Whitehead. The following quotation is from his last book, called *Modes of Thought*, from 1938:

> Nothing is more interesting to watch than the emotional disturbance produced by any unusual disturbance of the forms of process. The slow drift is accepted. But when for human experience quick changes arrive, human nature passes into hysteria. For example, gales, thunderstorms, earthquakes, revolutions in social habits, violent illnesses, destructive fires, battles, are all occasions of special excitement.

> There are perfectly good reasons for this energetic reaction to quick
> change. My point is the exhibition of our emotional reactions to the
> dominance of lawful order, and to the breakdown of such order. When
> fundamental change arrives, sometimes heaven dawns, sometimes
> hell yawns open. (Whitehead [1938] 1968, 95)

This tradition of thought has much deeper roots than Whitehead's
philosophy. Back in the seventeenth century, Spinoza made a similar point
in the preface to his *Theologico-Political Treatise* ([1670] 1951, 3). He draws a
contrast between well-structured and rule-bound situations, and situations
of doubt in which people are "driven into straights where rules are useless."
It is probable that he had in mind the situations of war and religiously
inspired conflict that were endemic before and during his lifetime and that
affected him personally. In well-structured circumstances, he suggests, the
human mind tends to be "boastful, overconfident and vain." Most people,
"when in prosperity, are so over-brimming with wisdom (however inexperi-
enced they may be), that they take every offer of advice as a personal
insult". Put these same people in the straights of more chaotic circumstances, however, and Spinoza finds that they "know not where to turn, but
beg and prey for counsel from every passer-by." They fluctuate "pitiably
between hope and fear" and become superstitious and generally "very
prone to credulity." Here Spinoza suggests that the same people can show
very different characteristics—have very different opinions, values and
feelings, for instance—as they cross the line between these two types of
situation.

What I call the *liminal affectivity* that Spinoza here invokes arises from the
fact that forms of process that were taken for granted have been perturbed
or disrupted. Since human subjectivity is intricately woven into the forms of
shared meaning that make up our various social practices, any significant
disruption to a social form of process will shock and uproot the psychic
constitution of those who participate, and disrupt the capacity for standard
forms of coordinated communication. To return to my theme of turning, in
these situations it usually feels, at least at first, as if our lives have taken a
sharp turn for the worse. This turn or swerve can of course be conceived
as a *passage,* and we should recall that for Spinoza affects are nothing but
the experience of passage or transition. Suffering and distress, to quote
from Spinoza's *Ethics* (1677, 138), are "passive states of transition... wherein
the mind passes to a lesser perfection," whilst joy and merriment are also
passive transitions, but transitions in which the passage is "to a greater
perfection." We must not forget, then, that for Spinoza, affects *are* experiences on the turn, or experiences of the turn.

But these situations of doubt and crisis described by Spinoza and Whitehead are just one kind of liminal occasion. I call them *spontaneous liminal occasions* to the extent that they concern things that passively happen to us rather than things we actively and self-consciously enact by and for ourselves. Although the distinction is analytic and never actually encountered in pure form, spontaneous liminal occasions can be usefully contrasted with what I call *devised* or self-generated liminal occasions. These are liminal experiences that we *do to ourselves and to each other*. Those who know the liminality literature will be aware here that I am influenced by Victor Turner, who wrote of unstaged and staged liminal situations, and also by Árpad Szakolczai (2000; 2009; 2016), who contrasts "real life" liminal situations with those that are "staged" (see also Thomassen 2014). I depart from Turner, however, in that the metaphor of "staging," although very vivid and useful, is overly limited to the model of the theater. The same is true of all so-called dramaturgical theoretical vocabulary within the social sciences, and of most theory whose keyword is performance or performativity. Let me explain why.

When Ritual Turns into Theater

The theater, as we know, is a relatively recent cultural form (it came into existence in the late sixth century BC in Athens). It is just one means amongst others for creating devised liminal experiences, and obviously in the case of theater it makes sense to call these experiences staged liminal experiences (Szakolczai 2013). It makes sense because the theater has a clear and architecturally instantiated division between an audience that observes from the auditorium or *theatron*, and players who act on the stage. But, arguably, it was precisely this division between *theatron* and stage that constituted what was novel about the emergence or invention of theater.

Cambridge Ritualist Jane Harrison did the decisive historical work on this topic, building on some of Nietzsche's ideas about the birth of tragedy. In a book on Ancient Greek religion published in 1903, Harrison shows how both the *theatron* and the stage emerged from a third and more mysterious space designated for the Chorus (see Harrison 1913). In ancient theater, the Chorus may originally have been composed of singers of the *Dithyramb*—a ritual song sung in honor of the god Dionysus. In the original Dionysian rituals, it is likely that everybody would participate, and so a fixed distinction between actor and observer would be problematic. But Harrison reasons that through time some members of the Chorus would split off and offer real-time interpretations, commentaries or embellishments of the Dithyramb sung by the Chorus. These new activities of the actors would be observed by a new category of spectators who were not obliged to participate. The spectators could simply enjoy the interpretations, commentaries and embellishments that would soon supplant the Chorus and become the main action of tragedy and comedy in the new medium of the theater. The psychosocial importance of the emergence of theater can hardly be overstated (but for a critique of the Cambridge Ritualist thesis see Rozik 2002). When theater emerged, it became, along with philosophy and democracy, one of the three fundamental novelties that define the classical period (roughly 500–336 BC).

I have discussed the emergence of Greek theater to explain why I consider the expression *"staged" liminal experience* to be too limited, and prefer instead the word "devised" or "self-generated." Harrison's work shows the dependence of theater upon a much older means for self-generating liminal experience, namely ritual. In fact, we might say that Harrison is fascinated with ritual at the historical moment that it is *on the turn*. In other words, she focuses precisely on the historical point at which ritual begins to mutate into theater or become theater. Ritual, as I have emphasized, is *not* divided into a group of actors who perform for a group of spectators. To call those who participated in the ancient rites of Dionysus "actors" who "perform" is to seriously misunderstand the *sacred* nature of their activity. Unless the ritual has degenerated into mere formal ceremony, it is not a matter of playing a part, but of *becoming other* through ritualistic means, and thereby encountering forces that are taken very seriously indeed. Likewise, the others present are not detached spectators enjoying the spectacle from the critical distance of their designated location, but more or less active participants who both witness and contribute to the process of becoming. As Kurakin (2018, note 14)—inspired by Durkheim—puts it, there is no arbitrary observer in ritual: "every particular participant of the ritual… is doomed to perceive the object or event, collectively turned to the sacred, as sacred." If ritual is a device for self-generating liminal experience of a predominantly *sacred* kind, then theater is a device for self-generating liminal experience of a predominantly *aesthetic* kind, exploiting the critical distance afforded by the *theatron*.

Liminal Affective Technologies

Ritual and theater are therefore quite different and not to be confused, and yet they share a fundamental similarity such that we might well say, following Harrison, that at a certain point ritual *turned into* theater. Since ritual existed long before 500 BC it can be considered the older of the two forms, and yet the two can coexist; theater might also turn into ritual, and there might also be a zone of indiscernability between them (Artaud's *Theatre of Cruelty* could be considered an effort to reconnect theater with ritual, for example, and certainly religious rites can easily turn theatrical, often to the anger of purists). In my recent work, I specify the fundamental similarity between ritual and theater as "devices" for self-generating liminal experience by calling them *liminal affective technologies.* They are, in other words, means or *media* through which we can self-generate liminal experiences of becoming, and manage, navigate and enjoy the liminal affectivity that is brought into play. In using the word "technology" I am extending the ordinary use of this word, much as Michel Foucault (2000) did when he wrote of "technologies of the self" (perhaps inspired by Marcel Mauss's [1935/2006] essay on "techniques of the body"). Any technology, as Niklas Luhmann (1990) points out, operates with a difference between the reduced complexity of repeatable cause–effect relationships, and "uncapped" causal relationships that have not yet been determined (see Andersen and Stenner 2020). Considered in this way, a technology is a "dodge to live" achieved by bringing uncapped cause–effect relationships into a form that produces reliably repeatable effects. But usually we think of technology as a means for producing reliably repeatable effects with respect to material forms in the so-called external world. A lever, for instance, is a technology for shifting weighty substances, and a sail a technology for harnessing the power of the wind.

Liminal affective technologies, by contrast, are about summoning and working with subjective, affective experience in order to occasion transformations. This is less a matter of reliably triggering and directing uniform causal process than of *undoing* the structural limits that usually produce conformal effects. To use a lovely turn of phrase from Norbert Elias, they involve "the controlled decontrolling of emotional controls" (cited in Wouters 2007, 232). Liminal affective technologies can in this sense be traced to, and build upon, more spontaneous liminal experiences and activities like play and daydreaming, both of which presume a certain "release" from the more structured routines of daily life. Both ritual and theater have obvious links to children's (and perhaps even animal) play. Ritual, for example, has a certain "excessive" and "repetitive" quality irreducible to mere survival or utilitarian functionality, and evocative instead of superfluous energy, enjoyed for its own sake. As with play fighting, we enjoy ritualistic acts irrespective of their "external" use-value. Ritual, in this sense, is at root a means for exciting affectivity, and it can diverge into the serious emotions of the religious sacred, or into playful fun, or any mixtures thereof. The concept of liminal affective technologies thus also allows me to express the difference between ritual and theater, since they are *different* liminal affective technologies. Continuing my theme of the turn, we might say that religious ritual is a technology for turning affectivity into sacred experience, whilst theater is a technology for turning affectivity into aesthetic experience.

Ritual and theater are, of course, not the only liminal affective technologies. Sports and games, viewed from this perspective, can be thought of as technologies for turning affectivity into *ludic* experience. Nor is theater the only aesthetic technology, since we must include each of the other arts: music, painting, dance, and so on. So, I have identified three broad types of liminal affective technology, corresponding to the *sacred*, the *aesthetic*, and the *ludic* (see Stenner 2017b). It is interesting to observe the extent to which the *aesthetic* and the *ludic* types both have a close relationship to ritual. Ritual can be considered the matrix of the arts and sport to the extent that it contains and nourishes them in embryonic form. The masks of theater were born out of ritual, but ritual also encompasses elements of dance, music and story-telling as well as sport-like tests of skill and endurance. Just like ancient theater, the old Olympic Games were originally a thoroughly sacred affair. In sum, we might say that, historically speaking, sacred ritual takes a turn towards the ludic and the aesthetic forms, which spring from it like seeds from a pod. But, even when independent, the arts and sport never quite lose the tinge of religious significance. It is not accidental, taking literature as an example, that Thomas Mann directly identified his novel *The Magic Mountain* with a rite of passage, describing it as "a novel of *initiation*": "In a word, the magic mountain is a variant on the shrine of the initiatory rites, a place of adventurous investigation into the mystery of life" (Mann 1953, 728). To the extent that a novel implicates its readers (and writers) in an experience that is transformative and not just "entertaining," that work of art can be said to function as a liminal affective technology (Szakolczai 2016; Stenner and Greco 2018). Through an analysis of Christopher Nolan's *Inception*, Stenner and Zittoun (2020) make a similar case for film.

In construing these different kinds of media as liminal affective technologies, I am drawing attention to the ways in which they work to self-generate emotional experience and deploy that experience within a project of transformation. When we listen to a piece of music we really like, for example, or when we play an instrument ourselves, we produce emotional effects, both for ourselves and potentially for others. If we are unmoved by a theater performance, or a movie, we are left disappointed. These activities share with ritual the common aim of producing *moving* experiences that are somewhat out of the ordinary and that are conducive of psychosocial transformation. Most scientific psychology of affect misses the entirety of these self-generated or devised affective experiences. It concentrates instead on a somewhat atavistic view of affects as raw survival mechanisms, wired into our brains through evolution to equip us for survival: fear for flight, anger for a fight and love for some other f word. In drawing attention to devised liminal affectivity and the technologies through which it is summoned, however, my intention is not to deny the brutal realities that may have been faced by our cave-dwelling ancestors, for whom, we are told, nature appeared in the raw with tooth and claw. In fact, the true value of the distinction between spontaneous and devised liminal occasions is the productivity of the *contrast* it permits. There is no pure spontaneous and pure devised experience—rather, everything falls somewhere in between. Indeed, it could even be said that liminal affective technologies function precisely at the *turning point* between the two. On the one hand, the liminal experience self-generated through liminal affective technologies helps us to navigate and manage the spontaneous liminality that might fall upon us. On the other hand, the spontaneous liminal experiences cry out, as it were, for symbolic expression, precisely because they challenge and transform the taken-for-granted order of daily life. New symbolism must be invented where old symbolism fails, and it is my thesis that the liminal affective technologies help us to create that symbolism and to drag it into emergence from the edge of semantic avail- ability. To evoke my theme of the turn once again, we might say that liminal affective technologies serve to turn a crisis into a drama, disabling toxic distress into thought-provoking tragedy.

Inconclusion: Some Contemporary Forms of Liminal Affective Technology

With the big theoretical picture behind us, I wish to bring the argument to a close by outlining some of the contemporary forms that liminal affective technologies are taking. It seems to me that the basic forms of ritual, art and games of various kinds are increasingly being instrumentalized to play a functional role in managing transitions within organizations of various kinds from schools to corporations (Zittoun 2007; Fuchs et al. 2014; Andersen and Pors 2016; Slater and Coyle 2017; Nissen and Solgaard

Sørensen 2017; Berg and Staunaes 2018; Zittoun and Rosenstein 2018). I would suggest that many of the institutional efforts to induce "change" in people and practices today can be usefully understood as liminal affective technologies (or what Berg and Staunaes 2018, modifying my terminology a little, call "liminal motivational technologies").

A key element of liminal affective technologies is their capacity to *potentialize* the emergence of unanticipated novelty, and in this respect, there is a close relationship between them and what Niels Åkerstrøm Andersen, Justine Pors, Hanne Knudsen and others working within the sphere of public management have called "potentialization technologies" (Andersen and Knudsen 2015; Andersen and Pors 2016). Examples would include things like managerial performance arts, 360 degree interviewing, sand-pits, future games, artistic interventions in therapeutic settings, Psychological Informed Planned Environments, and even cross-professional speed-dating. Potentialization technologies are used when there is a perception that some type of change is needed in an organization, and yet the nature of that change is not yet clearly specified. Methods are therefore needed to help people to "think outside the box" and to "expect the unexpected." The preferred methods tend to take the form of role-play games, pedagogical activies, and artistic (especially theatrical) interventions (Stenner and Andersen 2020). These serve to suspend the usual patterns of activity, and to generate unusual situations with distinct affective resonances. Drawing upon Luhmann's sociological theory, Andersen and myself reflect upon potentialization technologies as a species of liminal affective technology (Andersen and Stenner 2020). For example, in Denmark an organization called *Sisters Academy* use a technique that they specifically link to liminality theory, as well as to performance art and activism. One of their projects from 2013 was called "School in a Sensual Society." *Sisters Academy* would enter a school during the holiday period and transform its environment using techniques of light, sound, and set design. When the teachers and pupils returned it felt like a different place, and the teachers were then encouraged to experiment with their teaching based on the principle that aesthetics are of pivotal value. The ambition is to effect—or at least to suggest—an institutional transformation through the deliberate staging of a liminal occasion. This would be an example of "potentializing" by means of a liminal affective technology.

But liminal affective technologies are not limited to the occasioning of "fun" or "creative" situations in which some type of change has to be induced in participants who may well be reluctant. They can also be about managing and shaping the spontaneous affectivity generated by "real-life" liminal experiences. Eduardo Moreno, for example, studied the affective dimensions of deceased organ donation practices in Catalonia (Stenner and Moreno 2013). The entire deceased organ donation system in Spain is a complex *dispositif*, but we were particularly interested in the workings of small groups called *transplant coordination teams.* In the Spanish health-care system, these are composed of teams of physicians and other medical professionals whose role is to bring together all of the components—from the technical to the emotional—necessary for organ transplantation. A key role is to interview the closest available relative of the deceased in order to secure consent for harvesting the organs of their recently deceased loved one. The team members are trained to carefully manage the affectivity unleashed by these circumstances, and to use the resulting emotions to steer the relative towards a decision concerning consent, in full knowledge of the highly sensitive and transformative nature of the event being, as it were, "stage-managed."

The advantage of considering interventions, methods and techniques like these as liminal affective technologies is not just that it draws our attention to their relationship with rituals and their ludic and aesthetic off-spring, hence situating them within a broader genealogy. It also draws our attention to what we are trying to become when we use these technologies, and to our responsibility in actually enabling those becomings. This issue is increasingly important within our contemporary geopolitics, where global flows of capital threaten to impose a permanent situation of change upon practically all forms of human existence (Szakolczai 2016).

References

Andersen, Niels Åkerstrøm, and Hanne Knudsen. 2015. "Playful Hyper-responsibility and the Making of a Performing Audience." *Soziale Systeme* 19 (2): 433–55.

Andersen, Niels Åkerstrøm, and Justine Pors. 2016. *Public Management in Transition: The Orchestration of Potentiality*. Bristol: Policy Press.

Andersen, Niels Åkerstrøm, and Paul Stenner. 2020. "Social Immune Mechanisms: Luhmann and Potentialization Technologies." *Theory, Culture and Society* 37 (2): 79–103.

Angerer, Marie-Luise. 2017. *Ecology of Affect*. Lüneburg: Meson Press.

Angerer, Marie-Luise, Bernd Bösel, and Michaela Ott, eds. 2014. *Timing of Affect: Epistemologies, Aesthetics, Politics*. Zürich: Diaphanes.

Berg, Helle, and Dorthe Staunaes. 2018. "Governing through Intermediary Spaces: Reforming School and Subjectivities through Liminal Motivational Technologies." In *Critical Analyses of Educational Reforms in an Era of Transnational Governance*, edited by Thomas S. Popkewitz, Elisabeth Hultquist, and Sverker Lindblad, 197–212. New York: Springer.

Brown, Steve, and Paul Stenner. 2001. "Being Affected: Spinoza and the Psychology of Emotion." *International Journal of Group Tensions* 30 (1): 81–105.

Clough, Patricia. 2010. "Afterword: The Future of Affect Studies." *Body and Society* 16 (1): 222–30.

Clough, Patricia, and Jean Halley, eds. 2007. *The Affective Turn: Theorizing the Social*. Durham, NC: Duke University Press.

Craib, Ian. 1997. "Social Constructionism as a Social Psychosis." *Sociology* 31 (1): 1–15.

Curt, Beryl. 1994. *Textuality and Tectonics: Troubling Social and Psychological Science*. Buckingham: Open University Press.

Elliott, Anthony, and Stephen Frosh, eds. 1995. *Psychoanalysis in Context: Paths between Theory and Modern Culture*. London: Routledge.

Foucault, Michel. 2000. "Technologies of the Self." In *Ethics: Essential Works of Foucault 1954–1984, Vol 1*. London: Harmondsworth Penguin.

Fuchs, Mathias, Sonia Fizek, Paulo Ruffino, and Niklas Schrape, eds. 2014. *Rethinking Gamification*. Lüneburg: Meson Press.

Greco, Monica, and Paul Stenner, eds. 2008. *The Emotions: A Social Science Reader*. London: Routledge.

Greco, Monica, and Paul Stenner. 2017. "From Paradox to Pattern Shift: Conceptualising Liminal Hotspots and their Affective Dynamics." *Theory and Psychology* 27 (2): 147–66.

Green, André. 1999. *The Fabric of Affect in the Psychoanalytic Discourse*. Translated by Alan Sheridan. London: Routledge.

Gregg, Melissa, and Gregory J. Seigworth, eds. 2010. *The Affect Theory Reader*. Durham, NC: Duke University Press.

Hemmings, Claire. 2005. "Invoking Affect: Cultural Theory and the Ontological Turn." *Cultural Studies* 19 (5): 521–47.

Harré, Rom, ed. 1986. *The Social Construction of Emotions*. Oxford: Blackwell.

Harrison, Jane E. 1913. *Ancient Art and Ritual*. Oxford: Oxford University Press.

Kurakin, Dmitry. 2018. "The Cultural Mechanics of Mystery: Structures of Emotional Attraction in Competing Interpretations of the Dyatlov Pass Tragedy." *American Journal of Cultural Sociology* 7 (1): 101–27. doi: 10.1057/s41290-018-0057-y.

Leo, Russ. 2016. "Affective Physics." In *Passions and Subjectivity in Early Modern Culture*, edited by Brian Cummings and F. Sierhuis, 33–50. London: Routledge.

Leys, Ruth. 2011. "The Turn to Affect: A Critique." *Critical Inquiry* 37 (3): 434–72.

Luhmann, Niklas. 1990. "Technology, Environment and Social Risk: A System Perspective." *Industrial Quarterly* 4 (3): 223–31.

Mann, Thomas. (1953) 1999. "The Making of the Magic Mountain." In *The Magic Mountain*, 717–29. Translated by H.T. Lowe-Porter. London: Vintage.

Mauss, Marcel. (1935) 2006. "Techniques of the Body." *Economy and Society* 2 (1): 70–88.

Massumi, Brian. 1995. "The Autonomy of Affect." *Cultural Critique* 31 (2): 83–109.

Nissen, Morten, and Solgaard Sørensen. 2017. "The Emergence of Motives in Liminal Hotspots." *Theory and Psychology* 27 (2): 249–69.

Rozik, Eli. 2002. *The Roots of Theater: Rethinking Ritual and Other Theories of Origin*. Iowa City: University of Iowa Press.

Sedgwick, Eve Kosofsky, and Adam Frank. 1995. "Shame in the Cybernetic Fold: Reading Silvan Tomkins." *Critical Inquiry* 21 (2): 496–505.

Sewell, William. 1992. "Historical events as transformations of structures: inventing revolution at the Bastille." *Theory and Society* 25 (6): 841–81.

Slater, Rory, and Adrian Coyle. 2017. "Time, Space, Power and the Liminal Transformation of the Psychologised Self." *Theory and Psychology* 27 (3): 369–88.

Spinoza, Baruch. (1677) 1989. *Ethics: Including the Improvement of the Understanding*. Translated by R.H.M. Elwes. New York: Prometheus Books.

———. (1670) 1951. *A Theologico-political Treatise*. Translated by R. H. M. Elwes. London: Dover

Stenner, Paul. 1992. *Feeling Deconstructed? With Particular Reference to Jealousy.* University of
   Reading, UK: Doctoral Dissertation.
———. 1993. "Discoursing Jealousy". *In Discourse Analytic Research: Repertoires and Readings of
   Texts in Action*, edited by Erica Burman and Ian Parker, 114–33. London: Routledge.
———. 2017a. *Liminality and Experience: A Transdisciplinary Approach to the Psychosocial.*
   London: Palgrave.
———. 2017b. "Being in the Zone and Vital Subjectivity: On the Liminal Sources of Sport and
   Art." In *Culture, Identity and Intense Performativity: Being in the Zone*, edited by Tim Jordan,
   Kath Woodward & Brigid McClure, 10–31. London: Routledge.
———. 2018. "Bridging the Affect/Emotion Divide: A Critical Overview of the Affective Turn."
   In *Affect Theory and Rhetorical Persuasion in Mass Communication*, edited by Lei Zhang and
   Carlton Clark, 34–55. London: Routledge.
Stenner, Paul, and Niels Åkerstrom Andersen. 2020. "The Emotional Organization and the
   Problem of Authenticity: The Romantic, the Pedagogic, the Therapeutic and the Ludic as
   Liminal Media of Transition." *Systems Research and Behavioral Science.* Online first, April
   28. https://doi.org/10.1002/sres.2687.
Stenner, Paul, and Monica Greco. 2018. "On the Magic Mountain: A Liminal Affective
   Technology?" *International Political Anthropology* 11 (1): 43–60.
Stenner, Paul, and Eduardo Moreno. 2013. "Liminality and Affectivity: The Case of Deceased
   Organ Donation." *Subjectivity* 6 (3): 229–53.
Stenner, Paul, and Rex Stainton Rogers. 1998. "Jealousy as a Manifold of Divergent
   Understandings: A Q Methodological Investigation." *European Journal of Social Psychology*,
   28 (1): 71–94.
Stenner, Paul, and Tania Zittoun. 2020. "On Taking a Leap of Faith: Art, Imagination and
   Liminal Experiences." *Journal of Theoretical and Philosophical Psychology.* Online first,
   March. https://doi.org/10.1037/teo0000148.
Szakolczai, Árpad. 2000. *Reflexive Historical Sociology.* London: Routledge.
———. 2009. "Liminality and Experience: Structuring Transitory Situations and
   Transformative Events." *International Political Anthropology* 2 (1): 141–72.
———. 2013. *Comedy and the Public Sphere: The Rebirth of Theatre as Comedy and the Genealogy
   of the Modern Public Arena.* London: Routledge.
———. 2016. *Permanent Liminality and Modernity.* London: Routledge.
Thomassen, Bjorn. 2014. *Liminality and the Modern.* Farnham and Burlington, VT: Ashgate.
Tomkins, Silvan S. 1963. *Affect, Imagery, Consciousness, Vol. 1: The Positive Affects.* London:
   Tavistock.
Turner, Victor. 1969. *The Ritual Process: Structure and Anti-structure.* New York: Aldine
   Transaction.
Van Gennep, Arnold. (1909) 1961. *The Rites of Passage.* Chicago: University of Chicago Press.
Whitehead, Alfred North. (1938) 1966. *Modes of Thought.* The Free Press: New York.
Wouters, Cas. 2007. *Informalization: Manners and Emotions Since 1890.* London: Sage.
Zittoun, Tania. 2007. "Symbolic Resources and Responsibility in Transitions." *Young* 15 (2):
   193–211.
Zittoun, Tania, and Adeline Rosenstein. 2018. "Theatre and Imagination to (Re)Discover
   Reality." In *Handbook of Imagination and Culture*, edited by Tania Zittoun and Vlad
   Glaveanu, 223–42. Oxford: Oxford University Press.

ALGORITHM AWARENESS

MAPPING BACK

EXTERNALIZED ANTICIPATION

ARTIFACTUALITY

EXTERNALIZED INTROSPECTION

2

Algorithm Awareness: Towards a Philosophy of Artifactuality

Gabriele Gramelsberger

This contribution argues that while mankind is experiencing a decentering within its own media universe, a new agency has emerged: "algorithm awareness." By looking into recent technological developments, this new agency is analyzed as enabling two automated capabilites that can be called "externalized anticipation" and "externalized introspection." With these modes of "mapping back" information on users, it becomes necessary to conceptualize what is here called "artifactuality"—a hybrid form of information that is derived neither from purely statistical nor purely individual data.

1. Media Transforming into Iconoclastic Sensor Technologies

The very nature of media has been substantially changed by the introduction of computers, by the digitization of media itself, by the miniaturization of circuitry, and by the ubiquity of the myriad inter-connected objects in the proliferating Internet of Things. Of course, the consequences of these shifts are subject to many reflections in contemporary media theory and philosophy. These shifts have been addressed, for instance, by Patricia Clough and Nigel Thrift's concept of the "technological unconsciousness," referring to Jacques Derrida's idea of technicity "as bearer of unconscious thought" (Clough 2000, 17; Thrift 2004), by Mark Hansen's concept of the new "firstness" of database sensoriality (2016), by William Uricchio's proclamation of the "algorithmic turn" (2011), and Lev Manovich's "command of software" (2013). However, these shifts can also be reconstructed as media's transformation into sensor technologies driven by three major developments: (1) the shift from infor-mation technology (IT) to consumer Internet-IT with the introduction of the World Wide Web in 1991; (2) the shift to Mobile-IT with the introduction of smart phones in 2007 and the fostering of social networks—both partly replacing the Internet-IT and (3) the more recent shift into Aware-IT, which has also been addressed as the Internet of Things, interconnecting billions of smart objects worldwide (gartner.com 2019).

Aware-IT currently comprises more than six billion sensor- and algorithm-equipped objects continuously measuring and gathering the data of individuals and their surrounding environment. It is the realization of Mark Weiser's vision of "ubiquitous computing," based on technologies that increasingly merge with the environment and are capable of sensing everything (1991). Aware-IT is massively changing the human–media interrelationship. Media, anthropologically rooted in human senses, have been dominated by images and sounds. In particular the television age of the 1970s and 1980s, and the Internet-IT of the 1990s and 2000s, have broadcast and generated countless "Techno-Bilder," as Vilém Flusser has dubbed them, creating the "techno-imaginäre Welt" (1997, 27). In this techno-imaginary world the human subject has increasingly become only one element in the "network imagination" of teletechnology (Heath 1991, 294). However, we can now observe that these image-based technologies and their network imaginations have been taken over by algorithm-driven sensor technologies. These sensor technologies are iconoclastic, because they replace image and sound with pure data, thus marginalizing the phenomenological orientation of media towards the human.

Iconoclastic sensor technologies decenter man in his own media universe through the takeover of machinic and algorithmic imaginations operating beyond human thresholds. Data-based business models of internet platforms, search engines, and social networks are telling examples of this trend, exploiting the hyperfluidity of algorithms for the background algorithmical analysis of user-data. What is exploited is the widening temporal gap between humans and media (Gramelsberger 2016, 2020). While, in *Das Kapital* (1867), Karl Marx described the human capacity to transform nature through labor, and defined capital as the source of surplus value when invested in labor power, today's investment of data capitalism in the fluidity of media allows the temporal surplus of machines to be exploited as the new capital. This new capital is used to generate financial surplus value by algorithmically analyzing the movement of users in the digital world. Investment in server farms, supercomputers, fast broadband technologies, and advanced algorithms pays off.

2. Algorithm Awareness of Sensor Technologies

While algorithms and sensors are transforming media into iconoclastic technologies, the agency of objects and humans is also undergoing fundamental changes. The complex interrelationship between humans and objects is a major topic in human–machine communication studies and interface studies, but also in science and technology studies (STS). Since the 1980s, STS has been interested in the agency of objects as parts of social networks. This object-agency has been considered namely by Bruno Latour's and John Law's actor–network theory (Latour 1988, 1999), but also by Donna Haraway's concept of the "cyborg" (1985). Some more recent approaches also try to overcome the "ontology of separate things," as addressed for example in Lucy Suchman's book on *Human-Machine Recon-figurations* (2007, 257), and in studies on "agential realism" by Karen Barad (2007) and on "sociomateriality" by Wanda Orlikowski and Susan Scott (2008). However, these theories don't consider the new coalition of objects, sensors, and algorithms introducing a new mode of agency.

This new mode of agency can be called "algorithm awareness." Algorithms have become context-sensitive agents by collecting enormous amounts of individual data and by profiling us. Thus, context-aware algorithms can present us with personally tailored news feeds, products, and sugges-tions. Well-known examples are search engines producing different results for the same request, because they consider individual search profiles (adaptive media). However, algorithm awareness is not only an effect of context awareness: it links the individual to the global and the general in an unseen way. An interesting example is the decoding of individual DNA. In order to make DNA analysis cheap, today's DNA analyzers have to be fast. The problem with this is that due to the accelerated speed the "personal genome" one gets back is only partly individual. The error quote of fast DNA analyzers is quite high and algorithms are replacing missing or broken individual parts of DNA with statistically relevant genes. As long as the person falls under the statistical main cohort, this is not an issue. But, if the gene is meant to trigger a disease, the statistical insert becomes a problem (Gramelsberger 2017).

3. Externalization and Mapping Back

The DNA example makes clear the fact that algorithm awareness not only marginalizes the phenomenological orientation of media towards humans and challenges humans' agency and autonomy, but also confronts us with a new and hybrid mode of individual information externalized by technology, statistically averaged by algorithms related to many users, and mapped back on us by everyday user applications. "Mapping back" is an intrinsic ability of aware technology and technology-based media.

Traditionally, the philosophy of technology has interpreted technology as an extension of the human body. In particular, Ernst Kapp investigated technology as forms of organ projections (1877). Kapp, however, reflected on late nineteenth century technology—basically a collection of tools and instruments. Nevertheless, his ideas were adopted in the twentieth century by Marshall McLuhan, trying to grasp the transition from the Gutenberg galaxy to the electronic age:

> If a new technology extends one or more of our senses outside us into the social world, then new ratios among all of our senses will occur in that particular culture. It is comparable to what happens when a new note is added to a melody. And when the sense ratios alter in any culture then what had appeared lucid before may suddenly become opaque, and what had been vague or opaque will become translucent. (McLuhan 1962, 41)

The opaqueness of the "technological unconsciousness" (Clough 2000; Thrift 2004) has its roots in the extensions of senses by technology, because the projections are not organ projections, but cognitive projections.[1] Although the idea of organ- and mind-extending projections is debatable, the power of externalization as a function of extension is a dominant aspect of technology. However, in the age of algorithms

---

1   However, Ernst Kapp also wrote about extensions of mental life (Kapp 1877, chapter 12, 13).

the "projections" are mapped back on us in two ways: as externalized anticipation and externalized introspection.

On the one hand, algorithm awareness leads to externalized anticipation. Analyzing and profiling individual data is driving the new business models of data analytics exploiting the widening temporal gap between humans and media—as outlined above. Data analytics, however, searches for correlation patterns in vast data samples in order to predict trends. A questionable application, for instance, is the prediction of an individual's likelihood for committing a crime, or "predictive policing." A major player in this field is PredPol, which claims that "in contrast to technology that simply maps past crime data, PredPol applies advanced mathematics and adaptive computer learning. It has resulted in predictions twice as accurate as those made through existing best practices by building on the knowledge and experience that already exists" (predpol.com 2016). According to the company's homepage, the crime-predicting software in use is the descendant of an earthquake-forecasting system that uses the same algorithms.[2] But, the predictivity of earthquake-forecasting algorithms works differently than guessing in the context of human anticipation and expectation. There is little empirical evidence that supports the claimed benefits of predictive policing (Meijer and Wessels 2019).

On the other hand, algorithm awareness leads to externalized introspection. Speech analysis, pattern recognition, and automatized emotion analysis are examples of the increasingly externalized introspective abilities of current technology. An example of externalized introspection is emotion recognition. Face recognition algorithms—common tools in every surveillance architecture—can be easily extended with emotion analysis abilities. These emotion analyses are based on a taxonomy of our facial expressions, which was developed by Paul Ekman and Wallace V. Friesen in the 1970s, and named the Facial Action Coding System (FACS) (Ekman and Friesen 1976). Today FACS is used for automatic facial expression recognition (Cohn and De La Torre 2015). However, a machinic understanding of emotional expression is based on the tracking of facial features by pattern recognition of shapes, corners, and contours. These shapes and features are decoupled and translated into abstract mathematical features like light/dark-neighborhood coefficients of a pixeled grid. At the end of the transformation process coordinates of mesh vertices define the shape of a

---

2   However, not only the Los Angeles Police Department or the Metropolitan Police in London are using predictive policing. In 2015 Bavaria introduced the Pre Crime Observation System (Precob) programmed by the Institute of Pattern-based Prediction located in Oberhausen.

face, and the decoupled information can now be used to run various interpretations of it, for instance emotion analysis of the expressive patterns of one's face.

Affective computing, as it has been called by Rosalind Picard, "is a new area of research, with recent results primarily in the recognition and synthesis of facial expression, and the synthesis of voice inflection. However, these results are just the tip of the iceberg; a variety of physiological measurements are available which would yield clues to one's hidden affective state" (Picard 1995, 24; 2000; Clough 2007). A recent application of affective computing is SEMAINE, an EU-project devised to create a Sensitive Artificial Listener. This artificial listener can "interact with humans with a virtual character, sustain an interaction with a user for some time, and react appropriately to the user's non-verbal behavior" (semaine-project.eu 2016). Of course, affective computers can only recognize what we feel if we express our feelings "correctly"—that is in terms of a machinic understanding of emotion expression.

4. Towards a Philosophy of Artifactuality

The hybrid mode of individual and statistically averaged information, the algorithmic predictivity for anticipating human behavior, and the machinic understanding of externalized introspection such as emotion recognition are examples of the new mode of representation of individuality. The status of this kind of information is "artifactual"—it is neither a pure artifact, nor can it be considered the personal fact of an individual (Gramelsberger 2016a). It is a mixed mode of both: individual information and statistically averaged information. It transgresses the traditional form of statistics, because it is linked to predictivity for individuals and it directly maps the artifactual information back on us. Artifactuality is a new mode of entanglement between humans and technical objects. On the one hand, technical objects have become a technical sphere embedded in our everyday world. The ubiquitous and embedded character of this proliferating technical sphere has been addressed as "environmentalism" (Hörl and Burton 2017). On the other hand, the entanglement has become an epistemic entanglement of artifactual information. Without iconoclastic sensor technologies artifactual information wouldn't exist.

Understanding this new mode of knowledge, which is increasingly dominating everyday life, is part of a philosophy of artifactuality. Such a philosophy tries to grasp the very nature of artifactual knowledge. The examples have shown that the underlying logic of artifactuality is driven

by algorithms and the concept of the computer. Artifactuality results—
and this is my main hypothesis—from the introduction of the logic of
computers and algorithms into research, technology, and everyday life.
This logic is a mix of mathematical, logical, and data logical operations due
to the underlying machine instructions, which constitute the distinct epistemology of computer-based applications. The artifactual effects result
from it, transforming human forms of activity—practical activities as well
as cognitive ones—into assemblages of mathematical, logical, and data
logical operations, and thus externalizing and confronting us with these
transformed versions of human activities by mapping them back onto us.

"Mapping back" is the most problematic aspect of artifactual knowledge,
because the distinct operative epistemology of mathematical, logical, and
data logical operations is alienating human understanding. Mapping back
can also be understood as humans adapting towards algorithmic and
machinic imaginations: artifactual imaginations of ourselves. However,
these artifactual imaginations of ourselves are also computationally
enhanced, algorithmically accelerated, and statistically averaged
imaginations of ourselves. A philosophy of artifactuality has to conceptualize this new mode of knowledge, but also the new mode of human–
object agency providing more agency to algorithm- and sensor-equipped
objects.

References

Barad, Karen. 2007. *Meeting the Universe Halfway: Quantum Physics and the Entanglement of Matter and Meaning*. Durham, NC: Duke University Press.

Clough, Patricia T. 2000. *Auto-Affection: Unconscious Thought in the Age of Teletechnology*. Minneapolis: University of Minnesota Press.

Clough, Patricia T., ed. 2007. *The Affective Turn: Theorizing the Social*. Durham, NC: Duke University Press.

Cohn, Jeffrey F., and Fernando De La Torre. 2015. "Automated Face Analysis for Affective Computing." In *The Oxford Handbook of Affective Computing*, edited by Rafael Calvo et al., 131–149. Oxford: Oxford University Press.

Ekman, Paul, and Wallace V. Friesen. 1976. "Measuring Facial Movement." *Environmental Psychology and Nonverbal Behavior* 1 (1): 56–75.

Flusser, Vilém 1997. *Medienkultur*. Frankfurt a M.: Fischer.

Gartner, Inc. 2019. "Gartner Says 5.8 Billion Enterprise and Auto-motive IoT Endpoints Will Be in Use in 2020." Accessed May 12, 2020. https://www.gartner.com/en/newsroom/press-releases/2019-08-29-gartner-says-5-8-billion-enterprise-and-automotive-io.

Gramelsberger, Gabriele. 2016. "Es schleimt, es lebt, es denkt. Eine Rheologie des Medialen." *ZMK Zeitschrift für Medien- und Kulturforschung* 7 (1): 155–68.

———. 2016a. "Studies in the Technological and Mathematical Unconsciousness. Towards a Philosophy of Artifactuality in Research and Technology." Presentation July 27, 2016. Munich: Technical University Munich.

———. 2017. "Big Data-Revolution oder Datenhybris? Überlegungen zum Datenpositivismus der Molekularbiologie." *NTM Zeitschrift für Geschichte der Wissenschaften, Technik und Medizin* 25 (4): 1–25.

———. 2020. "Aware-IT/Care-IT: Die Folgen des technologisch Unbewussten für unser Subjektverständnis." In *Digitale Technologien zwischen Lenkung und Selbstermächtigung: Interdisziplinäre Perspektiven*, edited by Carmen Kaminsky et al., 40–54. Weinheim: BELTZ Juventa.

Hansen, Mark B. 2016. "Appearance In-Itself, Data-Propagation, and External Relationality: Towards a Realist Phenomenology of 'Firstness'." *ZMK Zeitschrift für Medien- und Kulturforschung* 7 (1): 45–60.

Haraway, Donna. 1985. "Manifesto for Cyborgs: Science, Technology, and Socialist Feminism in the 1980s." *Socialist Review* no. 80: 65–108.

Heath, Stephen. 1991. "Representing Television." In *Logics of Television: Essays in Cultural Criticism*, edited by Patricia Mellencamp, 267–302. Bloomington: Indiana University Press.

Hörl, Erich, and James E. Burton, eds. 2017. *General Ecology: The New Ecological Paradigm. Theory*. London: Bloomsbury Academic.

Kapp, Ernst. 1877. *Grundlinien einer Philosophie der Technik: Zur Entstehungsgeschichte der Kultur aus neuen Gesichtspunkten*. Braunschweig: George Westermann.

Latour, Bruno. 1988. "Mixing Humans and Nonhumans Together: The Sociology of a Door-Closer." In *Social Problems* 35 (3): 298–310.

———. 1999. "On Recalling ANT." In *Actor Network and After*, edited by John Law and John Hassard, 15–25 Oxford: Blackwell.

McLuhan, Marshall 1962. *The Gutenberg Galaxy: The Making of Typographic Man*. Toronto: University of Toronto Press.

Manovich, Lev. 2013. *Software Takes Command*. New York: Bloomsbury.

Marx, Karl. 1867. *Das Kapital: Kritik der politischen Ökonomie. Kritik der politischen Ökonomie. 1. Band: Der Produktionsprocess des Kapitals*. Hamburg: Otto Meissner. (*Capital: A Critique of Political Economy. Volume I: The Process of Production of Capital*. Chicago: Charles H. Kerr & Company 1909).

Meijer, Albert and Martijn Wessels. 2019. "Predictive Policing: Review of Benefits and Drawbacks." *International Journal of Public Administration* 42 (12): 1031–39.

Orlikowski, Wanda J., and Susan V. Scott. 2008. "Sociomateriality: Challenging the Separation of Technology, Work and Organization." *The Academy of Management Annals* 2 (1): 433–74.

Picard, Rosalind W. 1995. *Affective Computing*. MIT Media Laboratory Perceptual Computing Section Technical Report No. 321, November 26, 1995. Boston: Massachusetts Institute of Technology.

———. 2000. *Affective Computing*. Cambridge, MA: MIT Press.

PredPol. 2016. *Homepage*. Accessed 2016, July 12. www.predpol.com.

Semaine. 2016. *Project Homepage*. Accessed 2016, July 12. www.semaine-project.eu.

Suchman, Lucy A. 2007. *Human-Machine Reconfigurations: Plans and Situated Actions*. Cambridge: Cambridge University Press.

Thrift, Nigel. 2004. "Remembering the Technological Unconscious by Foregrounding Knowledges of Position." *Society and Space* 22 (1): 175–90.

Uricchio, William. 2011. "The Algorithmic Turn: Photosynth, Augmented Reality and the Changing Implications of the Image." *Visual Studies* 26 (1): 25–35.

Weiser, Mark. 1991. "The Computer for the 21st Century." *Scientific American* 265 (3): 94–104.

AFFECTIVE MEDIA

EMOTION REGULATION

AFFECTIVE DIFFERENCE

EMOTIONAL GRANULARITY

AFFECTIVE COMPUTING

PSYCHOPOWER

3

Affective Media Regulation: Or, How to Counter the Blackboxing of Emotional Life

Bernd Bösel

This contribution argues that with the emergence of affective media, affect or emotion regulation is undergoing a decisive transformation, because it is increasingly facilitated by automated systems that process users' affect expressions and encourage certain behaviors to maximize their happiness. It further develops the notion that affective media regulation itself demands regulations in a legal and sociopolitical sense. This argument is developed in four stages. (1) A brief overview of the terms "affect regulation" (Norbert Elias) and "emotion regulation" (Allan Schore; James Gross) in sociology and psychology provides some insight into the increasing centrality of these concepts and their position within the Foucauldian genealogy of the "security principle" (Frédéric Gros). (2) The term "affective media" is defined with recourse to

Kittlerian/Winklerian media theory as pertaining to affect-responsive media, or media capable of processing affect. (3) The near-total reliance of present affective computing applications on Paul Ekman's contested, if not outright refuted, theory of universal basic emotions leads to some serious doubts about its possible effects on users and their "emotional granularity" (Lisa Feldman Barrett). (4) Picking up on arguments made by critical algorithm studies, Shoshana Zuboff's critique of "surveillance capitalism," and legal scholars' fight for a "right to reasonable inference" by automated systems (Sandra Wachter and Brent Mittelstadt), a wide-ranging discussion of the dangers and pitfalls of blackboxing emotional life through affective media is encouraged.

1.   Affect Regulation

The title of this contribution combines two concepts that for heuristic reasons demand some separate considerations: "affect regulation" and "affective media." This section will start with a brief overview of the terms "affect regulation" and "emotion regulation," which have been used in sociology and psychology for some decades now and refer to an individual's capacity to self-regulate affects or emotions, following the assumption that some affective episodes a subject might experience necessitate a decrease of their psychophysical effects, while some social situations demand an increase of emotional expressivity and intensity.[1]

In the 1930s, the German sociologist Norbert Elias established the hypothesis that *The Civilizing Process* largely depends on the progressional strengthening of individuals' capacities of affect regulation. According to

---

1   The question of how a terminological difference between affects and emotions might be articulated will be addressed in section 3, "Affective Difference."

him, "as the social fabric grows more intricate, the sociogenic apparatus of individual self-control also becomes more differentiated, more all-round and more stable" (Elias 2000, 369). Constraints from the outside are replaced by internal constraints in an ongoing process of subjectification. In Western society, the "web of actions grows so complex and extensive, the effort to behave 'correctly' within it becomes so great, that beside the individual's conscious self-control an automatic, blindly functioning apparatus of self-control is firmly established" (367f.). One historically decisive step within this ongoing process was, according to Elias, the monopolization of physical force. By transferring the right to exert force to the state, citizens were pressured to develop habits and routines that would hold their more violent desires and urges at bay. Sociogenesis thus goes hand in hand with psychogenesis, the modeling or patterning of the psychic apparatus,[2] which requires an ever "higher degree of automaticity" (369).

The metaphor of an "apparatus" is most probably owed to the influence of Sigmund Freud, whose terminology one encounters frequently over the course of the text.[3] But apart from his clear nod to Freud and the psycho-analytical notion of unconscious defense mechanisms, the way that Elias presents his socio- and psychogenetic theory points toward an ongoing technologization of affect regulation as well. Not only does he rely heavily on comparisons of psychic life in a functionally highly differentiated society with the dangers and pitfalls of partaking in a modern, urban traffic system (368), he even resorts to a striking metaphor when he asserts that "as the conveyer belts running through their existence grow longer and more complex, individuals learn to control themselves more steadily; they are now less a prisoner of their passions than before" (374). This image of a technical device as something that pervades modern human life,[4] and in doing so gives the individual capacity for self-control a clear direction,

---

2   This is a strong parallel to Gilbert Simondon's concept of "psychic and collective individuation" (see Combes 2013, 25–30). For a comparison between Elias', Freud's, Weber's, and Adorno's respective solutions of how to cross the "psycho-social divide," see Cavalletto (2007).

3   For a comparison of Freud's *Civilization and Its Discontents* and Elias' *The Civilizing Process*, including some heavy criticism of their respective speculations, see Redner (2015).

4   The conveyor belt was invented in the late 19th century, but only with Henry Ford's introduction of the conveyor-belt assembly line in 1913 was a turning point for industrial production reached. Charlie Chaplin's iconic depiction of the industrial worker whose movements and perceptions get entirely reprogrammed by such an apparatus (in *Modern Times*, 1936) is one of the strongest commentaries on the purported neutrality of technology. It is conceivable that Elias saw that movie and

shows that Elias was acknowledging technology as a realm that influences and transforms psychological mechanisms (moreover, the metaphor "mechanism" that had been used to describe psychological processes since at least the 19th century proves that technology has already been recognized as a medium). Although Elias did not elaborate further on this pre-computer age image, it reads like a premonition of things to come. By resorting to modern traffic and production systems, he almost develops a cybernetic stance towards the regulation of affects and psychological processes. From a discourse analytical view, his frequent use of the term "control," both as noun and verb, exacerbates that impression. Historically speaking, the conception and development of automatic systems of control was only one step away, with the Macy Conferences that inaugurated the cybernetic movement starting in 1946 (Pias 2003; 2004). Generally speaking, there is no reason to assume that Elias' general thesis of the civilizing process requiring increasingly "higher degrees of automaticity" would come to any sort of halt with the development of computerized systems.

Apart from that, the attention that Elias devoted to processes of regulation—in this case of affects and desires—can also be understood as an informative example of what Georges Canguilhem once described as a general adoption of the concept of regulation that had become increasingly central in late 19th-century biology and had from then spread into social sciences (2017).

Recently, the historical scope of regulation—both as an idea and as a melting pot of techniques of governance—has been reconsidered by Frédéric Gros in his Foucault-inspired genealogical narrative concerning *The Security Principle* (2019). Gros distinguishes four separate dimensions as well as ages of security: (1) the spiritual age, when security was still understood as "tranquility of mind" (via the translation of Greek *ataraxia* into Latin *securitas*, which literally means "being free of care/concern"); (2) the imperial age, when security basically meant "absence of danger," which was to be brought about by a millenarian Empire (an idea that came into its own in the High Middle Ages); (3) the modern age, when security was mostly understood as a set of nation-state guarantees that circle around the notion of sovereignty; and (4) the biopolitical age, when instead of the sovereign state, the life of the individual is considered untouchable, so that "everything that is involved in the life of civil populations becomes an object of security" (Gros 2014, 23f.). In the context of this contribution,

that the scene in question inspired him to coin this image of "conveyor belts running through existence."

it is of particular significance that Gros also mentions "affective security" among the many newly defined biopolitical security concerns. Referring to child psychologists Margaret Mahler and Donald Winnicott, he thereby suggests that a child "must feel surrounded by a protective barrier, safe from external threats" so as to guarantee continuous and regulated "flows of communication and affection" between the caregivers and him- or herself (25). The term "flow" delineates what is probably the main concern of biopolitical security—Gros speaks of "flow control" (27) as the (decentralized) control of movements and communications; be it crowds at airports, train stations and borders, be it money, information, or affect, the flow of all these objects must be regulated at all times. Thus, with the perspective provided first by Foucault and now by Gros, we can understand this shift of interest to questions of control and regulation as a general and global shift in the dynamics of power—as a transition from older forms of power to what is now usually called biopower, as well as to what Bernard Stiegler proposed to dub "psychopower" (Stiegler 2010; van Camp 2012).

Given the scope of this transformation of the meaning of "security" throughout so many areas of political and social life—the ongoing securitization of territories, populations and properties through innovative techniques and technologies—it is somewhat surprising that within psychology, the term "regulation" has gained prominence rather late. Although questions of affective security have pervaded psy-disciplines from the outset, terms like "affect regulation" or "emotion regulation" only seemed to come into their own in the 1990s. In 1994, the neuropsychologist Allan Schore published his seminal *Affect Regulation and the Origin of the Self*, which integrates a neuroscientific approach with psychoanalytic theories of attachment. Schore hypothesizes that "the infant's affective interactions with the early human environment directly and indelibly influence the postnatal maturation of brain structures that will regulate all future socioemotional functioning" (1994, xxx). In other words, the capacity to self-regulate one's affects and emotions is said to be largely constituted through the interaction style of the primary caregiver. Any self-regulation of affect thus has a "dyadic origin" (31), meaning that auto-regulation is based on hetero-regulation in such a fundamental fashion that it complicates the whole notion of affective autonomization.

There is a second strand of psychological research that raised the term "regulation" to prominence. In the late 1990s, clinical psychologist James Gross introduced the concept of "emotion regulation" in a series of papers, and with the publication of the *Handbook of Emotion Regulation* (2007), the term obviously gained a central status in empirical psychology.[5] Gross's definition of his basic term, in contrast to Schore, is focused on the adult person when we writes that "emotion regulation refers to shaping which emotions one has, when one has them, and how one experiences or expresses these emotions" (2014, 6). Regardless of how these different approaches come about, they at least seem to imply a fully conscious, experienced, and more or less self-reflective person. This is best shown by referring to his schematization of five general ways to regulate one's emotions (Gross 1999, 559f.): (1) situation selection, which refers to approaching or avoiding certain people or experiences that are likely to elicit a certain emotion; (2) situation modification, which refers to "modifying the local environment so as to alter its emotional impact"; (3) the deployment of attention, which can influence the way an emotion unfolds once it has begun to take its effect; (4) cognitive change, meaning a re-evaluation of the situation can alter its emotional significance; and (5), the modulation of physiological responding (like controlling one's breath), which can alleviate the impact of even strong emotions. Whereas the first two tactics concern an individual's way of referring to his or her environment, the other three focus on modifications in the psychophysical system. The question of which tactics are used is of utmost importance, because if one would exclude situation selection and modification, one would reduce emotion regulation to an "inner" mechanism and thereby radically individualize and de-politicize it. It is especially important to keep the political question in mind when emotion regulation is being automatized through the use of responsive or adaptive media—which finally brings us to the second term that this contribution's title alludes to.

2. Affective Media

Even though the expression "affective media" has been used by scholars around the globe increasingly over the last few years, a clear-cut definition is, to the best of my knowledge, something yet to be arrived at. Theater scholar David Saltz once assigned affective media a specific place in his taxonomy of live media and described them as "nondiegetic" and "most often auditory," as in background music on stage and in film, but also including visual means of communicating emotions a character might feel (2001, 125).[6]

---

5   It is worth noting that Schore's research does not even get a mention in the *Handbook*, which can be read as a clear indication about how radically disconnected from each other the various psy-disciplines seem to be.

6   Understood in this sense, "affective media" and "atmospheric media" could probably be used interchangeably.

In 2012, in a special issue of the journal *Feminist Media Studies* on "mobile intimacy," the editors coined the term "affective mobile media" (Hjorth and Lim 2012), but did not bother to elaborate on it further. In recent communication studies, "affective media" has become just another phrase for "collaborative Web 2.0 technologies" (Jutel 2017, 337), more commonly known as social media.

So how can the term "affective media" be defined in a meaningful way? Rosalind Picard, figurehead of the affective computing research field, gives us a decisive hint, as she occasionally uses the more generic "affective media" when writing about her own research (2014). In contrast to the above-mentioned usage of this term, her approach refers to media that do not just elicit affects and emotions (which is something that could be attributed to virtually any medium), but that purportedly detect emotions and generate emotional expressions.

To get a better grasp of the specific quality of Picard's (albeit fleeting) use of the term, Friedrich Kittler's classical definition of what he called the "three basic functions of media" might be of help. According to the German literary-scholar-turned-media-theorist, technical media work in three ways: they transmit, they store, and they process (Kittler 1999, 244). Now, conceptualizing storage and transmission of information (or affect—even though this is admittedly not at all Kittler's focus) as basic media functions is a rather uncontroversial move. Writing, for example, stores information, and thus makes it accessible across time; it also transmits information to readers at a distance from the location where the writing took place, thus making it accessible across space. But what about the third media function, processing? Within Kittler's writing, it is clear that he introduces it always in conjunction with the computer (and its internal central processing unit). Adopting this more specific, computer-based media function, we can now come up with a working definition: *Affective media are computational media capable of detecting signals from humans, interpreting them as affects, and using this interpretation for interactive purposes.* Thus, affective media are affect-responsive media, or media capable of processing affect.

Having come up with a working definition, the main thesis of this article can now be developed further. *With the emergence of affective media, affect or emotion regulation is undergoing a decisive transformation, as it increasingly becomes externalized.* Thus regulation decreasingly depends on habitual techniques of either self-regulating one's emotions or regulating the emotions of others (like caregivers do), and is increasingly facilitated by automated systems that process our affective expressions and nudge us toward certain behaviors and, thereby, a purportedly more satisfying personal life. *With the advent of affective media, we are standing at the beginning of what can be called affective media regulation, understood as media-assisted, automatic affect regulation of individuals as well as populations.*

Still, as handy as the adoption of Kittler's third media function may be, it entails further questions. Intuitively, the term "processing" might seem to explain itself, but the closer one looks, the more difficult it becomes to grasp it clearly. As media scholar Hartmut Winkler (2015) has pointed out in his monograph *Prozessieren*, it is rather surprising that the exact meaning of "processing" has remained unquestioned for decades, which is why he dubs it the "neglected" third media function. It will be informative to recapitulate some of Winkler's findings, as they may provide insights into what the processing of affect by technical media actually means.

Stressing that "processing" is not just a term that pertains to something computers do, Winkler explores the concept in all its semantic richness. To process can just mean to handle or to manipulate something in the neutral sense of the term. Its most simple meaning covers the material transmission of something: an item of mail, an order, a commodity. In the widest sense of the term, all processes that involve media thus encompass some type of processing. But, of course, things get much more interesting when there is some kind of change involved—when "processing" pertains to some kind of alteration or modification of the very object that is being processed. Winkler thus comes to his definition of processing as "interfering modification" (Winkler 2015, 31).[7] This allows him to further differentiate between a generic concept of modification, which includes for example the work of film editors who manipulate film strips and thereby literally create a new product, and a more specific concept that Winkler limits to the "manipulation of words and numbers," as done by authors as well as computers. Both dimensions of "interfering modification" include material aspects, even if the output is not itself a material product, as is the case with computational processes. Moreover, every interfering modification is at the same time a kind of transformation (33–37), or an alteration of a pregiven form.[8]

Following these basic considerations, which include non-computational processing practices, it is possible to get a better idea of what computers

7   "Eingreifende Veränderung" in the original German version.
8   In some cases, if the source material cannot be said to have had a form by itself, interfering modification can also mean the conferral of form, or in-formation in the processual sense of the term (Winkler 2015, 74–77).

specifically do: they rearrange data by following mechanical and syntactical procedures. They transform input data into output data. In the case of computer programs that are deliberately designed to create output that is meaningful for users, we can say that the rearrangement equals a transformation of data into symbolically mediated information (114f.). By turning to affective media, we can try to make sense of Winkler's descriptions and at the same time test whether they provide us with a better understanding of what technologies like affective computing actually achieve.

The source material for affective media processing encompasses a whole array of data. In principle, all modes of affective expression are exploited: facial expressions, body movements, speech prosody, texts, and interactions with software, as well as physiological states or changes, such as heartbeat, skin resistance, muscle tension, respiratory rate, and electrical brain activity (Healey 2015). To measure physiological signals, sensors that have to be worn on the body are required, which of course makes everyday usage more difficult. But "affective wearables" have come a long way since Rosalind Picard first propagated their use for affect detection (1997, 227–46). The emergence of smartphones and specialized self-tracking gadgetry makes the fulfillment of Picard's hopes and promises more likely. Apart from this passive tracking of body data, so-called active tracking is still being used, which means intentional input by the user, such as in "mood tracking" applications (Pritz 2016), which depend on active feedback (e.g., through an emoticonized answer to the app's question about the user's current mood).

Andrew McStay, who has spoken with more than 100 interviewees within the emotional artificial intelligence (AI) community, reports in his monograph *Emotional AI: The Rise of Empathic Media* that there is a very strong bias against users' self-reporting when it comes to the goal of emotion detection. Many developers seem to share the "belief that understanding of affect through observation, neuroscience and biometrics is innately more objective" (McStay 2018, 60) than what individuals might say when asked about their current emotional status. Obviously, this focus on technology-assisted observation entails a rather behavioristic view, if with a twist, because "the conscious self is not denied, but instead not trusted" (60). The underlying assumption is that machines, at least in principle, if not in present reality, can detect what an individual is experiencing more accurately than the conscious self of that individual is able to.

This trust in machinic sentience is based on a well-publicized strand of contemporary psychology: the theory that there is a fixed set of genetically programmed basic emotions and that these emotions all have distinct and recognizable expressive features. The most famous proponent of this theory is Paul Ekman, who claims to have discovered the universal facial expressions of six basic emotions, and who developed the Facial Action Coding System, which has been adopted by a large part of the affective computing community.[9] Affective media applying this method are connected to ever-expanding databases of examples of tagged facial emotions. They track muscles and movements around the mouth, nose and eyes and identify so-called action units that are then used to infer which emotion(s) are present and to what extent.

Criticism of this technological adoption of a theory that is far from uncontested among researchers has been made both without and within the affective computing field (Tuschling 2014; Lisetti and Hudlicka 2015). McStay sums up the reservations about Ekman's universalist and reductionist approach accurately and concludes "that facial coding is not neutral because it is laden with social theory that informs the weighting of expression classifiers, algorithms and interpretation of the data" (2018, 71f.). This acknowledgment is founded in social constructionist theories of emotion, which McStay subdivides into a "strong constructionist view" that argues against the whole idea of innate basic emotions, and a "weak constructionist view" that admits to the existence of basic emotions but stresses that this explains little, considering how inseparable emotional life is from social and cultural practices that inevitably inform emotional expressions. While refraining from strong claims regarding the implementation of automated facial coding in affective, or, as he calls it, "empathic media," McStay wisely asserts that such applications "present a clear articulation of emotional life" (69). In other words, affective media process and transform physiological data into meaningful, but biased emotion categories.

3. Affective Difference

Facial coding may be the most common automated emotion detection method, but it's by no means the only one. Voice-based methods are used increasingly via smartphone apps, and given the logistical advantage they have over facial observation (which requires that a camera be positioned

9   "Using this model, expert FACS coders analyze a facial expression frame by frame to identify groups of active muscles and then apply well defined rules to map these muscle activation patterns into discrete emotion categories" (Bianchi-Berthouze and Kleinsmith 2015, 156).

in front of the user's face), they may become even more influential in the future. Apart from that, voice-based affect analytics may also profit from the widely shared assumption that it is much more difficult to deflect detection of arousal, worry, fear, or other affective states in one's speech than it is to control one's facial muscles. The same applies to trackings of physiological data.

But regardless of the exact method affective media use, emotion detection is rooted in the assumption that emotions cannot be entirely concealed but are always accompanied by involuntary physiological movements or signals—in other words, that they "leak" (McStay 2018, 55). Likely the best metaphor for this idea has been brought forward by psychologist and neuroscientist Lisa Feldman Barrett. In her book *How Emotions Are Made*, she recapitulates the global quest for what she calls "emotional fingerprints"—the idea that each emotion has a "distinct pattern of physical changes, roughly like a fingerprint" (Feldman Barrett 2017, 3).[10] If this assumption were true, then the purported skills of affective media to correctly identify these emotions when they occur would at least epistemologically stand on solid ground. The question would then just be how accurate detection software works, as in principle it would be perfectly conceivable that emotions could be automatically and validly detected and labeled. But Feldman Barrett questions this very assumption, and her research can be regarded as the most encompassing attack of what she calls the "classical view of emotion" yet. According to her, the search for universal physiological and/or neurological markers has rather produced evidence to the contrary, namely that with emotional expressiveness "variation is the norm," and that emotion fingerprints are nothing but a myth (23). Her anti-Ekmanian account draws its plausibility from her own research, which for a long time followed the classical view of emotions, i.e., that each emotion is accompanied and even constituted by a "collection of movements on the inside and outside" (x) of a body—a concept that she sums up with the image of the brain as a container for several distinct emotion circuits that function just like electrical circuits in a machine.

After first having unsuccessfully applied this theory in her research, and after having then conducted a comprehensive meta-analysis of, as she claims, "every published neuroimaging study on anger, disgust, happiness, fear, and sadness," Feldman Barrett and her team of researchers concluded that there is "little to support the classical view of emotion," that "no brain

---

10   For a concise definition of the "fingerprint hypothesis" and its localization in the
      autonomous nervous system, see Siegel et al. (2018).

region contained the fingerprint for any single emotion," and further that even considering "multiple connected regions at once (a brain network)," no such fingerprints can be found (20–22). Leaving the classical view behind, she holds that emotions are socially constructed and that with the probable exception of the feelings of pleasure and pain, there are no telltale signs that would reliably indicate to an observer what the observed subjects may be experiencing at any given time.

After making a case for a strong constructionist view of emotions, Feldman Barrett reserves the term "affect" for "the general sense of feeling you experience throughout each day" (72). This simple conception of feeling includes just two aspects: valence, as the dimension of pleasantness or unpleasantness, and arousal, as the dimension of agitation or calmness. Affect is registered through the sense of interoception, of feeling the internal state of the body. As such, it accompanies a sentient body during its whole life span. It represents the body's overall condition and thus helps to regulate what Barrett calls the "body budget": "Your affective feelings of pleasure and displeasure, and calmness and agitation, are simple summaries of your budgetary state" (73). They do not indicate intentionality, like emotions are usually said to do. But they lead us to "believe that objects and people in the world are inherently negative or positive," which means they are estimated to impact the body budget either to its disadvantage or advantage (75).[11] This should come as no surprise since bodies are not closed systems: they rather exist in constant processual exchange with their environments and especially with their "affective niche" (73), meaning the things and persons in the surroundings that are predicted to have an impact on the overall body budget.

Where affect is the constantly fluctuating feeling of a body's condition, emotion is, according to Feldman Barrett, a kind of meaning-making that interprets those physical feelings on the basis of acquired emotional knowledge. It goes without saying that such knowledge is socially constructed and varies within parameters like culture, language, milieu, class, gender, ethnicity, religion, family-based values, and so on. "Emotions are not reactions to the world; they are your constructions of the world" (104)—this is how Feldman Barrett sums up this shift in understanding emotions

---

11   Readers of Spinoza will most likely recognize that this conception of bodily affect mirrors the Dutch philosopher's definitions of what he calls the three basic affects: the *conatus*, or striving to maintain the body's capacities, joy if these capacities are increased, and pain if they are decreased (Spinoza 2018).

on the basis of what could be called "affective difference."[12] In other words, brains process and transform physiological data into meaningful, but probably (and necessarily) biased emotion categories—just like affective media do, as was explored at the end of the preceding section. It must be stressed that "processing" here also means "meaning-making," and that "to make meaning is to go beyond the information given" (126). This is done by applying categories that have been gathered over the life span. Feldman Barrett sums up her theory with an instructive example:

> When you experience affect with unpleasant valence and high arousal, you make meaning from it depending on how you categorize ... If you categorize the sensations as fear, you are making meaning that says, 'Fear is what caused these physical changes in my body.' When the concepts involved are emotion concepts, your brain constructs instances of emotion. (126)

The more emotional categories individuals have at their disposal, the more accurate the categorization of their affective states is at any given moment. The term that Feldman Barrett proposes for the ability to experience one's affective states in a more or less finegrained way is "emotional granularity" (3). In psychology, the observation of patients who were unable to verbalize feelings occasioned the creation of a construct called "alexithymia," which gained terminological status in 1976 (Taylor and Bagby 2000, 40). Alexithymia is a disposition (or condition) that makes it difficult to verbally express affective differences, whereas, on the other end of the spectrum, high emotional granularity is a solid basis on which to verbalize those differences, and even to create new concepts if those that are used in a given language do not seem sufficient for capturing recurrent contours of feeling.

We are now ready to ask a decisive—and probably provocative—question: *Is the externalization of affect regulation via affective media the fastest way of decreasing emotional granularity among its users, meaning that they will gradually lose (or not develop) their ability to verbalize their feelings in an adequate and versatile way? In other words, is the implementation of affective media regulation in reality the fastest road to collective alexithymia? And are we willingly approving a kind of "blackboxing" of affect regulation?* If we remember that affective media process physiological data and categorize them by using simple standard models of emotion and emotional expression, then we also have to acknowledge that such automated categorization

---

12   The obvious similarities and differences to Brian Massumi's distinction between "affect" and "emotion" (2002) cannot be further discussed here. For a discussion of this "affective difference" and its possible further conceptualization, see Bösel (2017).

creates a conceptual reality. Affective media regulation thus entails what we could call "self-fulfilling processing"[13]—a processing that fundamentally shapes emotional experience instead of just detecting it, as many developers want users to believe.

4.   Regulating Affective Media

The phrase "affective media regulation" can now finally be understood in yet another sense: as the regulation of affective media themselves, for instance through legal frameworks or through rules and cautions users develop and follow in their interactions with such media.

There are, of course, many reasons why regulative frameworks regarding the collection of so-called affective data should be implemented—first and foremost, the possible (and actual) abuse of such data through third parties, such as companies, governments, political parties, or fraudsters. In her widely discussed *The Age of Surveillance Capitalism*, Shoshana Zuboff refers, amidst many other examples, to the development of affective computing applications over the past twenty years and ultimately points out their susceptibility to exploitation. The basic argument of her book is that with the discovery of what she calls "behavioral surplus" by Google in the early 2000s, capitalism entered a new phase. Where classical capitalism worked on the premise of a lack of predictability among market patterns, surveillance capitalism utilizes technologies that give its strong actors the means to collect sufficiently precise data in order to predict the behavior of users and consumers. "Surveillance capitalism thus replaces mystery with certainty as it substitutes rendition, behavioral modification, and prediction for the old 'unsurveyable pattern'" (Zuboff 2019, 497). She gives Rosalind Picard some credit for having developed affective computing in both theory and practice with good intentions (285), but ultimately comes to the conclusion that Picard "did not foresee the market forces that would transform the rendition of emotion into for-profit surplus: means to others' ends." (291) In the course of successfully establishing her research area, Picard, perhaps inadvertently, became "part of this new dispossession industry" (287). The company Affectiva that she co-founded with her student Rana el Kaliouby quickly turned to conducting exclusively profit-oriented market research and discarding medical and assistive applications for which the affective computing project had been founded. Picard's departure from the company didn't halt its commercial momentum. El

---

13   I want to thank my colleague Sebastian Möring, who invented this rather fitting pun in a conversation with me, for his permission to use it here.

Kaliouby is very outspoken in her endorsement of technological solutions to the problem of how to optimize one's emotional life, promoting so-called emotion chips as standard modules in technical devices, capable of an ubiquitous and permanent "emotion scanning."

Considering how vast our knowledge of the deliberate misuse of per-sonlalized data has already become, regulatory mechanisms for companies that provide affect detection software seem an inevitability if one wants to preserve the conditions for personal autonomy that are pivotal in demo-cratic systems. Consumers and users should have the right to be informed about affective data being collected and their supposed emotional states being measured and tagged. Legal scholars have recently pointed out that data protection laws should not just make sure that subjects have con-trol over how their personal data are being collected and processed, but also how they are evaluated, meaning: What inferences are being drawn by AI? Such inferences are being used "to nudge or manipulate us, or to make important decisions (e.g., loan or employment decisions) about us" (Wachter and Mittelstadt 2019, 4). The authors clarify that inferences may have been the main factor in the ongoing debate on the ethics of AI all along: "Concerns about algorithmic accountability are often actually concerns about the way in which these technologies draw privacy-invasive and non-verifiable inferences that cannot be predicted, understood, or refuted" (4). They further argue that "a new data protection right, the 'right to reasonable inferences,' is needed to help close the accountability gap currently posed by 'high-risk inferences'" (7).

Biases in AI have been well publicized in the past few years (O'Neil 2016; Pasquale 2015). In the field of "artifical emotional intelligence," racialized bias has been reported in a study that looked into the emotional analytics of male basketball players' portrait photos: black faces were inferred as expressing more negative emotions than white faces (Rhue 2019). But the systemic bias begins even earlier, namely with the tagging of facial expressions or other sensory data as being indicative of a certain discrete emotional state itself. If emotional granularity, introduced by Feldman Barrett as the ability to verbally express one's affective states in a highly differentiated manner, is understood as being intrinsically valuable, then affective media that rely on contested—if not simply outdated—theories of supposed universal basic emotions contribute to what can be called emotional stereotyping, thereby inadvertently diminishing emotional granularity. This problem could at the least be alleviated by making it a legal requirement to point out which psychological models affect detection software puts into practice.

Regulating affective media would of course have to go beyond simply regulating how affects get detected, captured, and classified, and instead encompass the way affects get automatically elicited and modified. In this regard, affective media go much further than merely regulating affect in the sense of Norbert Elias, whose theory of the civilizing process revolved around increasing inhibition of affective expressions. Let us imagine for a moment that a fully attentive and affectively versatile digital personal agent does actually exist: How does it know in which direction to steer the person it is assisting? How is the emotional target state defined?

The literature on affective computing remains astonishingly vague on the question of what affective goals it is actually trying to achieve. In a discussion of the ethical aspects of affective computing, the utilitarian imperative of "maximizing net happiness" is readily cited (Cowie 2015, 338)—but without addressing the obvious question of how happiness is defined in the first place. Some researchers and developers in the affective computing arena have begun resorting to Martin Seligman's and Mihaly Csikszentmihalyi's (2000) "positive psychology" and accordingly call for "positive technology" (Riva et al. 2012) or "positive computing" (Calvo and Peters 2014), each of which would specifically be designed to increase users' well-being. With this focus on positive experience, issues like digital addiction, stress, frustration, or attention deficits, which have all been linked to digital environments and interfaces, are addressed and countered in a way that deserves some recognition. At the same time, this reliance on the seemingly helpful positive psychology framework ignores how much controversy it has caused from the outset (Kristjánsson 2013; Ehrenreich 2009; Miller 2008; Held 2004). But considering the enormous academic and commercial success, in addition to the sociopolitical acceptance of the positive psychology movement, the embracing of affective media by developers seems almost inevitable. This is why a broader engagement with concepts like "happiness," "well-being," and "human flourishing" is something to be desired.

Finally, one remark on the possible future of automated affect regulation. It has become something of a truism to point out the dangers and pitfalls of relying too heavily on digital services and devices, starting with the unwanted effects of not knowing what to do or how to do what one wants to do without help from our gadgets that didn't even exist a generation ago, and ending with serious digital addiction issues or possibly life-threatening mental health problems that are linked to social media usage. Nevertheless, the prospect of externalizing one's capacity for affect regulation apparently has not yet received widespread discussion or even attention.

This may change within the current media landscape, which is swift not only in promoting new technologies, but also in scandalizing them whenever a case of precedence raises serious concerns, even if one may wonder why this has not hitherto been the case. One reason may be that users of digital services are used to recommendation algorithms that work best when they suggest content that is sufficiently similar to what has produced positive affect before, and still offers something new or surprising. As long as algorithms work on that basis, users will not be seriously startled by the way they are influenced by their devices. As a result of their functional inconspicuousness, recommendation algorithms operate more or less below the radar of critical attentiveness. Programmed to elicit emotional responses, affective computing will likewise use cues that have proven successful in previous instances.

If you enjoy going for a walk, but haven't done so in a while, and your mood has become rather unstable, nudging you to pick up your positive habit again is a safe bet with regard to emotional well-being. Let us imagine, in contrast, affective media that influence you to behave in a way that is not at all in line with your habits and dispositions. A digital personal assistant that is not restricted in any way might come to the conclusion that "maximizing net happiness" would entail quitting your job, leaving your home, and tending sheep in the countryside. Or it might discourage you from further pursuing your political activism, because it might involve health risks, and, in the long run, will only foster your frustration with the global political situation.

As contrived as these examples might be, they hopefully point out that the blackboxing of affect regulation might lead to a serious disempowerment of moral and political subjects. Depending on how closely knit the ties between private companies working solely on capitalist terms and either ideological movements or governmental agencies become, influencing populations by steering each individual into a targeted emotional disposition might become an affordance readily provided by future affective media—which would mean that these media may become a serious threat to democracy. As with many other issues pertaining to the disruptive effects of new technologies, the conversation on how affective media should be regulated has yet to begin—and this conversation must encompass the legal and sociopolitical as well as the ethical levels.

References

Bianchi-Berthouze, Nadia, and Andrea Kleinsmith. 2015. "Automatic Recognition of Affective Body Expressions." In *The Oxford Handbook of Affective Computing*, edited by Rafael A. Calvo, Sidney K. D'Mello, Jonathan Gratch, and Arvid Kappas, 151–69. New York: Oxford University Press.

Bösel, Bernd. 2017. "Affektive Differenzen, oder: Zwischen Insonanz und Resonanz." In *Resonanzen und Dissonanzen: Hartmut Rosas kritische Theorie in der Diskussion*, edited by Christian Helge Peters and Peter Schulz, 33–51. Bielefeld: Transcript.

Calvo, Rafael A., and Dorian Peters. 2014. *Positive Computing: Technology for Wellbeing and Human Potential*. Cambridge, MA: MIT Press.

Canguilhem, Georges. 2017. *Regulation und Leben*. Berlin: August Verlag.

Cavalletto, George. 2007. *Crossing the Psycho-Social Divide: Freud, Weber, Adorno and Elias*. Aldershot: Ashgate.

Combes, Muriel. 2013. *Gilbert Simondon and the Philosophy of the Transindividual*. Cambridge, MA: MIT Press.

Cowie, Roddy. 2015. "Ethical Issues in Affective Computing." In *The Oxford Handbook of Affective Computing*, edited by Rafael A. Calvo, Sidney K. D'Mello, Jonathan Gratch, and Arvid Kappas, 334–48. New York: Oxford University Press.

Ehrenreich, Barbara. 2009. *Smile or Die: How Positive Thinking Fooled America & The World*. London: Granta.

Elias, Norbert. 2000. *The Civilizing Process: Sociogenetic and Psychogenetic Investigations*. Malden, MA: Blackwell Publishing.

Feldman Barrett, Lisa. 2017. *How Emotions Are Made: The Secret Life of the Brain*. London: Pan Books.

Gros, Frédéric. 2019. *The Principle of Security: From Serenity to Regulation*. London: Verso Books.

———. 2014. "The Fourth Age of Security." In *The Government of Life: Foucault, Biopolitics, and Neoliberalism*, edited by Vanessa Lemm and Miguel Vatter, 17–28. New York: Fordham University Press.

Gross, James J. 1999. "Emotion Regulation: Past, Present, Future." *Cognition & Emotion* 13 (5): 551–73.

Gross, James J., ed. 2007. *The Handbook of Emotion Regulation*. New York: Guilford Press.

Gross, James J. 2014. "Emotion Regulation: Conceptual and Empirical Foundations." In *The Handbook of Emotion Regulation. Second Edition*, edited by James J. Gross, 3–20. New York: Guilford Press.

Healey, Jennifer. 2015. "Physiological Sensing of Emotion." In *The Oxford Handbook of Affective Computing*, edited by Rafael A. Calvo, Sidney K. D'Mello, Jonathan Gratch, and Arvid Kappas, 204–16. New York: Oxford University Press.

Held, Barbara S. 2004. "The Negative Side of Positive Psychology." *Journal of Humanistic Psychology* 44 (1): 9–46.

Hjorth, Larissa, and Sun Sun Lim, ed. 2012. "Guest Editors' Introduction: Mobile Intimacy in an Age of Affective Mobile Media." *Feminist Media Studies* 12 (4): 477–84.

Jutel, Olivier. 2017. "Affective Media, Cyberlibertarianism and the New Zealand Internet Party." *Triple-C* 15 (1): 337–54.

Kittler, Friedrich A. 1999. *Gramophone, Film, Typewriter*. Stanford, CA: Stanford University Press.

Kristjánsson, Kristján. 2013. *Virtues and Vices in Positive Psychology: A Philosophical Critique*. Cambridge: Cambridge University Press.

Lisetti, Christine, and Eva Hudlicka. 2015. "Why and How to Build Emotion-Based Agent Architectures." In: *The Oxford Handbook of Affective Computing*, edited by Rafael A. Calvo, Sidney K. D'Mello, Jonathan Gratch, and Arvid Kappas, 94–109. New York: Oxford University Press.

Massumi, Brian. 2002. "The Autonomy of Affect." In *Parables for the Virtual: Movement, Affect, Sensation*, 23–45. Durham, NC: Duke University Press.

McStay, Andrew. 2018. *Emotional AI: The Rise of Empathic Media.* Los Angeles: Sage.

Miller, Alistair. 2008. "A Critique of Positive Psychology—or 'The New Science of Happiness.'" *Journal of Philosophy of Education* 42 (3–4): 591–608.

O'Neil, Cathy. 2016. *Weapons of Math Destruction: How Big Data Increases Inequality and Threatens Democracy.* New York: Crown Publishing.

Pasquale, Frank. 2015. *The Black Box Society: The Secret Algorithms that Control Money and Information.* Cambridge, MA: Harvard University Press.

Pias, Claus, ed. 2003. *Cybernetics—Kybernetik: The Macy Conferences 1946–1953, Bd. I: Protokolle.* Zürich: diaphanes.

———, ed. 2004. *Cybernetics—Kybernetik: The Macy Conferences 1946–1953, Bd. II: Essays und Dokumente.* Zürich: diaphanes.

Picard, Rosalind. 1997. *Affective Computing.* Cambridge, MA: MIT Press.

———. 2014. "Affective Media and Wearables: Surprising Findings." *MM '14. Proceedings of the 22nd ACM International Conference on Multimedia*, 3–4.

Pritz, Sarah Miriam. 2016. "Mood Tracking: Zur digitalen Selbstvermessung der Gefühle." In *Lifelogging*, edited by Stefan Selke, 127–50. Wiesbaden: Springer.

Redner, Henry. 2015. "The Civilizing Process—According to Mennel, Elias and Freud: A Critique." *Thesis Eleven* 127 (1): 95–111.

Rhue, Lauren. 2019. "Emotion-reading Tech Fails the Racial Bias Test." *The Conversation.* January 3, https://theconversation.com/ emotion-reading-tech-fails-the-racial-bias-test-108404.

Riva, Giuseppe, Rosa M. Banos, Cristina Botella, Brenda K. Wiederhold, et al. 2012. "Positive Technology: Using Interactive Technologies to Promote Positive Functioning." *Cyberpsychology, Behavior, and Social Networking.* 15 (2): 69–77.

Saltz, David Z. 2001. "Live Media: Interactive Technologies and Theatre." *Theatre Topics* 11 (2): 107–30.

Schore, Allan N. 1982. "Foreword." In John Bowlby: *Attachment: Attachment and Loss, Vol. 1.* New York: Basic Books.

———. 1994. *Affect Regulation and the Origin of Self.* Hillsdale, NJ: Lawrence Erlbaum Associates.

Seligman, Martin, and Mihaly Csikszentmihalyi. 2000. "Positive Psychology." *American Psychologist* 55 (1): 5–14.

Siegel, Erika H., Molly K. Sands, Wim Van den Noortgate, Paul Condon, et al. 2018. "Emotion Fingerprints or Emotion Populations? A Meta-Analytic Investigation of Autonomic Features of Emotion Categories." *Psychological Bulletin* 144 (4): 343–93.

Spinoza, Baruch de. 2018. *Ethics: Proved in Geometrical Order.* Edited by Matthew J. Kisner. Cambridge: Cambridge University Press.

Stiegler, Bernard. 2010. *Taking Care of Youth and the Generations.* Stanford, CA: Stanford University Press.

Taylor, Graeme J., and Michael R. Bagby. 2000. "An Overview of the Alexithymia Construct." In *The Handbook of Emotional Intelligence: Theory, Development, Assessment, and Application at Home, School, and in the Workplace*, edited by Reuven Bar-On and James D. A. Parker, 40–59. San Francisco: Jossey-Bass.

Tuschling, Anna. 2014. "The Age of Affective Computing." In *Timing of Affect: Epistemologies, Aesthetics, Politics*, edited by Marie-Luise Angerer, Bernd Bösel, and Michaela Ott, 179–90. Zürich: diaphanes.

van Camp, Nathan. 2012. "From Biopower to Psychopower: Bernard Stiegler's Pharmacology of Mnemotechnologies." In *CTheory*, www.ctheory.net/articles.aspx?id=706.

Wachter, Sandra, and Brent Mittelstadt. 2019. "A Right to Reasonable Inferences: Re-Thinking Data Protection Law in the Age of Big Data and AI." *Columbia Business Law Review* 2019 (2): 494–620.

Winkler, Hartmut. 2015. *Prozessieren: Die dritte, vernachlässigte Medienfunktion*. Paderborn: Wilhelm Fink.

Zuboff, Shoshana. 2019. *The Age of Surveillance Capitalism: The Fight for a Human Future at the New Frontier of Power*. London: Profile Books.

PSY DATA

BOTS

MENTAL HEALTH

BODY DATA

CHAT BOTS

CAPITALISM

From Social Data to Body Data to Psy Data: Tap, Tap, Tap

Oliver Leistert

Our networked condition under capital relations continues to open pathways to tap into new sources of value. Since the social media turn, the expansion of capital in the digital realm has successfully tapped into body data by way of products like Fitbit. More recently, the proliferation of psy data is underway with chat bots, backed by artificial intelligence to harvest the last remaining and intimate part of expressiveness that neoliberal subjects are producing: mental health apps are at the last frontier of capital's attempts to profitably govern its subjects. To understand these processes, a recap of Marxian theory and the use of some tools created by Félix Guattari will be undertaken.

The capturing mode of data sensing of all sorts has made every human body potentially a media outlet, delivering discriminable sections of the population as an inference of multi-modal data points. This is the subject of this text: how a body became media. And since there is nothing else but a body, this implies a psyche, too: body data and psy data under late capitalism's[1] networked condition. Both are captured under different registers and treated technically in different ways, but both nonetheless serve the same purpose: to prolong and further differentiate governmental technologies by reducing costs.

One such governmental technology is the diffusion of social media platforms. The exploitation of social media users and the selling of advertisements has shifted dramatically from old-fashioned advertising that took the pollution of the public sphere via billboards as a model—i.e., non-targeted broad sending of data towards unknown users—to a highly refined algorithmic discrimination down to the individual level (Andrejevic 2011). Such aggregated data points that constitute the subjects of datafication in the modality of algorithmic governmentality (Rouvroy and Berns 2013) are, broadly speaking, the current material background of ad techniques on the web and the main monetization strategy of this billion-dollar industry driven by technologists.

More recently, we can observe the advent of a new paradigm of data extraction and exploitation. A well-known example for the proliferation of body data is the fitness tracking industry, i.e. companies like Fitbit, which manage to deliver sensors for physical bodies, in combination with the tracking and sensing possibilities that the average smart phone or smart watch offers, as desirable gadgets for a contemporary urban subjectivity. If need be, users may add via their dashboards additional data to the data silos of the company. Fitbit's products can be used to track all sorts of body functions, and are widely used in sports and leisure activities to control the subject's performance and self-set goals,[2] but functionality varies a lot depending on the product.[3]

---

1   Indeed, we still don't know what a body can do. And we will never *know*.

2   There have been severe cases where military and spy personnel were trackable via their fitness app data. See https://www.bellingcat.com/resources/articles/2018/07/08/strava-polar-revealing-homes-soldiers-spies/.

3   See https://www.fitbit.com/. The market is still quite diverse and besides GAFA (Google, Apple, Facebook, Amazon) with Google Fit and Apple Health, and sport companies such as Nike, medical companies, such as (now defunct) BodyMedia, are also forming the field.

Until recently the sensing of body data has been the exclusive domain of the licensed medical industry, conducted under supervision of medical personnel. This kind of data, e.g., generated by heart monitoring machines, used to remain in its own sphere, legally separated from the internet economy. Strong data protection laws for medical data prevent further economic exploitation, at least in the European Union. Nonetheless, this market has grown dramatically in a few years, and with health insurers jumping on board the mental health app market, and inspired by huge investments of the European Union into so-called e-health programs, the prospects of this market have become more than promising.[4]

Body Data and the Networked Neoliberal Condition

The move from body data sensing techniques under the guidance of medical personnel, to body data sensing techniques under self-guidance and driven by the principles of value-extraction by markets, marks a turning point for the integration of body data into the global dataveillance cloud we have been subjected to since the turn of the century. I propose that, while sensing body data has been a medical practice for a long time (e.g., long-term EEGs), the genealogy of more recent developments points to a kind of data sensing that was established with the mass adoption of smart phones and commercial social networking. Once the ubiquitous, self-referencing digital narcissism and permanent exposition of affects, whose emblematic symptom is signified by the like button, had become a means of delegated self-governance and assessment, it was only a matter of time and capital's ceaseless drift towards expansion that signaletic material from the body would supplement the subject's desire to measure its inclusion and belonging to a data sphere of dividualistic aggregation. All the more so since the body data industry is targeting the governmentally self-governed subject in its desire to remain desirable, driven by fear of losing status. Our general networked condition is, therefore, intertwined with the advent of this surveillant assemblage that includes fitness and health trackers and their corresponding wetware.[5]

Body data are data sensed from bodily signals, such as pulse or blood pressure. These are a-signifying semiologies in Félix Guattari's terms, or

---

4   Since data protection and privacy laws differ vastly between the US, the EU, China, and India, I will not discuss the specifics of this topic here.

5   See Gerhard and Hepp (2018) for a discussion of self-tracking and the construction of a datafied self from the perspective of ethnography.

signaletic matter, devoid of signification (Guattari 2013). They contain a deterritorializing vector, in much the same way as other a-signifying signals, such as rhythms or computer code. The reterritorializing production of meaning takes place with the help of applications and calculations that render the pulse beats into a comparable unit against a normalized field, which can then be read by the subject and ascribed meaning. The process of signification remains exterior to the data sensed, and the data only become meaningful to the urban class consumer after correlations to statistics and norms, such as the body mass index (BMI), are made.

A possible point of intervention into this assemblage, to subvert and open it up, would be the interface between body data sensed and its further processing. But instead of further deterritorializing the body signals through creative relaying, such as opening a plane of consistency between other sensed pulses and imagining something else (e.g., to create a collective symphony), the prevalent purpose that the technologist's instrumentality of neoliberal investments gain from this signaletic virtuality is to impoverish it immediately by reducing it to a measurement against normalized BMIs or other biopower standards. I will return to this problematic use of technologies in capital relations.

The Poverty and Authoritarian Twist of Quantified-Self

The act of calibrating body data against such indexes as the BMI (a feature that is part of the Fitbit app), stems from the older regime of discipline that worked the individual as an indistinguishable item in a series (Foucault 1995). Contemporary norms and "the normal" are usually decoupled from this absolute, static index and become statistical matters of ranges within an acceptable threshold.[6] Body data sensing, from this perspective, integrates a *neodisciplinary regime* into the array of dynamic self-governance methods. With the return of this old norm-style, the recent authoritarian turn of neoliberalism finds its equivalent on the level of the production of subjectivity via body data. Here, neoliberal

---

6   George Canguilhem has shown in his doctoral thesis from 1943 how the difference between normal and normativity has been historically productive in the clinical fields (Canguilhem 1989). Foucault has written on the problem of norm, normal, and normativity extensively, see e.g., Foucault (2003). Maria Muhle has written a fine book on the problematic established by Canguilhem and reworked by Foucault (Muhle 2013). See Sellar and Thompson (2016) for a further discussion of control societies and norms, and in terms of algorithms, of course, all the works by Antoinette Rouvroy (e.g., 2011).

subjectivity is remodeled by a recourse to old paradigms such as mass measures and non-subjective, non-individual, abstract norms re-enter its value system. But this does not provoke an existential crisis for the contemporary paradigm, because the cult of the individual established by the current phase of capital expansion remains compatible with a serial body normativity derived from the masses of bodies: the very process of body data sensing overcodes this apparent contradiction (in value systems) between the idea of an undifferentiated item in a mass and the smart simulation of the singular subject. The technology provides an instantiation of what before was left to each body's own devices through the immediate immanence of the body's being. And it is precisely this bodily, self-dependent milieu that is captured by body and psy data sensing, over-coded and reworked into the transcendental value system of norms and normativity provided by the modern power-knowledge-subject complex.

Thus, the quantified-self's misery and poverty cannot be exemplified better than through its inability to let creative collective processes proliferate, such as a heartbeat symphony. Instead, all that is done with the captured body data is to dump it into the vectors of normalization. But there is a much broader context to consider here: while it certainly has some explanatory reach to describe self-quantifying subjectivities as just another hideous manifestation of neoliberal self-indulged control and narcissism, the *broader desire to feedback body data into data silos is not at all explained sufficiently within a framework of governmentality*, or a Foucauldian analytics of power, for that matter. This phenomenon, to my understanding, points towards a technoculture that is historically much older and more profoundly tied to the question of how to relate to the world, of Western ontologies so to say. It is a general condition of subjects in capitalist societies that one can recognize, at least schematically, in this case. In order to make this claim, I will have to turn to Karl Marx for a moment.

Capital, Abstract Value, Alienation

In a Marxian sense, the social relations that capital establishes are obscured and deceiving in everyday practice. According to Marx's analyses, under capital relations, an abstract power is at work behind the backs of the subject. This power is responsible for both the unprecedentedly rapid technological developments since the seventeenth century, and for the failure to transform technological developments into an emancipatory development for all human (and non-human) kind. This dialectical figure of technological progress without humanity's progress is what Marx identified in his analysis of capital as the most basic insight. And it is worth returning to his analysis for the sake of understanding the proliferation of sensed body and psy data.

To sum up Marx's analysis very briefly: the historicity of the commodity is rendered invisible under capitalist modes of production. Subjects are secluded from its history and from the practices that produced the rich, even abundant, materialism all around in a fashion unique to capital relations' mode of production, distribution, and consumption. This is what Marx called the fetish character of the commodity. Abstract value is the only mover of capital, while its use value—such as the concrete experience one may have with a product—remains irrelevant to capital. This is what I propose to call the *tragic bifurcation between a value of means without ends and a value of ends with appropriate means*. The original deterritorialization that capitalism uses to overcode all societal relations establishes a fetishism of the commodity not as a psychological condition, but as an organizing principle of societal relations as reification: things, not humans, seem to be at the center of all doings. And for capital, only abstract value matters. The commodified product as commodity is overcoded and deterritorialized, or, in the case of labor, concrete labor from the perspective of capital is abstract labor only. By separating the concrete world from the societal relations it takes over, determined by the abstract value (capital's[7] sole mover), capital produces a schizophrenic plane that Deleuze and Guattari have famously and extensively described in their two-volume book, *Capitalism and Schizophrenia* (Deleuze and Guattari 1983; 1987). Without owning the means of production and the products produced, and subjected to a being that is reduced to interchangeable points of action within the process of production, distribution and consumption, subjects are cut off, alienated from the cycle of production, exchange and consumption by the abstract movement of capital. Capital establishes a barrier that cuts through all relations and deflects them into new connections. Maurizio Lazzarato, a thorough reader of Guattari, has condensed this:

> In capitalism, subjectivity is submitted to a schizophrenic tension that causes it to tend towards modes of living that are both futuristic and archaic. On the one hand, it is sustained by a deterritorialization which undermines 'existential territories' (a way of living which would assure

7   The fetish character of the commodity is not linked to fetishism as a psychological dimension and concept, as discussed prominently by Freud. On the other hand, nothing stands in the way of letting both concepts of fetishism join forces. On the epistemic necessity of mingling all kinds of fetishism, see Donna Haraway's discussion of genes in Haraway (1997, 134–37).

professional and social security, ethnic and national identification, languages, values and cultures solidified in time etc.) and on the other hand, it is caught up in a neo-archaic reterritorialization (nationalism, Lepenism, a return to traditional values—work, family, ...). Guattari's insights remain of fundamental importance in this context as it is essential to being able to conceive of a way of escaping these simultaneously reactionary and hyper-modernist 'reconversions' of subjectivity. (Lazzarato 2008, 174)

Guattari has shown that the production of subjectivity is, at least since the end of World War II, a key operation of capitalism. Marx was equally fascinated by capitalism's production of subjects, but during his time, this production was a much more violent and disciplinary operation than it has become (in the West) today. This physical violence made it hard to acknowledge that industrial workers also internalized the disciplinary regime. Marx, as a proto macro-economist and sociologist, was barely interested in micrological or micropolitical events (a post-68 interest). He defined capital as consisting of two parts: fixed capital, i.e., the machines bought to produce, and circulating capital, such as the labor bought. Now, necessarily driven by competition, capitalists have to reduce unit labor costs in order to survive. To invest in fixed capital, in new machines, to reduce production costs, is the inevitable way to survive under the conditions of competition. But fixed capital is not productive in terms of abstract value: the sole source of abstract value remains the difference between the worker's life time spent—the concrete time at work—and what this turns out to be as invested circulating capital. This means, from a Marxian perspective, the only source of value is the worker's life time spent as labor power. The margin to realize profits equals negatively the rise in productivity of the machines. This is, in a very brief sketch, the tendency of the rate of profit to fall, a basic law of capitalism, as Marx coined it famously, and described it in the third book of "Capital".[8] And beyond its numerous problems and complexities, it provides at least one interesting insight, namely that technological development plays a difficult, ambivalent role for capitalism. Antonio Negri and Michael Hardt's[9] analysis

---

8   Moishe Postone has focused precisely on the intricate relation of abstract value and abstract time as the founding mover of capital and means of domination (Postone 2008).

9   Based on this tendency, many fantasies have bloomed that understand this as an even teleological claim by Marx that equals a verdict about the historical necessity of capital's proliferating crisis. My point is more humble: there is a need to integrate more and more into the realm of capital, or to widen its realm, as the productivity of

is very much based on the liberating prospects that cooperatively owned technologies entail (Hardt and Negri 2005).[10]

The immediate consequences of this basic law of capitalism are well known: outsourcing the production to cheap labor regions and expansion of the capitalist model into new frontiers—a continuation of the primitive accumulation and colonial enterprise. The capture of affects in social media silos is therefore just a logical consequence of capital's movement into new fields—because the worker's life time spent now includes the user's life time spent.

This expansion also proved to be a very subtle means of social control in line with the ideological necessity of individual freedom in liberal regimes. Differing from the disciplinary regime of the warehouses and Fordist production facilities, the call to participate in a dataveillance capture scheme is translatable into the rhetorical guise of choice. This cornerstone of liberalism, which has mutated in neoliberalism toward a few algorithmically prefabricated possibilities to choose from—most often all in a purely commodified way—down to the infantilizing "like" button, continues to serve and function as the mental token of liberation.

Capital and Body Data: An Alienated Techno-Culturalist Semiotic Drive

To capture body data and capitalize from it is a possible next logical step in the blind and inevitable process of the expansion movement of capital. Technology in the manifestation of products like Fitbit, and the networked condition of the body they invoke, make this possible. To look at sensed body data as an effect of the automatic movement of capital brings to the fore the deficiency of any description of technological developments as neutral or free from economic interests. On the other hand, to prioritize the relation of capital and technology entails the risk of totalizing this relation and of missing the many subtle processes that benefit from capital's dependency on technological investments and developments. These complexities cannot be captured by Marx's theory of value alone. Nonetheless, Marx's value theory continues to provide the most convincing

machines continues to grow; a need to tap into new sources of wealth, such as body data and psy data.

10   In fact, the rereading of the *Grundrisse* had sparked a complex discourse about the question of machines and the "general intellect," most prominently in Italy under the term post-operaismo. See Negri and Fleming (1991), Virno (2003), Virno (2008), or Lazzarato (1996).

explanation of the inability of capitalism to handle our planet and all life forms on it in a responsible way.[11]

But to return to the problematic of societal relations under capital's terms: I have referred to the alienation inherent to capital modes of production and consumption, including the relations of and amongst laboring subjects. And it is here where, although alienation might not be the best term for it, the sensed body data find their place, too—Fitbit belongs to the reproductive sphere. Subjects are using their "free time" to remain fit for their jobs, in fear of losing in the competitive game they are subjected to due to capital's ongoing reduction of circulating capital. Neoliberalism has been very successful in capturing time beyond the pure working hours. On the one hand, by a simple extension of working hours, on the other by the informal dissolution of the differences between work and leisure. Leisure time, as it was invented in and for the Fordist era, is history. As long as one is not truly offline, one is always at least "on hold." To sense body data then is a double operation of expansion into uncharted territories: first, it is a new passage for capital to tap into data from subjects outside of official working hours. Second, since the data sensed signify nothing but the bodies' condition in relation to other bodies or static norms such as the emblematic BMI, competition in the workplace leaks into the intimate sphere of body functions. Heart rates now become a possible indicator of job promotion. This is a twist that workplace surveillance could never have achieved itself. It was only possible via the loop into the value system of health. Thus, it is a logical development that companies start to offer free body data sensing devices to their labor force: body data become part of the curriculum vitae.[12]

The established capturing mode of body signals with networked technologies reproduces and prolongs an alienated techno-culturalist drive that colonizes the relation of the subject and its body as an option for commodification. While a Foucauldian genealogical approach on governmentality bears witness to the intrinsic linkages of power, knowledge and subjectivation, a Marxian perspective, by neglecting this productive and

---

11   Isabelle Stengers writes in her preface to the translation of *In Catastrophic Times*: "Today there is no need to assert, as I did at the time of writing *In Catastrophic Times*, that capitalism—some representatives of which claimed held the solution (so-called green capitalism)—is fundamentally irresponsible. In fact, unregulated capitalism and its allies have refused the role that should have been theirs. It was the route of direct confrontation that was taken, with the determined negation of global warming" (Stengers 2015, 8). On capital and ecology, see Moore (2015).
12   Fitbit products have become a common "free" gift from companies to their employers in order to extend the workplace surveillance scheme.

enabling relation between power and subjects, and by reducing subjects to mere effects of objective relations they are unable to grasp, offers, in a more direct way, a reworking of the processes of commodification that take place above and under the skin. It is only because the relations between subjects and technology are overcoded by capitalist modes of production, distribution and consumption, i.e., what Marx termed alienated, that body data sensing assemblages can become operative on a massive scale in the first place. In addition, the functionalist, post-structuralist approach emblematic in the concept of the assemblage renders visible the de- and reterritorializing flows of micropolitical codings that treat economy, desire and semiotics as one single matter of a becoming. Sensed body data seems to be a convincing case to blend Marxian capital movement as historical development and post-structuralist wetware network desires, because sensed body data are intrinsically linked to capital while at the same time being a pertinent item of a semio-capitalistic operation that Marxian tools alone cannot shed enough light on. This is even more the case once we turn to psy data, the golden valley of the mental health market.[13]

But Then There Is Psy Data—The Final Frontier

Psy data is the term I suggest for "mental health" and "affective" data collected within the current paradigm of capitalist datafication. My example for this new data paradigm is Woebot: a chat bot software that is connected with data silos and so-called artificial intelligence.[14] The mental health software Woebot acts like a trustworthy friend or companion. It is positioned at the frontier of the dataveillance complex and marks the entrance of Western subjectivities into a realm that until recently only China ventured out to conquer with their social surveillance politics called the social credit system.[15] Woebot, and many other mental health chat bots for that matter, work "better" the more data they gather and process. Users are asked to let Woebot sniff into all profiles by using the user's credentials to access Facebook, Twitter etc., accordingly. This seems to be a rational decision, since the analyst would be allowed to ask any question, too, and rightly expect an answer. The only problem here is that Woebot, of course,

---

13   Alienation remains an alien concept and carries much of the burden of Marx's reversal of Hegel. Thus, with it comes a problematic heritage of Sein and Schein, that I can only call upon here by naming it problematic. See Althusser (1969) and Althusser, Balibar, and Fernbach (2015) for the continued pertinent discussion of Marx's philosophy.
14   https://woebot.io/#features
15   https://en.wikipedia.org/wiki/Social_Credit_System

is not a psy-analyst and there is a cruel displacement at play (see Figure 1). The bot's possible answers rely on datafication of the subject's life. But this is not a mirror. Datafication is not representation, but only the production of dividuals, massive amounts of data points that can arbitrarily be combined. Second, the relationship between a subject and this bot app is heavily determined by the relation that subjects and their smart phones are engaged in and its degree and kinds of intimacy. This includes such basic and elementary effects as the screen's brightness and glow, which affects not only infants, but adults, too. And this goes up to the power relations that the subject as the apparent master of the phone cultivates and enjoys in this psy-setting.

[Figure 1] Screenshot woebot.io/#features (Source: http://woebot.io/#features)

The realm of signifying semiologies is the small part of reality that Félix Guattari despised for being the main functor that produces the reduced and infantilized subject of capitalism. It is here that the expansion of capital reaches its last frontier to tap into a subject. Once even the "conversations" about one's psychic status and well-being are part of the dataveillance cloud, the tapping of data has worked itself into the most inner utterances that subjects are able to signify—of course, without any proper semantic understanding thereof. The machine that seems to be listening and responding is only a reification of the alienated nature subjects are being subjected to in capital relations. As pointed out earlier, the relations that subjects can have with such technology, and even more so if this is such an intimate technology, are overcoded from the start by deterritorializing vectors of capital into modes of value extraction and reterritorialized by the infantile and regressive vectors capital sets in motion as a substrate—the psybot app.

The deceit that such bot apps operate on is in plain sight, but as the app taps into the subject's depressive or simple unhappy mental state—in a societal setting whose paradigmatic cultural gesture is a like button—the deceit meanders without much resistance into a successfully exploited social hack. And while there is no way to tell when the data on psy states that was entered into the app would return and shape, most likely imperceptibly, the possible choices the subject has, it is safe to say that conceptually the behaviorist paradigm of Woebot and other mental health apps is targeting only behavior and not well-being. Psy data are data that are supposed to support or rearrange the subject's functioning in her purported social setting. The harvesting of psy data adds another layer to body data, social media data, workplace surveillance data and older forms of data, such as travel data or insurance data.

So, there is body data and psy data, all fed into the dataveillance cloud and in a reciprocal, functional loop between bodies and data processing. Tapping into body functions and the most intimate emotional states, the algorithmic governmentality that Antoinette Rouvroy (2013) highlighted recently, is being supplemented by a variety of other governmental technologies. Their function is to keep the subject—which is the only source of value in a Marxian sense via her expenditure of life time as labor time—alive and well. Whatever depression, paranoia or simply refusal to work there may linger in her soul, her smart phone companion will readily assist in overcoding such obstacles to disciplinary neoliberalization.

References

Althusser, Louis. 1969. *For Marx*. London: Verso.

Althusser, Louis, Étienne Balibar, and David Fernbach. 2015. *Reading Capital: The Complete Edition*. London: Verso.

Andrejevic, Mark. 2011. "The Work That Affective Economics Does." *Cultural Studies* 25 (4–5): 604–20.

Canguilhem, Georges. 1989. *The Normal and the Pathological*. New York: Zone Books.

Deleuze, Gilles, and Félix Guattari. 1983. A*nti-Oedipus: Capitalism and Schizophrenia*. Minneapolis: University of Minnesota Press.

———. 1987. *A Thousand Plateaus: Capitalism and Schizophrenia*. Minneapolis: University of Minnesota Press.

Foucault, Michel. 1995. *Discipline & Punish: The Birth of the Prison*. New York: Vintagebooks.

———. 2003. *Abnormal: Lectures at the Collège de France 1974–1975*. London: Verso.

Gerhard, Ulrike, and Andreas Hepp. 2018. "Digital Traces in Context | Appropriating Digital Traces of Self-Quantification: Contextualizing Pragmatic and Enthusiast Self-Trackers." *International Journal of Communication* 12: 18.

Guattari, Félix. 2013. *Schizoanalytic Cartographies*. London: Bloomsbury Publishing.

Haraway, Donna J. 1997. *Modest_Witness@Second_Millennium.FemaleMan_Meets_OncoMouse: Feminism and Technoscience*. New York: Routledge.

Hardt, Michael, and Antonio Negri. 2005. *Multitude: War and Democracy in the Age of Empire*. Reprint edition. New York: Penguin Books.

Lazzarato, Maurizio. 1996. "Immaterial Labour." In *Radical Thought in Italy: A Potential Politics*, edited by Virno Paolo and Hardt Michael, 133–47. Minneapolis: University of Minnesota Press.

———. 2008. "The Aesthetic Paradigm." In *Deleuze, Guattari and the Production of the New*, edited by Simon O'Sullivan and Stephen Zepke, 173–83. London: Continuum.

Moore, Jason W. 2015. *Capitalism in the Web of Life: Ecology and the Accumulation of Capital*. New York: Verso.

Muhle, Maria. 2013. *Eine Genealogie der Biopolitik: Zum Begriff des Lebens bei Foucault und Canguilhem*. Paderborn: Wilhelm Fink.

Negri, Antonio, and Jim Fleming. 1991. *Marx beyond Marx: Lessons on the Grundrisse*. New York: Pluto.

Postone, Moishe. 2008. *Time, Labor, and Social Domination: A Reinterpretation of Marx's Critical Theory*. Revised. Cambridge: Cambridge University Press.

Rouvroy, Antoinette. 2011. "Technology, Virtuality and Utopia: Governmentality in an Age of Autonomic Computing". In *Law, Human Agency, and Autonomic Computing: The Philosophy of Law Meets the Philosophy of Technology*, edited by Mireille Hildebrandt and Antoinette Rouvroy, 119–40. New York: Routledge.

Rouvroy, Antoinette, and Thomas Berns. 2013. "Gouvernementalité algorithmique et erspectives d'émancipation: Le disparate comme condition d'individuation par la relation?" *Réseaux* 177 (1): 163–96.

Sellar, Sam, and Greg Thompson. 2016. "The Becoming-Statistic: Information Ontologies and Computerized Adaptive Testing in Education." *Cultural Studies ↔ Critical Methodologies* 16 (5): 491–501.

Stengers, Isabelle. 2015. *In Catastrophic Times: Resisiting the Coming Barbarism*. London: Open Humanities Press.

Virno, Paolo. 2003. *A Grammar of the Multitude: For an Analysis of Contemporary Forms of Life*. Semiotext(e) foreign agents series. Cambridge, MA: Semiotext (e).

———. 2008. *Multitude between Innovation and Negation*. Los Angeles: Semiotext(e).

AFFECTIVE MILIEU

INTENSITY

RELATIONALITY

MIMESIS

TECHNICAL SENTIENCE

5

Affective Milieus: Intensive Couplings, Technical Sentience, and a Nonconscious In-between

Marie-Luise Angerer

The developments in media technology at the dawn of the twenty-first century are characterized by an understanding of once separate entities as radically open systems. Human and animal bodies, and technical and natural environments, are connected in complex ways via processes of organic sentience and algorithmic sensors: signals are transposed into data, which are in turn exchanged (in the form of information) between the bodies and their surroundings, creating a pool of data from which political, economic, social, and ethical conclusions are drawn. Donna Haraway's companion species, Lynn Margulis's symbionts, and Myra Hird's micro-ontology all point to processes of contagion, infiltration, and multiple agencies that call not only for a thinking in relations but for a thinking "as

embedded, embodied and even … as the very 'stuff of the world'" (Åsberg, Thiele, and van der Tuin 2015, 152).

In the early 1980s, Donna J. Haraway positioned humankind between animals and machines, stating in her *Cyborg Manifesto* ([1985] 1990), that in an age of increasingly porous borders between natural and artificial organisms, hybrids and cyborgs begin to emerge: animal and human, human and machine. Hybrids, however, are neither figures of the future nor prototypes for science fiction films and computer games, but pointers to the here and now. Today, similarities, gradual differences, and relations between humans and others have become more important, making humankind into one species among "significant others" (Haraway 2003). This places the emphasis on the constitution of the networked human body, which is no longer understood as an autopoietic system that merely exchanges energy, but is instead conceived of as a "biomediated-body" (Clough 2010, 2) that processes information.

At the dawn of the twenty-first century, the relations between bodies and environments are being channeled via information technology. Body data communicate with environmental data, neuronal signals control body and ambient temperatures, and the *little sisters* (as Siri and other digital voice assistants are referred to by Rosalind Picard, the founder of affective computing, in order to play down fears of big data [see Picard 1997]), increasingly organize and intervene in everyday routines. Such digital assistants are now being enthusiastically placed at the side of humans as *new Others,* as farsighted planners and sensitive agents, *non- or para-humans* who will outdo or replace humans even in those moments where they (still) differ from machines. Until the end of the twentieth century, affect/ emotion was considered as the human dimension that could be neither calculated nor entirely bypassed. Today, algorithms have long since begun to intervene (via affective computing) to connect humans and machines on a psycho-cybernetic basis. This is not the end of humankind (the kind of physical and mental overcoming aimed for by transhumanism) but it certainly shifts the human away from the centuries-old fictitious center of humanism, requiring humans to organize new (affective) milieus with non-, para-, or post-human Others. Rather than being created via social or political networks, these new milieus will be constantly produced, shifted, and reconfigured via complex sets of links.

Media Fabrics: Process and Relation

Georges Canguilhem has traced out the history of the concept of milieu, describing how, in the second half of the eighteenth century, it moved from mechanics into biology, where it came to denote the fluid, the medium through which life comes into being and develops. The milieu is that which connects two bodies, "it is their milieu; and insofar as the fluid penetrates all the bodies, they are situated in the middle of it [au milieu de lui]" (Canguilhem [1965] 2008, 99). Canguilhem argues that the nineteenth century repeatedly returned to the concept's mechanical past, strikingly demonstrating his point with the example of Auguste Comte and his *Philosophie positive* ([1830–1842] 1896), according to which the living organism is influenced by its milieu and its variables (such as air, water, and light), while the influence of the organism itself is negligible. The only organism Comte credits with the ability to actively intervene in its milieu is the human organism (see Canguilhem [1965] 2008, 101).

At the beginning of the twentieth century, however, this mechanistic view began to shift. Jakob von Uexküll presented his theory of *Umwelt*, in which, alongside humans, he gave a prominent place to animals with their various specific realities. In basic terms, his approach states that an organism's specific qualities create its own specific *Umwelt*, how this *Umwelt* is perceived by the organism, and how the organism intervenes in it. At the same time, each organism is nourished and preserved by its *Umwelt* in a distinct way (see Uexküll [1909] 2011). We find this view again in the writings of Gilles Deleuze and Félix Guattari, where work on the "melodic complexes" between nature and culture (Deleuze and Guattari [1980] 2002, 219) is described against the backdrop of Uexküll.

In 1929, a decade after Uexküll's *Theoretical Biology* ([1920] 1926) , his contemporary Alfred N. Whitehead published the foundation of his process philosophy under the title *Process and Reality* (Whitehead 1978). In it, he formulated the foundations of a relational cosmology that abandoned any categorical distinction between nature and culture, no longer focusing on the place of humankind within either one. Instead, he introduced a radical linking of nature and subjectivity that makes no claim to primacy. Whitehead uses the term "superject," by which he means the form of subjectivization resulting from a diverse network of processes. With his concept of *prehension*, positing appropriation and abstraction as the basic modes of perception, Whitehead emphasized a *blind emotion* that operates without consciousness (see Whitehead 1978, 162ff.). Haraway borrows this concept in her *Companion Species Manifesto* (2003), rendering it as "graspings" (Haraway 2003, 6). In this sense, *prehension* can be understood as a growing together of relations in which everything and everyone comes into being in a process of mutual grasping, meaning there can be no subject and no object prior to this process.

This explains Haraway's interest in evolutionary biologist Lynn Margulis and her endosymbiont hypothesis, elaborated since the early 1960s (see Margulis and Sagan 1995). This theory is based on an assumption that as life developed, one single-cell organism was absorbed by another, becoming part of an increasingly complex organism. Correspondingly, the components of human cells can also be traced back to these original single-cell organisms—the pairing of host and parasite functions via the mechanism of contagion. In this model, individuals (i.e., all organisms larger than bacteria: animals, plants, fungi, etc.) are symbiotic systems, viewed as tightly interwoven, integrated microbe communities. For Margulis, then, most new species have emerged not as the result of random mutations but via the accumulation of bacterial symbionts (see Margulis 1981).

We can return here to the concept of milieu as described by Canguilhem for the nineteenth century, with reference to Auguste Comte and the exchange of energy in thermodynamic bodies. As sociologist Patricia T. Clough explains in her essay "The Affective Turn" (2010), this model was definitively replaced by that of the "biomediated body" at the end of the twentieth century. While the organic, thermic body exists in a state of exchange with its surroundings in order to stock up on energy and maintain itself as an autopoietic system, the "biomediated body" is viewed as an open system converting energy into the information needed to survive in what I propose to call a *MediaNature*. In this model, the reconfiguration of matter as information is described from two angles: from the viewpoint of molecular biology, and with the help of new visualization technologies. With such images and 3D scans, it becomes possible to look inside the body in new ways. This visible, interchangeable, malleable image of the body—one that can be morphologically altered in any way—corresponds with a molecular self (image). In her book *Immaterial Bodies* (2012), Lisa Blackman examines these various developments and explains that biomedicine, too, has long since stopped viewing the body as a singular entity, focusing instead on "the proliferation and emergence of technologies and practices which enable the enhancement, alteration, and even invention of new bodies" (Blackman 2012, 7). These shifts will have a serious and lasting impact on our understanding of body images, she writes, because "these technologies enable the body to travel beyond the boundary of the skin recast as mobile information to be altered, engineered, and transformed within laboratory and computational settings" (7). In this context, she also mentions the sociologist Nikolas Rose, who in his works has traced the development of such a mobile concept of life that has long ceased to be compatible with the image of the body as a closed entity.

In my book *Desire After Affect* ([2007] 2014) I examine the substitution of the psychoanalytically charged concept of desire with that of affect in both theory and practice, arguing that this replacement has far-reaching implications for the way we think the human and, more broadly, our being-in-the-world. As one example, I discuss the work of philosopher Luciana Parisi, who introduces a definition of desire conceived of not as a mental dimension but as a force which, in its most recent stage of development, is defined as nanotechnical desire (Parisi 2008). Parisi frames this desire as an energy, a driving force behind affective contagion. In her essay *Techno-ecologies of Sensation,* she develops the concept of contagion further, applying it via an "extension of feeling" (Parisi 2009, 188) to an environment replete with technology. In this transposition, desire becomes a life force (comparable with Spinoza's *conatus*), but it also becomes a general capacity for feeling as found in the tradition of sensualism.

Gradations of Sensitivity

For a philosophical reflection on the ongoing convergence between information technology and biotechnology, Isabelle Stengers (2011) suggests a reference to the encyclopedist and materialist Denis Diderot. Firstly, with regard to a general transposition of sensing onto technical nature, he could be read as a direct descendent of a monistic naturalism. Secondly, however, Diderot is someone who does not impose dogmas (either epistemological or ontological), instead appealing to his readers to take practice seriously and to look carefully at what happens, where, and how (Stengers 2011, 373). This focus on practice—what Haraway might call *Staying with the Trouble* (2016)—also applies in the case of transformations such as the emergence of distributed sentience—, when algorithms are cast as sentient beings and when "smartness" denotes a comprehensive capacity to both encode and decode feelings.

In his sensualist epistemology, Diderot views sentience as a fundamental capacity with only gradual differences of degree, increasing from inanimate matter to passive and then active sentience. In *D'Alemberts Dream* ([1769] 1965) Diderot debates with mathematician and physicist Jean-Baptiste le Rond d'Alembert, with whom he co-published the *Encyclopédie*, about the classical question of what might constitute the difference between a human being, an animal, a marble statue, and a clavichord. In a famous passage, he states:

> We humans are instruments gifted with sensation and memory. Our senses are simply keys that are struck by the natural world around us, keys that often strike themselves—and this, according to my way of thinking, is all that would take place in a clavichord organized as you and I are organized. There is an impression that has its cause either inside or outside the instrument; from this impression a sensation is born …. (Diderot [1769] 1965, 101 [translation modified])

But is it really possible to transpose Diderot's comparison between a human and a clavichord onto what Luciana Parisi calls "technosensation"? What Parisi describes here is a kind of "tactile exchange" between agents such as bacteria, viruses, and cells as they transfer information via chemical processes such as quorum sensing,[1] biofilm formation, and sporulation. She draws these examples from the micro-ontological approach of environmental scientist Myra Hird: "Bacterial communities … perform collective sensing, distributed information processing, and gene-regulation of individual bacteria by the group" (Hird 2009, 42). Hird has adapted Haraway's concept of companion species to her concept of co-evolution and co-enactment among non-species, demonstrating that bodies operate in an intra-active fashion on a cellular level in both genetic and morphological terms. The concept of intra-action was introduced by Karen Barad to stress, with reference to Nils Bohr's quantum theory, that rather than two poles entering into a relation within one another, it is relationality itself that causes them to emerge as poles (see Barad 2007). Unlike Barad's epistemological model, Hird's micro-ontology takes a radically asymmetrical approach: its basic assumption is that the biosphere does not need humans to survive, while humans depend on the biosphere. In this way, she inverts the power structure between parasite and host: for Hird, the human is the parasite, the biosphere the host. Activities taking place inside and outside the human body clearly have no need for a subject that is aware of them, acting instead beneath or beyond the threshold of perception—a zone to which, as I will discuss in more detail below, a concept of the nonconscious might be applied.

---

1   Quorum sensing denotes the ability of unicellular organisms to employ chemical communication to measure the cellular density of their population. It allows cells to activate specific genes only when cellular density exceeds or falls below certain thresholds. See https://en.wikipedia.org/wiki/Quorum_sensing (accessed 13 November 2018)

But let us return to Parisi. She transfers this bacterial exchange model to techno-sensorial processes that interconnect environmental and body data. Parisi's techno-ecology is partly founded on bacterial exchange and communication, but she also introduces Whitehead's concept of pre-hension, using it as a first stepping stone towards affective thinking. With the help of this concept, she stresses, it becomes possible to understand mathematical computation and information processing in actors and agents as open and reversible rule-based systems,

> not only because they are responsive to the physical environment which they seek to simulate, but more importantly because their discrete operations become infected and changed by informational randomness. The apparent opposition between affect and com-putation is here dissolved to reveal that dynamic automation is central to the capitalization of intelligible functions. (Parisi 2014, 184)

This makes it abundantly clear that the affective dimension is added here as a joker, allowing her to juggle between visceral, biological, cognitive, and technical processes. Data become "affective data" (Parisi and Hörl 2013, 39) because they are affected via their own movements, in the sense of an infection or contagion. The same goes for the abrupt switch to sentience: in Parisi's idiom, a "techno-ecology of sensation" (40) simply means that energy is translated into information. But what is the difference between a technical sensor and a sentient being as described by Diderot?

The ongoing restructuring and infra-structuring of the environment, cities, and bodies by media technology poses us with the challenge of rethinking both the technical and the organic sides of the equation as relational and processual, in turn obliging us to extend our definition of sentience, long seen as the exclusive preserve of humans, and possibly animals, to include the non-organic and the technical. The graded model of sentience pro-posed by Diderot lends itself to this, but possibly also to a concept of inten-sity like that discussed by Alfred N. Whitehead and later by Gilles Deleuze and Félix Guattari.

Intensities

Intensity is one of the central concepts in Gilles Deleuze's *Difference and Repetition* (1968). Deleuze and Guattari define intensity as a variable inscribed in becoming, an element of sensory experience without which mental development is totally inconceivable.

> Between the intensive and thought, it is always by means of an intensity that thought comes to us. The privilege of sensibility as origin appears in the fact that, in an encounter, what forces sensation and that which can only be sensed are one and the same thing. … In effect, the intensive or difference in intensity is at once both the object of the encounter and the object to which the encounter raises sensibility. (Deleuze and Guattari [1968] 1995, 145)

The particularity of an intensity, they write, is to be "constituted by a difference which itself refers to other differences" (154). In *A Thousand Plateaus*, Deleuze and Guattari describe series and structures that are present simultaneously, constantly changing, switching, connecting, exchanging, and redistributing intensities. It is no coincidence that they refer to Spinoza and his conception of bodies as determined by stillness and motion, by speed and slowness. Affects appear here as "becomings" (Deleuze and Guattari [1980] 2002, 256), described as the latitudes of a body: *"Latitude is made up of intensive parts falling under a capacity, and longitude of extensive parts falling under a relation"* (257, italics in original).

What takes place here between latitudes and longitudes on the plateau of the senses, Whitehead attributes to the dense texture of reality that oscillates between subject and object in order to establish "how order in the objective data provides intensity in the subjective satisfaction" (Whitehead 1978, 88). For Whitehead, intensity is directly connected with the question of survival. To organize this survival, nature must produce societies "which are 'structured' with a high 'complexity' but which are at the same time 'unspecialized'" (101). This means that the question of intensity is a question of the "ordered complexity of contrasts" (100). With this definition, we can turn back to Diderot's gradations of sentience, especially since Whitehead himself details the various grades of complexity and structuring from inorganic to organic societies (see 103ff.).

In one extremely vivid passage, Whitehead describes how humans, as "enduring objects with personal order" (161), experience their lives, their surroundings, their existence. Half awake, sleeping, dreaming, remembering, concentrating on feelings—"a torrent of passion" (161)—the human individual is oblivious to all else. What stands out in our consciousness, then, is not "basic facts" but rather the "derivative modifications which arise in the process" (162). The consequences of neglecting this basic distinction, as Whitehead stresses, are "fatal to the proper analysis of an experient occasion" (162). The most primitive form of experience is emotional, a "blind emotion" (162), and in the higher stages of experience this corresponds to "sympathy, that is, feeling the feeling in another and feeling conformally *with* another" (162). With reference to primitive feeling, Whitehead speaks of "vector feelings" and "pulses of emotion" (163) that are partly responsible for providing contrast. Here again, then, we have contrasts that are responsible for an intensity that has little in common with feelings, as we are used to calling them. Whitehead is very clear on this: feeling in human and animal experience is not merely emotion, but has always already been "interpreted, integrated, and transformed into higher categories of feeling" (163). Even so (and this could be helpful in thinking about affective milieus) the "emotional appetitive elements in our conscious experience are those that most closely resemble the basic elements of all physical experience" (163).

The vector system used by Deleuze and Guattari with reference to Spinoza appears in Whitehead's work as "dimension of narrowness and dimension of width" (166). The dimension of narrowness is that of the "intensities of individual emotions," while the dimension of width results from the higher stages of complexity. The "ocean of feeling" (166) permitted by "savoring the complexity of the universe" is due to the dimension of width, while the "emotional depths at the low levels have their limits" (166). Consciousness is defined by Whitehead here as "supplementary feeling" (165), which does not necessarily contain a "conceptual feeling" (165) where contrasts are allowed or rejected.

In spite of the brevity of this account, I hope it makes two things clear: firstly, the subordinate role of what is introduced as consciousness, and secondly a concept of intensity and sensation defined not in opposition to this consciousness, but as passing through it in different stages of complexity. Intensity as contrast, as the difference of difference, leads to the next question, that of the production of encounters, non-encounters, attractions, and repulsions.

Affective Mimesis

In his 1946–47 lecture series, entitled *Machine and Organism*, Canguilhem spoke about technology "becoming biological," and concluded by referring to recent efforts made at the Massachusetts Institute of Technology under the label "bionics"—studying biological structures that might serve as models for technology. "Bionics," he writes, "is the extremely subtle art of information that has taken a leaf from natural life" (Canguilhem [1965] 1992, 69). Today, nanotechnology is learning from nature, copying what nature has always been capable of. In his afterword to the German edition of

Gabriel Tarde's *Monadology and Sociology* ([1893] 2012), Michael Schillmeier understandably argues that Tarde's monadology is well suited to helping us understand nano-research. For Tarde's monads are not windowless like those of Leibniz, but rather performative and open, differing from but also resembling one another in their belief and their desire (see Schillmeier 2009, 109). Tarde himself speaks of a "need for society" that is common to humans, trees, and stars (Tarde [1893] 2012, 14ff.). This reflects a "tendency of monads to assemble" (34). And this assembly takes place via the movement of imitation that occurs on both the micro and the macro level. Deleuze and Guattari refer to this Tardian concept of imitation as a "flow" that is moved by belief and desire.

> What, according to Tarde, is a flow? It is belief or desire (the two aspects of every assemblage): a flow always consists of belief and of desire. Beliefs and desires are the basis of every society, because they are flows and as such as 'quantifiable'; they are veritable social Quantities, whereas sensations are qualitative and representations are simple resultants. Infinitesimal imitation, opposition, and invention are therefore like flow quanta marking a propagation, binarization, or conjugation of beliefs and desires. (Deleuze and Guattari [1980] 2002, 219)

In Tarde's model, then, movement and sensation are the two main pillars (comparable to Spinoza's vectors), which he translates as belief and desire. The monad, his smallest unit, constitutes an interconnected difference that creates an environment for itself, creating small and large societies via imitation on both micro and macro levels. This in turn can be compared with Margulis' host–parasite model, as described above, in which each renewal takes place via assemblies that carry their earlier phase into the next.

Is it possible, today, to see a resurrection of Gabriel Tarde's monadology with its psychomorphism in a kind of "media-techno-morphism" that organizes itself via "sensory" coupling disguised as affective mimesis? This would bring together all of the aspects considered in isolation above: *Umwelt*, sensitive capacities, intensities, affections, desire. So why is it that these aspects are coming together today as an "affective milieu"? Not because of any noticeable return of emotion, and not because particular attention is now being focused on the notion of intensity (see Kleinschmidt 2004) as Tristan Garcia's book *The Life Intense* ([2016] 2018) seems to suggest. Instead, this milieu must be understood as an intrinsic connection, which, rather than linking humans, animals, and others in new ways based on information technology, causes them to emerge from these connections as contrasts (as defined by Whitehead). Garcia conceives of intensity as a technical coupling, but he does so exclusively in terms of electricity, equating today's often-heard imperative to live an intensive life (with regard to social media, event culture, experience of nature, social status, etc.) with the electrification of the modern, enlightened age. The invention of the lightbulb, attempts to measure bolts of lightning, and the hysterical fad of Mesmerism all point to an irreducible moment: point zero. In the course of the nineteenth century, this point was located in technology, in nature, and in humans, allowing it to be introduced as the ineluctable/unsurpassable degree of intensity. Today, however, Garcia claims to observe the exact opposite: the more humans try to intensify their lives—via all manner of pleasures like sport, wellness, yoga, and a healthy diet—the more exhausted they feel. In recent years we have become used to such descriptions of an exhausted society and the fatigued self, a phenomenon habitually blamed on the media. But Garcia believes he can name the culprit: electronics (as opposed to electricity, which, as a natural phenomenon, affects humans) is responsible for the end of intensity—it has robbed electricity of its intensification. Because "[i]n the electronic age, data is transmitted by electric current, but electricity no longer excites our imagination; now it is little more than a commodity capable of transporting information" (Garcia [2016] 2018, 134). Intensity is now only a means, not an end: "Our obsession thus imperceptibly shifts away from intensity and instead becomes attached to information" (136). Because information depends not on the intensive but on the extensive, every piece of information, be it text, image, or sound, is broken down and reassembled. Translated into Spinoza's language it would read: *capacity* (latitude, including affects) is replaced by the question of *relations* (longitude, extensive). The ethical dilemma described by Garcia as a consequence of all this is an ontological barrier (the bar that separates signifier and signified in Lacan, and crosses out *le grand A(utre)*, A): life versus being, says Lacan, life versus thinking, says Garcia: "Living makes us intense," he writes, "but thought makes us equal" (Garcia [2016] 2018, 142).

But what if this radical separation between living and thinking has long since ceased to function? Or to put it differently: what if the radical bar (Lacan) has been an ideology of the twentieth century with its obsession with the hegemony of language? What if, instead, a kind of intermediate stage has opened up, an in-between area not occupied by the kind of preconscious described by Freud, but having become a zone of the *nonconscious* where technology and organic sensation intra-act? N. Katherine Hayles has introduced the term "nonconscious cognition," which, as she writes, "provides a bridge between human, animal, and technical cognition, locating them on a continuum rather than understanding them as qualitatively different capacities" (Hayles 2017, 67). But this gradation between human and animal, between human and technology, needs one decisive extra step, which is lacking in Hayles' account, and which I would like to call an *affective translation*. If we understand affect not as something related to the body or as something opposite to emotion, but as a conceptual term or—as Whitehead defines feeling—as "a mere technical term" (Whitehead 1978, 164), we might get an impression of this nonconscious as a zone of ongoing translational processes, from bodily processes via technical signal to meaning and vice versa, where affect operates as connecting, disconnecting, and/or translating movements (see Angerer 2017, 27). This experience is affective and nonconscious.

Translated from German by Nicholas Grindell

References

Angerer, Marie-Luise. (2007) 2014. *Desire After Affect*. London: Rowman & Littlefield International.

———. 2017. *Ecology of Affect: Intensive Milieus and Contingent Encounters*. Lüneburg: meson press.

Åsberg, Cecilia, Kathrin Thiele, and Iris van der Tuin. 2015. "Speculative Before the Turn. Reintroducing Feminist Materialist Performativity." *Cultural Studies Review* 21 (2): 145–72.

Barad, Karen. 2007. *Meeting the Universe Halfway: Quantum Physics and the Entanglement of Matter and Meaning*. Durham, NC: Duke University Press.

Blackman, Lisa. 2012. *Immaterial Bodies: Affect, Embodiment, Mediation*. Los Angeles: Sage.

Canguilhem, Georges. (1965) 1992. "Machine and Organism." In *Incorporations*, edited by Jonathan Crary and Sanford Kwinter, 44–69. New York: Zone.

———. (1965) 2008. "The Living and its Milieu." In *Knowledge of Life*, 98–120. New York: Fordham University Press.

Clough, Patricia T. 2010. "The Affective Turn: Political Economy, Biomedia, and Bodies." In *The Affect Theory Reader,* edited by Melissa Gregg and Gregory J. Seigworth, 206–28. Durham, NC: Duke University Press.

Comte, Auguste. (1830–1842) 1896. *The Positive Philosophy of Auguste Comte*. London: Bell & Sons.

Deleuze, Gilles. (1968) 1995. *Difference and Repetition*. New York: Columbia University Press.

Deleuze, Gilles, and Félix Guattari. (1980) 2002. *A Thousand Plateaus: Capitalism and Schizophrenia*. London: Continuum.

Diderot, Denis. (1769) 1965. "D'Alembert's Dream." In *Rameau's Nephew and Other Works*, edited by Ralph H. Bowen, 92–176. Indianapolis: Hackett.

Garcia, Tristan. (2016) 2018. *The Life Intense: A Modern Obsession*. Edinburgh: Edinburgh University Press.

Haraway, Donna J. (1985) 1990. "A Manifesto for Cyborgs: Science, Technology, and Socialist Feminism in the 1980s." In *Feminism/Postmodernism*, edited by Linda J. Nicholson, 190–233. New York: Routledge.

———. 2003. *The Companion Species Manifesto: Dogs, People, and Significant Others.* Chicago: Prickly Paradigm Press.

———. 2016. *Staying with the Trouble: Making Kin in the Chthulucene.* Durham, NC: Duke University Press.

Hayles, Katherine N. 2017. *Unthought: The Power of the Cognitive Nonconscious.* Chicago and London: The University of Chicago Press.

Hird, Myra J. 2009. *The Origins of Sociable Life: Evolution After Science Studies.* Basingstoke: Palgrave Macmillan.

Kleinschmidt, Erich. 2004. *Die Entdeckung der Intensität: Geschichte einer Denkfigur im 18. Jahrhundert.* Göttingen: Wallstein.

Lee, Jasmin, Jien Wu, Yinyue Deng, et al. 2013. "A Cell-cell Communication Signal Integrates Quorum Sensing and Stress Response." *Nature Chemical Biology* 9: 339–43.

Margulis, Lynn. 1981. *Symbiosis in Cell Evolution: Life and its Environment on the Early Earth.* San Francisco: Freeman.

Margulis, Lynn, and Dorion Sagan. 1995. *What Is Life? The Eternal Enigma.* London: LDN.

Parisi, Luciana. 2008. "Die Nanogestaltung des Begehrens." In *Gender Goes Life: Die Lebenswissenschaften als Herausforderung für die Gender Studies*, edited by Marie-Luise Angerer and Christiane König, 63–93. Bielefeld: transcript.

———. 2009. "Technoecologies of Sensation." In *Deleuze/Guattari & Ecology,* edited by B. Herzogenrath, 182–199. Basingstoke: Palgrave Macmillan.

———. 2014. "Digital Automation and Affect." In *Timing of Affect: Epistemologies, Aesthetics, Politics,* edited by Marie-Luise Angerer, Bernd Bösel, and Michaela Ott, 161–77. Berlin: diaphanes.

Parisi, Luciana, and Erich Hörl. 2013. "Was heißt Medienästhetik? Ein Gespräch über algorithmische Ästhetik, automatisches Denken und die postkybernetische Logik der Komputation." *Zeitschrift für Medienwissenschaft: Medienästhetik* 8: 35–51.

Picard, Rosalind. 1997. *Affective Computing.* Cambridge, MA: MIT Press.

Schillmeier, Michael. 2009. "Jenseits der Kritik des Sozialen: Gabriel Tardes Neo-Monadologie." In Gabriel Tarde, *Monadologie und Soziologie,* 109–53. Frankfurt: Suhrkamp.

Stengers, Isabelle. 2011. "Wondering About Materialism." In *Speculative Turn: Continental Materialism and Realism,* edited by L. Bryant, N. Srnicek & G. Harman, 368–80. Melbourne: re.press.

Tarde, Gabriel. (1893) 2012. *Monadology and Sociology.* Melbourne: re.press.

Uexküll, Jakob von. (1909) 2011. *A Foray into the Worlds of Animals and Humans, with A Theory of Meaning.* Minneapolis: University of Minnesota Press.

———. (1920) 1926. *Theoretical Biology.* New York: Harcourt Brace.

Whitehead, Alfred North. 1938. *Modes of Thought: Six Lectures Delivered in Wellesley College, Massachusetts, and Two Lectures in the University of Chicago.* New York: Macmillan.

———. (1929) 1978. *Process and Reality.* New York: Free Press.

PANOPTICON

CYBERNETICS

SYNHAPTIC

TOUCH

VISION

6

Synhaptic Sensibility

Pierre Cassou-Noguès

The concept of a "synhaptic sensibility" expresses a new relation between sight and touch that comes to power with new haptic and synhaptic technologies. These technologies work on a variety of haptic data and change our affective relationship with each other and with ourselves. They transform our affective live. With regard to the power of political and social control synhaptic technologies are local and imply a synchronized multiplicity. This puts them in opposition to the centralized invisible oversight that characterizes the model of the panopticon. Therefore "synhaptic sensibility" can help to understand how "control societies" are related to the current transformation of the properties of touch and sight and to the communication of affects.

The Man with Butterfly Hands

In his "Letter on the Blind," Denis Diderot relates a dialogue with a blind man. At one point, the unnamed blind man from Puisaux is asked whether he would like to have eyes, that is eyes that see. "If it were not for curiosity," he replies, "I would just as soon have long arms: it seems to me my hands would tell me more of what goes on in the moon than your eyes or your telescopes" (Diderot 1916, 77). Diderot does not comment on the blind man's answer. There is no way to tell whether this repartee is true or whether it was invented by Diderot. Usually, it is interpreted as showing that touch gives a fuller, and more affective, presence than sight: all that touch would lack is distance. But, if one considers the situation seriously (well, not exactly seriously, but with a sort of stubbornness), one must realize that such long arms would be completely unpractical in daily life.

Imagine moving around in a crowded room with arms that can reach to the Moon! If they are to be as useful as eyes, these arms would have to be extendable, elastic or telescopic, so that they could adjust to the distance of the object to be touched. In fact, the best scenario would be to have flying hands that were remotely controlled. One could imagine such hands, in a story. Maybe Diderot's character would have some kind of implant in his brain, or his brain would have been rewired so that he can move his flying hands at will: he imagines moving his natural hand and it is his flying hand that takes off in the desired direction. Some experiments in neuroscience involve such apparatus: the subject imagines moving his arms, an implant or an EEG helmet catches the signal in the brain of the patient, and the signal can be used to move the cursor on the screen.[1] Or maybe the character was born with these flying hands, like a kind of superhero or extra-terrestrial being. In any case, let us admit that he moves his flying hands just as easily as I move my hands. Would it be enough?

The character is standing in a crowded room; Diderot and his people are asking him about his blindness and his Bluetooth hands. To recognize a newcomer, who does not say a word, the blind man would have to touch the stranger's face, which the other might resent. The hands would be as useful as eyes only if the blind man could use them to sense other people without them feeling too uncomfortable. So, ideally, the hands should be invisible and without weight, like transparent butterflies, which could land on my skin, feel my face, without me feeling their touch. If the butterfly

---

1   For instance, an EEG pong game. http://people.ece.cornell.edu/land/courses/
    ece4760/FinalProjects/f2015/vkm22_nk437/vkm22_nk437_old/vkm22_nk437/
    main.html

hands were light enough, I would be no more aware of them than I am aware of someone watching me from behind. If, in a crowded room, I were to look in a mirror and notice someone staring at my back, I would feel uncomfortable. In the same way, I would feel some kind of itch on my cheek, and I would realize the man is feeling my face with his flying hands. I might ask: "Why are you doing this?," as I might ask someone looking at me with persistence: "Why are you staring at me?"

Now, the butterfly hands, the long arms that Diderot's blind man wished for, become more interesting, and one can imagine various uses for them, and various questions for the man. What relation for instance would he have to other people's affects? Would he feel joy, or sadness through his hands? Would affects communicate to him? Or, being able to touch without being touched, would he remain remote to the emotions he could feel in others?

However, the butterfly hands have one major flaw compared with sight. When I enter a crowded room, I see all the people in the room at once (or most of them—some may be hidden behind others), and the general architecture of the room, and where is the cold buffet for instance, and my friends, whereas the man with the butterfly hands, if he is blind, would be able to feel things, and faces, or bodies, at a distance, but only one by one. It would take him a long time to feel everything there is, and take in through his hands the shape of the room, and figure out who is there and where the buffet is.

Let us then add one more technological fantasy to the butterfly hands: there are not only two of them, but many, flying in a swarm. Now, when the man enters the room, he sends his many hands through the room, they feel the floors, and the walls, and the people, and the food on the buffet. Then, after a few moments, he would know as much as—or rather more than—I do simply using my eyes. Of course, it would take him a few moments—his hands would have to trail all over the room. And it would take a powerful mind to be able to reconnect, and synchronize all the information, the tactile feelings that his many hands transmit to him. Maybe his brain is a super-computer, or it is linked to a super-computer.

In any case, the impression, the "view" that he gets of the room, so to speak, is still different from the one that I perceive with my eyes. Obviously, it is made of tactile rather than visual contents. It contains aspects that I would not usually see, like body temperatures. It probably involves a more intimate relationship with the people in the room. But this "view," which is not strictly speaking a view, also has a different structure. The impressions that these many hands give our superhero (or maybe super-villain—we don't know what he will do with his hands) are still local, and temporal. Each hand feels a trail of sensations, like when I move my hand on the table and feel the roughness of the wood and the slight bumps that mark the joints between the planks, one after the other. The man has to reconnect all the local impressions in a structured view that the eye gives me at once. Or maybe he does not need to reconnect these impressions and can live, and manage, in a world that is made of many disjointed local impressions. Maybe he knows in this way enough about his surroundings to be able to orientate, and interact with things and people. In fact, we can give a visual equivalent of this. Imagine that I see the room through many cameras scattered about: there is one on the buffet, and one on the left corner, and one on the ceiling above a group of people talking, etc. I look at all the images that these cameras record on a multitude of windows on the screen of my computer. Of course, now I am separated from the room by a screen, and I have lost most of the affective presence of the people that I can see, but my multi-angled vision has a structure similar to the experience of the man with the butterfly hands. It is made of visual impressions rather than tactile impressions, but these have a similar structure. We both have multiple flows of two-dimensional impressions (tactile or visual) that we must recombine, resynchronize in order to identify particular objects. It is as if both "views" were produced by a single sense, technologically mediated, and which can operate with visual as well as tactile contents. I will call this sense, or this way of perceiving, "synhaptic." I will discuss this term at length below.

Now, my point in this paper, which the parable of the man with the butterfly hands intended to illustrate, is that contemporary technology transforms our sensibility so as to give birth to a new sense, a new way of perceiving, whose structure can be filled with visual, tactile or in fact auditory impressions (it seems we cannot taste, nor smell through our computers), but which has properties that none of our natural senses have. It is different from vision, as it is different from touch. It represents a transformation of sight and of touch which supersedes both of them, and operates with visual as well as tactile contents.

As I will illustrate through the course of this paper, the technologies that bear on our sensibility, and in particular on our touch, are *de facto* affective technologies: they *transform our affective relationship* with each other and with ourselves, for this affective relationship essentially operates through touch. Thus, the properties of touch, the way it operates, the kind of con-tact it involves in space and in time, its reciprocity (if I touch your hand with my hand, you touch my hand with your hand) represent key elements in the communication of affects. Transforming the properties of touch is transforming our affective life.

Now, when I say that contemporary technology is giving birth to a new "synhaptic" sense, it is not that someone, some mad scientist, a kind of Dr. Griffin (to take up the character of H. G. Wells, in the novel *The Invisible Man* [1897]) is working in his home laboratory on a pair, or a swarm, of butterfly hands. One does not necessarily need these hands. The security man who is sat in front of his screens, with a dozen cameras giving him various views of the underground parking, is already perceiving the surrounding space synhaptically. His perception of the parking lot has visual contents, but these visual contents share the same structure as the butterfly hands in the above parable. I will mention below several devices that actually transform the properties of touch so as to enable it to operate at a distance and without reciprocity, and in this way make it part of a synhaptic sensibility.

I believe that contemporary technology produces a synhaptic sensibility. Nevertheless, I wish to add a caveat to this claim. I do not claim to be a scientist (nor a physicist, nor a sociologist, nor a natural scientist, nor a human scientist) or to be able to predict where we, or technology, are going. I only claim to be a philosopher, and if I can say anything about what is, it is through the domain of the possible. As I defend elsewhere (see Cassou-Noguès 2010; 2016; 2018) I believe that philosophy or, to be more precise, metaphysics does not describe the Real but the Possible, as it is opened up by fiction, stories that work. Some stories work, some do not work: that is to say, we adhere to some stories and not to others. One cannot imagine any situation in a story that works. Though I cannot develop these claims here, stories that work, stories to which one adheres at a certain time and place, delimit a certain domain of the possible which, to me, is exactly the domain on which metaphysics relies.

Thus, to be more exact, my claim would be that contemporary technology makes possible a synhaptic sense, which represents a different form of perception and enables another kind of communication of affects and another form of surveillance. I will mention below real devices, but in principle, as a metaphysician, I could dispense with examples or make them up or lie about them, as long as these examples work as stories.

Sensibility Extended, from Descartes to Wiener

At the beginning of his *Dioptrique*, René Descartes illustrates his theory of vision with an experience of blindness. Imagine that you are walking at night on a path in the forest, without light. You would use a stick to feel the obstacles on your way.

> No doubt you have had the experience of walking at night over rough ground without a light, and finding it necessary to use a stick in order to guide yourself. You may then have been able to notice that by means of the stick you could feel the various objects situated around you, and that you could even tell whether they were trees or stones or sand or water or grass or mud or any such thing. It is true that this sensation is somewhat confused and obscure in those who do not have long practice with it. But consider it in those born blind who have made use of it all their lives: with them, you will find, it is so perfect and so exact that one might almost say that they see with their hands or that their stick is the organ of some sixth sense given to them in place of sight. (Descartes 1988, 153)

Of course, it is a bit surprising to introduce a theory of vision using the example of a blind man. But, in Descartes' world, vision is a sort of touch. Descartes' world is filled with particles. There is no emptiness. A light, such as a lamp, emits particles that push other particles in a line which eventually reaches the eye. Or this line of particles pushing each other bounces on the table, which resists and sends another stream of particles on a line which reaches the eye. So, the eye feels the pressure of these particles, and from this pressure the mind produces an image: the lamp, and the table on which the lamp is placed, just like the hand feels the pressure of the stick that hits a stone on the road, and the mind deciphers in this pressure the form of a stone. Thus, the analogy between vision and touch is certainly justified in Descartes' world.

However, in this passage, technology, a rudimentary technology (we have just picked up a branch on the road and cut off all unnecessary leaves), also appears as a means to transform and extend our sensibility. More precisely, technology seems to bring together, or bring closer, sight and touch. Through the stick, touch can operate at a distance. It becomes a sort of sight. Sight and touch are not defined by their contents (what I see, colors for instance, and what I touch, smoothness or roughness)—they are defined by their properties: touch is a sense of contact. But, precisely, technology can modify these properties and, in this way, transform our sensibility or invent new senses that have the same contents (in the end, it is always colors, or textures) but have different properties and extend our relationship to the external world: the stick gives us a sense of distance that works in the dark.

Now, technology and science have changed since Descartes' time, and the blind man's stick may no longer be the right paradigm for our technology. In fact, the example of the blind man's stick points to a limit in the Cartesian technology that we have surmounted. To put a long story short, one thing that has changed is that we have discovered that perception is information, and information can be coded and inscribed on various material supports, so as to be transported, and possibly transformed, before it is again decoded. Thus, the contents of my perception, the sounds that I hear, are produced from certain variations of pressure in the air around me. But there are ways to abstract the structure of these variations, to replicate this structure on another support that can be transported in space or in time, and to produce again the same variations of pressure in the air, so that I will again hear the same sound, or not exactly the same sound, for in these operations of coding, transportation and decoding, some information may be lost and covered up by noise. The gramophone, the telephone, the photograph, are all examples of such processes. None works perfectly. Something is lost in these operations. At first, the photograph was black and white. We could not code colors. Then it was two-dimensional. But even the best virtual reality devices do not produce perfect vision. One still can see the pixels, or the colors are a bit wrong.

These operations also enable us to deliberately transform the message while it is coded. Or they enable us to decode the message into the contents of another sense. For instance, I can represent sounds as a moving curve on a screen or, as in the "hearing glove" on which Norbert Wiener was working, sounds can be represented by tactile variations, which the subject could understand as a language, just as those who are not deaf understand sounds as a language. Though it never really worked, Wiener hoped that his hearing glove would enable a deaf person to follow a conversation on the tips of her fingers.

The same operations also enable us to code information that we do not naturally perceive in the content of one of our senses. The radar codes the reverberations of sounds that we do not hear in terms of vision. In his novel *L'homme truqué* ([1921] 1990b), Maurice Renard imagines a man whose technological eyes would see electric circuits and electromagnetic fields.

Although the gramophone, the telephone, the photograph, and Renard's novel precede cybernetics, it is really Norbert Wiener who, relying on the example of the telephone, puts in place the theory of perception as information, which can be coded, transported, and decoded (cf. Cassou-Noguès 2014).

Now, the preceding examples are mainly concerned with sight and hearing, images and sounds, but the same theory of perception as information also works for touch. The tactile message, so to speak, can also be coded, transported, and decoded. As Descartes foresaw, with the image of the blind man feeling with his stick the obstacles on the road, touch can operate at a distance. But it is no longer a matter of "things," or particles, pushing each other. Information when coded can be transported in many different ways, through electromagnetic waves for instance. The stick could be broken in two parts, one in the hand of the blind man and one trailing on the road. The information gathered by this end of the stick would be transmitted by, say, Bluetooth to the other end, and the blind man would feel pressures and vibrations in his hand so as to discern the obstacle on the road at a distance, at any distance. There are two consequences that concern the extension of our sensibility.

First, in practice, the stick of the blind man could only have a limited length, whereas the tactile message suitably coded can be transported at any distance, in space or in time. There is no limitation in principle. We could touch at any distance, in space and in time. I will call this *telehaptics*. But, second, the operations of coding and decoding, the breaking up of the blind man's stick, enable us to separate action and reaction—to disconnect touching and being touched. When we shake hands, I touch your hand and you touch mine, or my hand touching yours is also touched by your hand. The extension of touch through the blind man's stick does not change this reciprocity. If the blind man walking on the road hits a passer-by with his stick, this person is touched, and would look up to the blind man, and maybe angrily grab the stick: he would feel the blind man's hand resisting on the other hand of the stick. Being touched is still touching. But we can now interrupt this reciprocity with precision. This is at the basis of what I call *synhaptics*.

Haptic Technology

TeslaTouch is a system developed by Disney Research[2] that enables the user to touch various materials on a screen: paper, sand, the fabric of a cloth, etc. The user moves her finger on the screen and feels the texture of the material. The system seems to have been designed for online shopping. Equipped with such a screen, the virtual customer would be able to touch her clothes before buying them. In a sense, the device abstracts the texture from the reality of the object so as to transport it through space, or time.

Cybergrasp, developed by the company Cyberglove, is a glove that enables the user to take a virtual object in her hands.[3] The user wears a virtual reality mask in which she sees an object. Equipped with the glove, she can raise her hand and actually grasp the object. The glove has joints which fit to the knuckles of the fingers and are governed by small motors that can stop the hand that tries to close on the object. In this way, the glove forces the hand to remain in the position the hand would have if it held the object that the user sees in her VR mask. The user then feels the shape of the object in her hand, and the specific resistance that the object would have: holding a virtual tennis ball, the user would be able to squeeze it, whereas a glass vase would feel absolutely impenetrable. The system renders the shape and the elasticity of the objects. The texture is lost. As the glove introduces resistance into the movements of the fingers but not those of the arm, the objects that the user grasps and moves around seem to be weightless.

Various other tactile devices are used by museums to enable visitors to virtually touch objects from the gallery—a Greek vase from the tenth century BC, for example. All these systems participate in what I call telehaptics: the possibility of touching at a distance through space or time (for after the system has been put in place, if the vase was broken the user would still be able touch it). It is like a telephone, which enables the user to speak, or hear, at a distance from their interlocutor. Of course, some qualities, some aspects of the thing that it is touched are lost in the process, or transformed, just like my friend's voice on the telephone. The blind man's stick, from Descartes' *Dioptrique*, has been indefinitely extended, extended and improved—the blind man could break the Greek vase with his stick, whereas the user of TeslaTouch won't stain the cloth with her finger. She touches the cloth but this touch has no effect on the thing. The reciprocity

2   https://la.disneyresearch.com/publication teslatouch-electrovibration-for-touch-surfaces/
3   www.cyberglovesystems.com/cybergrasp

of touch is already in question. Certainly, the glove might wear out through her touch. But her touch has no effect on the object that she touches. She does not touch the glove. She touches a vase through the glove, like she might look at it through her glasses, if she were short sighted. We do not usually see our glasses. We see through them. In the same way, the glove is relatively transparent. It represents a prosthesis enabling a new kind of sensitive experiment, opening a new sense (a sort of sixth sense, to take Descartes' expression) that has new properties.

The Hugshirt is a kind of T-shirt that fits tightly to the body. One notices bizarre patches, on the arms and the shoulders. These patches (which are placed on those parts of the body that touch when two people hug) can both record and simulate a hug. That is, they are able to record the pressure and body temperature when the user hugs herself, and they can also impress pressure and warmth on the skin of the user when she is sent a hug at a distance. So, if two friends, A and B, wear Hugshirts, A hugs herself and, through her phone, sends the hug to B, whose Hugshirt will then slightly squeeze and warm her so as to make her feel A's hug. If A does not wear her Hugshirt, she can still send a hug through her phone. If she has recorded previously the parameters of her hug, this will be the hug that her friend receives. If not, it will just be a standard hug.

In this way, hugging can be done from any spatial or temporal distance:

> The Hug Shirt™ records a hug like you would record a movie and delivers the data to your mobile ... Sending hugs is as easy as sending a text message or chatting, and you are able to send hugs while you are on the move, in the same way and to the same places you are able to make phone calls (Rome to Tokyo or New York to Paris).[4]

The system illustrates the idea of perception as information perfectly. A tactile impression (and a tactile impression that is felt in an affect of empathy) is turned into a message, a piece of information, which can be coded. As such, it is transported and decoded and felt again on the body of the receiver. Of course, the message may be impoverished, or transformed in the process, just as the voice on the telephone.

Hugging is both touching and expressing one's love or sympathy, communicating an affect without words but through touch. The communication of emotions that language makes possible through space and time has been extended to something more immediate, operating below language and through a mute touch. We could record our hug to send it to our loved

---

4   https://cutecircuit.com/the-hug-shirt/#after_full_slider_1

ones after we are dead. It is not that we would hug from beyond the grave, as palpable ghosts: we would simply hug from the past.

To me, the uncanny aspect of the Hugshirt does not lie in this distance, which may be unusual for touch but to which we are accustomed in the realms of sound and vision. We are not surprised at being able to look at the photograph of someone who is long dead, or hearing her voice on a tape, or hearing her play the piano on a record. However, what is sent through the Hugshirt is not my hug to my friend but rather my hug to myself. It is my hug to myself that I record on my Hugshirt and then dispatch. It seems that these tactile messages, these affects, that I send to my friends are all directed towards myself. It is a bit like sending a selfie, where I am smiling to myself as I appear on the screen of my phone. I hug myself and send it to my friend. It is through this relationship to myself (maybe it is already a kind of auto-eroticism) that I can relate to others. In contemporary technology affective communication (when it takes place outside language) seems to be irremediably self-centered.

The same kind of mechanism used for the Hugshirt also appears in sex toys. There are different products, such as Max and Nora developed by Lovense. Max is a plastic vagina, and Nora is a plastic penis. The two devices are connected to the phones of the users. The movements that the man gives to his Max are transmitted to the woman's Nora, and vice versa, so that both devices are animated in rhythm and by the same kind of vibrations. They can be linked with a chat app like Skype so that both users can see each other. "Our interactive sex toys allow couples to have long distance sex. ... The toys will respond to your movements and send the feedback to your partner."[5] Or, on the video featured on the website, "They may not shorten the miles that keep you apart, but when you use Lovense toys, you just might not notice." As already noted, the distance may be in fact spatial and temporal. Just as with the hug, which can be recorded and sent again later on, "the moves of each session [with Max and Nora] and audio can be recorded and played back any time you want."

The same thoughts apply to the Hugshirt as to these sex toys. Both devices stage the same kind of distance between the users while allowing them to remain in contact. They make possible the nonverbal communication of affects at a distance. They are self-centered. What the user transmits to his/her partner is a movement that is directed towards him/herself. The communication with the other operates through self-eroticism.

5   www.lovense.com/long-distance-sex-toys

But there is something more. The Hugshirt was first introduced in 2002, and obviously has not been a commercial success. In the same way, on the webpage of Lovense, when one looks at the photographs of the young and happy couple chatting on their phones, and then sees the drawings of the two sex toys vibrating beside them, it is difficult not to find something uncanny in the association. The photographs are sleek and carefully produced with nice lighting and sweet colors, of the kind you would see in romantic movies. The bright pink dildo is so incongruous that it seems to have been added as a prank. It's as if the two sets of images belong to different realities. And, in fact, they do. The only hint on the website of Lovense is a short review (the last of a long list but clearly visible nevertheless): "I had a client that did love Max for him and Nora for me. Great toys."[6] It is signed: @AlluringAli25. However, searching for Lovense on YouTube, one discovers several videos on the topic, "how to boost your webcam girl's income by using Nora," and dozens on "Lush," another dildo produced by Lovense, which this time works only one way: it is remotely controlled by phone, or through the internet, and is used in sex chat. This product is only one among many. They enable the client to control the vibrations of the dildo while the webcam model is using it. Among the devices mentioned, these remote-controlled dildos are the only ones that have been commercially successful. Precisely because they do not belong to "telehaptics": they do not provide touch at a distance. The client does not touch anything (except the phone, or the mouse of the computer)—he/she only defines the way the model is touched. Again, the reciprocity of touch is broken.

Invisible Versus Intangible

In a sense, the invisible man is as old as philosophy. In Plato's Republic, Socrates tells the story of a shepherd from Lidia, Gyges, who finds a magical ring that makes him invisible: he will kill the king then marry the queen and become king himself (Plato 2006). The example of Gyges is used to raise a moral issue: Would we do good if we could do bad and not be caught?

H. G. Wells has added another twist to the story. In the novel *The Invisible Man*, Griffin, a physicist, invents a complicated chemical process that makes him invisible—but living as an invisible man in Edwardian Britain is not as easy as it seems…

6   www.lovense.com/long-distance-sex-toys

The invisible man sees but cannot be seen. He is absolutely transparent. Scientifically, he is an aberration. If the man is transparent, his retina should retain nothing of the rays of light that go through him, so he should be blind. We do not know anything that is absolutely transparent in the real world. A panel of glass may seem to be transparent, if it is perfectly clean and if one's gaze is orthogonal to the panel. But if you take it in your hand, you will see the angles. If it was round, without angles, then it would deform shapes, so you would know there is something between you and the object you are looking at. However, in the story, the invisible man is absolutely transparent, and he is not blind: he sees, but he cannot be seen.

Now, let us try to imagine an intangible man, who could touch but not be touched, as the invisible man can see but not be seen. What would happen if I tried to shake hands with the intangible man? He would feel my hand in his but I would not be able to feel his hand in mine? So how could he hold, press or caress my hand, without me feeling his hand? It seems it is impossible. Indeed, a few years after Wells' novel was published, Maurice Renard Renard ([1912] 1990a) attempted to write a parallel story, *L'homme au corps subtil*, in which a physicist hopes to become intangible. But, when he can no longer be touched he loses his sense of touch in turn. He has become a sort of ghost. It is as if the invisible man had become blind in trying to make himself invisible. It seems there is no way to imitate in the realm of touch the invisibility of the invisible man. In fact, there are no stories, at least no story with the aura of Wells' novel, featuring such an intangible being in this sense (if there were, we would know, as we all know about the invisible man). Of course, there are stories about ghosts that cannot be touched, but they cannot touch either. There are stories about beings whom you should not touch: *Noli me tangere,* don't touch me, says Jesus Christ, after his resurrection. It's as if the invisible man was rendered invisible because one must lower one's gaze before him. There are beings that are almost intangible, like an ant crawling on my arm that I do not feel because my sensibility is too gross. It would be as if the invisible man was invisible because I am myopic.

Thus I claim (see Cassou-Noguès 2010 and 2016) that we cannot imagine, or write a story about, a character who would be intangible as the invisible man is invisible: a character that could touch but not be touched as the invisible man can see but not be seen. Considering that fiction opens up the possible on which philosophy is based, as I mentioned earlier, I take this asymmetry to prove that touch and vision, as we naturally experience them, have different properties: touch has a reciprocity that does not belong to vision. It is possible to see without being visible but it is impossible to touch without being tangible.

It is precisely this reciprocity of touch that contemporary technology interrupts. Contemporary technology makes it possible to touch without being touched, or to be touched without touching. Wearing a Hugshirt, when I am sent a standard hug, I am touched without touching. When my hand is in the cybergrasp glove, I touch objects (say, a Greek vase from a museum) without leaving any trace on these objects: the hand that touches is intangible. Or take the man with the butterfly hands, in our parable at the beginning of the story. Even if I could feel his hand on my arm, I would think I was being touched by a bizarre device, a kind of plastic butterfly. But the man himself who moves his butterfly hand off my arm remains intangible for me. Or, for a last example, take the drone. A pilot may use a drone to reach a target, or to "touch" it, in a sense. The drone may be shot down but the pilot themselves is not touched as the target is touched. As with our butterfly hands, a drone is a means to touch a target that cannot touch you.

All these devices should be considered as prostheses. Of course, by a particular turn of attention, I can perceive the prosthesis as such. When I wear glasses, I don't usually see them. But, if they are new for instance and I am not used to them, or if there is a mark on the lens, I suddenly see the frame. In the same way, I might feel the fabric of the Hugshirt if it irritates my skin, or, if my hand is sweating, I might feel the slippery joystick that enables me to drive the drone. In these instances, when the prosthesis does not work properly, we have a tactile relationship with the prosthesis, and this relationship has a reciprocity. However, when the prosthesis works properly, I perceive through the prosthesis, which opens up a new relationship to another object, that is a new sense with different properties. I can't feel the joystick in my hand—I only perceive the target, which I can touch without being touched. None of these examples present an intangible character exactly similar to the invisible man, but they illustrate various ways in which contemporary technology breaks down the reciprocity of touch.

The character of an invisible man has been used to raise various philosophical problems. Plato's problem is moral. In Wells' novel, as in Paul Verhoeven's *Hollow Man* (2000), there is the problem of madness: would the interruption of the relationship to myself that I have in the mirror (when I can no longer see myself as I see others) lead to some kind of desperate solitude and, in the end, madness? There is also the problem of social invisibility, where invisibility is no longer power but weakness. In Ralph Ellison's novel (1952), the invisible man is the figure of the African American in the context of the 1950s. It could be a beggar, or a hotel doorman whom no one looks at: people go in without looking at the man holding the door—he is invisible.

However, the concept of invisibility that pervades our imagination and has been used in these various perspectives is a relatively recent one. Despite Plato's story, before the age of cinema invisibility usually took on a different form. At least, the version of the story of Gyges that is most often represented in paintings (especially Dutch paintings from the seventeenth century) is not that of Plato but that of Herodotus. In Herodotus's *Histories* (2013), Gyges is a friend of the king Candaules. The king is proud of his wife and wants to show her to Gyges. So, he helps Gyges to hide in their bedroom where he can see the queen undress. Paintings usually represent the moment when the queen sees Gyges looking at her from behind the bed. They exchange a glance. In Herodotus' story, the queen will then convince Gyges to kill the king and marry her, thus making him king himself.

Of course, the position of Gyges in this story, being visible but hidden from the queen, until they exchange this glance, tells something of the position of the spectator looking at the painting, who herself sees the queen undressing and is hidden, in a sense, though not invisible. One can also wonder how a painting could have represented Gyges, in Plato's story, as an invisible man. To my knowledge, it has never been tried. It may be cinema, and James Whale's film of 1933 (*The Invisible Man*, Universal), which turns our attention from one version of Gyges to the other. Whale finds a way to represent the invisibility of the invisible man in the famous scene in which Griffin takes off his bandage, and his clothes, and disappears altogether.

Though these points should be discussed more at length, one could relate the age of painting to a certain form of invisibility: the invisibility of the hidden spectator. One could relate the age of cinema to another form of invisibility, invisibility as transparency: the invisibility of the invisible man. Now, the digital age would be associated with a fantasy of intangibility. We no longer dream of invisibility. It seems that in contemporary discourse, invisibility is rather a social invisibility, on the model of Ellison's *Invisible Man*: it is weakness rather than power. Power would be the ability to not leave "traces": hide the IP of my computer, and the numbers of my credit cards, etc. But leaving no trace is being intangible.

Synhaptic

In his book on touch and Jean-Luc Nancy, Derrida denies that touch evades technology and, possibly thinking of Descartes' blind man and his stick, he situates technology in the space [espacement] in between the two sides of touch, in between the hand that touches and the object that is touched, or in between the skins that touch (Derrida 2000, 337). This idea is perfectly illustrated by the Hugshirt. When they "hug" each other, the two partners are separated by the whole apparatus of contemporary technology, smart shirts, sending signals to smartphones, sending signals to distant servers, and data centers that record the hug before sending it back to a distant server, a smartphone, a smart shirt. This is telehaptics: touch at a distance mediated by technology. But it is an anecdotal aspect of contemporary technology. In fact, whatever the reason (because they are too expensive or because we are not really interested in them), the devices that enable tele-haptics are not commercially successful. My claim is that, rather than tele-haptics, contemporary technology enables a dissociation of the reciprocity of touch and, in this way, the emergence of a new synhaptic sensibility. In fact, it brings touch towards vision. But, conversely, vision is also brought towards touch.

In *Mille Plateaux*, Deleuze and Guattari rely on a distinction between haptics and optics. Obviously, haptics is related to touch, and optics to sight. But haptics and optics are not defined by this relation to touch and to sight, nor is this relation exclusive (Deleuze and Guattari 1980, 601ff.). Haptics and optics are defined by their properties. Haptics are local, optics global. Sight gives a global impression of the room, whereas, when I put my hand on the table, I have only a local sensation of the texture of the wood. In fact, to form a global impression of the object, I have to coordinate a multiplicity of local sensations. In this sense, close sight, when I bring my eye close to the object, is also haptic, for it also gives a local impression of the object.[7]

Now, contemporary technology relies on a local use of sight: local but multiple. Take the watchman in a parking lot. He would sit in front of a screen, divided in several windows where various cameras show him key points of the parking lot. He does not use his sight as someone entering a room, or a restaurant, and taking a global view of the place would. His sight is multi-focal. It is a multiplicity of local views. Translated into the realm of touch, it is as if he had multiple hands placed on an object, each giving him

---

7   It is true that though touch gives a local impression of the object, it also informs us of some atmospheric quality (temperature, moisture) that seems to be lost in close vision. In this regard close vision would be even more "local" than touch.

a local sensation of the object. He must then reconnect these multiplicities in order to form an idea of the object.

Thus both touch and sight become what I call synhaptic. Following Deleuze and Guattari, I define our synhaptic sensibility by its properties rather than by its contents. First, our synhaptic sensibility has the reciprocity of vision: I can sense without being sensed. This requires a technical transformation of touch. Second, our synhaptic sensibility is local as touch: it is "haptic" in Deleuze and Guattari's sense. Third, it is multi-focal, like the different windows on the screen of the security guard of a parking lot. This multiplicity may imply contents coming from different senses. The security guard may be listening to the radio on his computer while he is gazing at his screen. Or he may be listening to a playlist that another user of the musical platform may have assembled several days before. There are various ways of reconnecting these multiplicities, but all of these connections are related to time. Or, more precisely, they require content coming from different moments in time to be placed in relation to one another in order to form one present, or recapture an actual state of the object. When the security guard is listening to a playlist, he relates a stream of music programmed in the past to the present images of the parking lot (the music itself having been recorded at yet another time). If he notices someone trying to steal a car, he might rewind the footage from the different cameras in order to find out how the thief entered the parking lot. He is now trying to find out who the thief is, to see his face. To do this, the watchman needs to reorganize different temporal flux, and isolate in those images that relate to the same object, the thief. Thus, our technological sensibility implies a multiplicity of flux—these always need to be synchronized and there are various way to operate this synchronization: What is happening in the parking lot now? Who is the man I see on camera 3?

I use the word "synhaptic" to express this idea that our technological sensibility is haptic (though it has not the reciprocity of touch). It is local and implies a synchronized multiplicity. More precisely, I want to oppose synhaptics to panoptics. The panopticon is a prison imagined by Jeremy Bentham. The cells are situated in a circular building, and the guard is standing in a tower in the middle of the circle. The prison is built so that, from his vantage, the guard can see all the prisoners in their cells. The guard of the panopticon sees all that is happening. In *Surveiller et punir* (1975), Foucault considers the panopticon as the diagram of the disciplinary societies that have developed since the seventeenth century. In his "Postscript on the Societies of Control," Deleuze argues that we no longer live in these disciplinary societies, which could be represented by the panopticon. Surveillance, claims Deleuze, no longer takes place in a prison, or a factory, or at school. We no longer need these closed institutions. Surveillance takes place outside, in the "open air": "The conception of a control mechanism, giving the position of any element in an open environment at any given instant (whether animal in a reserve, or human in a corporation as with an electronic collar) is not necessarily one of science fiction" (Deleuze 1992, 7).

My point is that the difference between disciplinary societies, modeled on the panopticon, and our control societies is not only that surveillance takes place outside of institutions. Surveillance uses another kind of sense model in which there is no need to see everything. The guard (of the parking lot, of a prison, of a city) does not need to see everything: he only needs to see what is happening at key points. Our cities are watched over by surveillance cameras but these do not capture the entirety of the city. The city is not a panopticon. If, for some reason, I wish to track a certain person who appears on the camera on the subway platform, I will rewind the images of the entrance to the station to find out when exactly the man got in. Then I will inspect all the cameras around the entrance: I catch the man on a camera belonging to a bank. Here I can see his face. I put it in the Google bar (let us say). I find the man's profile on LinkedIn. I now know who his friends are, and his colleagues, and where he went on holidays. Whether I am a policeman, or a computer doing data analysis, his profile will not give me everything about the man but it will give me a set of parameters, key elements that I can use to conclude whether the man is likely to steal a handbag, or whether he will buy the new phone that I advertise on the commercial screen of the subway. Again, I do not need to see everything, in an overall view, like when I enter a crowded room and look around to find out who is there, or like the keeper of the panopticon in his tower. I have a multiplicity of local, "haptic" data, and I isolate relevant elements in this data so as to perceive the actual state of my object. In this sense, I resynchronize these haptic data. Instead of the panopticon, we have a synhaptic sensibility.

As mentioned at the beginning of the paper, haptics is often considered to be the sense of affects. Indeed, some of the haptic technologies discussed above, the Hugshirt for instance, are related to the communication of affects. The same goes for our synhaptic sensibility in contrast to the panoptic model. The panopticon's guard observes the movements of his prisoners but has no access to their inner life. The synhaptic guard, or watchmachine, gaining access to relevant data, our profile on Facebook, the gallery of our photos on Instagram, our actual position, the books we read on Amazon, may know much more about us, our "preferences" and, indeed, some of our affects: at least those expressed by the emoticons we have tagged on our photos on Facebook. It may know, predict, or manipulate by sending us the right commercials. Synhaptic technologies are *de facto* affective technologies.

References

Cassou-Noguès, Pierre. 2010. *Mon zombie et moi: La philosophie comme fiction.* Paris: Seuil.
———. 2014. *Les cauchemars cybernétiques de Norbert Wiener.* Paris: Seuil.
———. 2016. "A Quasi-Phenomenology with Examples: The Invisible Man, the Posthuman and the Robot." *Iride, filosofia e discussione pubblica* 2: 299–314.
———. 2018. "Corrélationisme, spéculation et principe de présence" In *Choses en soi: Métaphysique du réalisme*, edited by Emmanuel Alloa and Elie During, 295–308. Paris: PUF.
Deleuze, Gilles. 1992. "Postscript on the Societies of Control." *October* 59: 3–7.
Deleuze, Gilles, and Félix Guattari. 1980. *Mille Plateaux.* Paris: Minuit.
Derrida, Jacques. 2000. *Le toucher, Jean-Luc Nancy.* Paris: Galilée.
Descartes. René. 1988. "Optics." In *The Philosophical Writings of René Descartes*, vol. 1. Translated by John Cottingham, Robert Stoothoff, and Dugald Murdoch, 152–76. Cambridge: Cambridge University Press.
Diderot, Denis. 1916. "Letter on the Blind for the Use of Those Who See." In *Diderot's Early Philosophical Works*, translated by Margaret Jourdain, 68–141. Chicago: Open Court.
Ellison, Ralph. 1952. *Invisible Man.* New York: Random.
Foucault, Michel. 1975. *Surveiller et punir.* Paris: Gallimard.
Herodotus. 2013. *Histories.* Translated by T. Holland. London: Penguin.
Plato. 2006. *The Republic.* Translated by R. E Allen. New Haven: Yale University Press.
Renard, Maurice. (1912) 1990a. "L'homme au corps subtil." In *Romans et Contes fantastiques*, 478–94. Paris: Laffont.
———. (1921) 1990b. "L'homme truqué." In *Romans et Contes fantastiques*, 737–95. Paris: Laffont.
Wells, Herbert G. 1897. *The Invisible Man.* London: Pearson.
Wiener, Norbert. 1950. *The Human Use of Human Beings.* New York: Houghton Mifflin.

Films

Verhoeven, Paul. 2000. *Hollow Man.* Columbia.
Whale, James. 1933. *The Invisible Man.* Universal.

HUMAN–ROBOT COLLABORATION

INTUITION

PROXIMITY

IMMEDIACY

TACIT KNOWLEDGE

[7]

Encoding Proximity: Intuition in Human–Robot Collaborations

Dawid Kasprowicz

The growing field of human–robot collaborations has raised questions of how to behave when interacting with speaking and moving technological objects. One key idea here represents the notion of intuition as the promise of natural and effortless interaction with non-living objects. But intuition also refers to a non-rational, affective mode of reasoning. This article argues that in human–robot collaborations, intuition is not exhaustive in the promise of fluid interactions. In showing how social expectations are encoded in collaborative practices, the text argues that intuition becomes a modus operandi for the programming and modeling of affects.

1.   Technics of "Natural" Feedback[1]

A body of two split ellipsoids, one ellipsoid mounted on top of the half-round of the other, with smooth edges and a light circle that expands and shrinks from the middle of the upper split-ellipsoid to signal a communication with the target person, an elderly lady. This strange-formed object is a social robot who at first sight reminds us more of a designer lamp kept in the back corner of the living room than of a private companion. But its producers, the American company Intuition Robotics, gave her a name and a voice. In the eyes of the company, ElliQ is this new member of the daily lifeworld for elderly people living alone, which can be placed between a design object and a living companion, between the non-living agent and the agent elderly people would like to talk to: "She sounds like a machine. She feels like a machine—but she has that one-of-a-kind personality that will help her users develop an enchanting feeling towards her." This intermingling of bodily passivity and social activity should form a core for users, as the company writes, "to intuitively understand the object in front of them so that they could naturally access this intelligence they perceive" (fig. 1).

[Figure 1] Intuitively to understand, the object ElliQ, Credits: Intuition Robotics

1   This article draws on ideas from another article dealing with the question of practices with robots, entitled "New Labor, Old Questions. Practices of Collaboration with Robots" (Kasprowicz [in preparation]).

ElliQ's main functions resemble those of Amazon's Alexa. She calls relatives, reminds us of dates in the calendar, and suggests activities for us from the collected user-data. ElliQ represents the revival of inanimate and lively objects, which "our primitive forebears" still had, as Sigmund Freud noted ([1919] 2003, 155), and which we re-establish today in our digitalized world. The notion of intuition plays a central role in this context. In the quote above, "intuitive" is used synonymously with the adjective "natural." Besides, the semantics of "intuitive" promise simple and effortless access to highly techno-sociological interactions. In all its semantic impact, intuition enables an assumedly unbiased and unmediated interaction with media. This function of the term has a long history in the field of human–computer interaction (HCI). Whether for an operating system or for the navigation of a homepage, an interface should be able to reduce complexity while at the same time referring to the symbols and processes of the user's experience. In the ideal way, the computer becomes itself the invisible machine in this interaction, hidden behind the operation of an intuitive, natural interface design (Norman 1998, 2011). One can call this intuition an *effect* because the success of the design can only be assured through the user's interaction.

However, with ElliQ as our example, intuition deals with something different, namely the formalization and coding of *affects*. Here, the social habitus of bodily proximity, gestures and haptics are discussed and transformed to target the human as the environment for a robotic system. Being intuitive therefore means creating an expected proximity that includes the potential affect of the human partner in the calculations of the robotic system. On the following pages, I will refer to a special field of human–robot interactions, so-called human–robot collaborations in industrial labor, to show how the notion of intuition transforms from a guiding concept for human–machine or human–computer interactions to a complex procedure entailing practices of modeling, simulating and materializing human–robot relationships. First, I will argue that within this transformation, intuition turns from the magical semantic of a "gut instinct" into a *modus operandi* to communicate social expectations, bodily routines and the tacit knowledge of labor between human and non-living agents. Secondly, I will use a case study of human–robot collaborations to demonstrate how these operations create a new interface that does not relate to displays or design objects, but to the space in between the heterogenous ontological agents. In this example, the operation is the robot's task of carrying a table with his human partner. Here, the coding of intuitive haptics not only regulates the sequence of actions but also the social status of each of the collaborators— either as the leader or the follower of the movement. But before we turn to the case study, I will go deeper into the problem of intuition as the natural and unmediated immediacy from a historical perspective.

2.   Mediated Immediacy—The Meaning of Intuition

In a general sense, a better understanding of what intuition might be can be given by explaining what it does not mean: a discursive formation to describe the world, to represent an idea, and therefore to activate something that mediates between the subject and the object—like concepts, images, or symbols. From this point of view, one could trace this idea back to Plato's "eidos." On the one hand, we can only think of the archetype through the image as a reproduced being that we can perceive. On the other hand, the image—as the "idea"—always belongs to the archetype and is derived from it at the same time. Here, the unity of being and the manifold of the sensually perceived world need something that mediates them.

However, regarding the modern age, the conception of a mediator for the transcendent world (whether it is the Platonic "eidos" or God's will), is suspended by the consciousness of a self. Intuition turns from the contemplation of God to an unmediated access to truth via the reasoning human self. This meaning of a clear, non-synthetic insight is made explicit in René Descartes' *Rules for the Direction of the Mind* when he writes:

> By 'intuition' I do not mean the fluctuating testimony of the senses or the deceptive judgement of the imagination as it botches things together, but the conception of a clear and attentive mind, which is so easy and distinct that there can be no room for doubt about what we are understanding. … intuition is the indubitable conception of a clear and attentive mind which proceeds solely from the light of reason. (Descartes after Williams [1684] 1996, xxiii)

As the philosopher Bernard Williams writes, the light of reason is similar to a classical Augustinian and Platonic sense of seeing intelligible things (1996, xxiii). In the philosophy of Immanuel Kant this god-given light of reason (or better: cognition) has nothing to do with intuition. For him, intuition means to synthesize the received manifold impressions of our sensibility to an apprehension. The intuitive use of reason is here, again, opposed to the discursive, which necessitates concepts. But—and this is an important turn—without explicit intuition, no conceptions of our apprehensions can be made. Finally, Kant's use of intuition defines access to the world that is only mediated through our sensibility—it neither depends on a *cogito* nor on a special quality of the world outside. Without our "sensible intuition" of the world, there can be neither any perception nor judgment of the world (Kant [1791] 1998, 288). However, all perceptions depend on two "axioms of intuition," as Kant calls them—the inner intuition of time, which combines the manifold sensations in the mechanism of causality, and the outer intuition of a "unity of space," which is based on the axioms of Euclidean geometry (262). These two "*a priori* conditions of intuition" ground the existence of our perceptions as the contingent "empirical intuitions" (284).

In these examples from Cartesian and Kantian philosophy, intuition maintains its enchanting power as unmediated access to *a* world or *to the* world outside. It comes together with an ambivalent status of something that is pre-conceptual, but which requires the discursive elaboration of a (self-)observing philosopher. This ambivalence continues throughout the 19th and 20th centuries, although here, intuition turns its meaning to a non-rational, non-analytic technique of reasoning. Philosophers like Henri Bergson see intuition as a method against the empirical and axiomatic definition of Kant. For Bergson, intuition opens up the questioning of the metaphysical absoluteness again ([1934] 1946, 32–34). The other significant approach comes from Edmund Husserl. Like Bergson, Husserl understands intuition as a method. But for him, it is the key to overcoming the Cartesian legacy of a world-constituting *res cogitans* on which all perceptions depend. Instead, Husserl calls for a "pure intuition" by which all external and historical circumstances are detached and only the unmediated, perceptual act of seeing can be used for statements about the world ([1929] 1977, 24). Whether as a concept for the unmediated access to our perception of the world or as a method for the genesis of knowledge, intuition keeps its ambivalent status and represents a special technique of thinking, which must be made explicit but that also withdraws from analytic concepts.

Today, this mixture is the dominating idea in the myriad books on business management. Economic success is something nobody can predict but nevertheless, some managers have a special talent for choosing the right option. Here again, it is a kind of "gut instinct" that enables some decision-makers to recognize a situation and then to decide more habitually than analytically, since they can't have access to all relevant information. The social scientist Herbert A. Simon termed this mode of intuitive decision-making "bounded rationality," and opened up the way for numerous theories and research projects on the affective constraints of *Homo oeconomicus* (1947, 1987; for a historical overview see Akinci and Sadler-Smith 2012, 109–16).

Another big influence on the question of decision-making and intuition in economics came from the psychologists Daniel Kahneman and Amos Tversky. Their research about gambling behavior in lotteries from 1981 showed an alternative to the Utility Theory. The premise of the Utility Theory is the *Homo oeconomicus* and rational mode of thinking, which can be derived from any economic situation if all conditions have been considered. But for Kahneman and Tversky, as for Simon, these models have been much too normative and ignorant about the hidden parameters influencing the human decision-making process (Kahneman and Tversky 1981, 5). Again, intuition is the hidden source underneath rational conclusions—it is, as Kahneman and Tversky write in one of their earlier publications, "our lay model of the world" (6).

In all its modes and meanings, whether as the intelligible insight into truth, or as the *a priori* for perceptions in space and time, whether as a method of metaphysics or as the "informal and unstructured mode of reasoning, without the use of analytic methods or deliberate calculation" (5), intuition represents both unmediated access to knowledge and a set of expectations for meeting the world. Thus, intuition does not only refer to a philosophical discourse, but it embraces the communication of different layers of a world, to paraphrase the term of Kahneman and Tversky. It is here where philosophers and engineers meet and where the construction of collaborative robots requires the formalization of those hidden, affectual layers.

3. Encoding Proximity: Man, Robot and the Interface

How does this relate to the actual questions around human–robot collaborations? First, the use of intuition in robotics aims to build up expectations of a direct and "natural" way of communicating with technical objects. The technics of gestures, signs and haptic commands open up a wide space of possible executions. The idea of a collaboration, as the agreement to pursue a single goal together, demands a mutual understanding between partners of the other's intentions, as well as the negotiation of one's own next movement. Hence, collaboration always implies not only the recognition of a partner's intentions but also the renegotiation of one's own intentions about the possible actions of the other, which are at the same time the variables for one's own movements. This mutual inclusion of the other, which Niklas Luhmann in his *Social Systems* called "interpenetration"[2] (1995, 213), entails another dimension of intuition in human–robot collaborations, in which gestures, signs and haptic commands have to be both "explicit and intuitive" (Gleeson et al. 2013, 349). It is here where the process of en- and de-coding proximity becomes crucial, because the practice of bodily routines and their assumed intuitive affect depends on the practice of formalizing movements and gestures to make them explicit. The Austrian-British philosopher and chemist Michael Polanyi called this the relation between "knowing-that" and "knowing-how." While the first designates the "proximal" term about the circumstances we are aware of but are not yet able to express, the second refers to the "distal" term that denotes the execution of the action (1966, 9–10).

In human–robot collaborations, the so-called tacit knowledge of the proximal must be modeled and materialized. An often-cited example of this logic is the task of carrying a table by two agents. In the following passages, I will describe the formalization of this tacit knowledge using the example of a project of a French group of robotic engineers from the University of Montpellier.

The goal of the project, which ran from 2009 to 2013, was to construct a robot that is able to execute simple tasks together with its human partner. In the group's project, to move the table with the human partner, the robot should not react to the fixed cues of a follower or a leader in the sense of stimulus-reaction chains. Instead, it should "recognize" the intentions of its human partner and interpret them so that it can anticipate the next movement and negotiate "its own programmed intentions" (Evrard and Kheddar 2009, 45). In this case, negotiating means to program subtle changes in body postures and movements to avoid uncomfortable table positions or too intrusive recommendations that could confuse the human partner. Hence, the formalization of haptics in the collaborative task of carrying a table does not refer to what autonomous agents *can do* in the first place, but how their haptics can be *en*coded to meet the social expectations of their partners. Encoding haptics of autonomous robots initiates the modeling of social values into a collaborative task.

2   It is important to indicate that for Luhmann, interpenetrations are intersystem relations that are environments for each other. Therefore, the collaborations are a mode in which the human becomes the environment of the robotic system. Moreover, one can't reduce interpenetrations to stimulus-response chains. Luhmann describes them as reciprocal penetrations that one can observe as the determination of the penetrating system by the receiving system. Each system does not react to the other but creates its own complexity with regard to penetrating systems (Luhmann 1995, 213).

For this collaborative setting, the French research group used a model called "homotopy switching," after the mathematical principle of homotopy (greek, homos=same and topos=place). A homotopy takes place between two topological spaces X and Y that are defined in the functions γ_0 and γ_1. If all points of the space X are identical and the same is the case for the space of Y, then the two functions γ_0 and γ_1 connecting the spaces are called homotopic. In a simple sense, these functions (which are also paths in a topological sense) have two parameters [0,1]—"0" for the initial condition with two topological spaces and "1" as the time that runs while the two functions deform into one another. The salient point is that X and Y are not only identical, but equivalent, defined by the two functions creating the homotopic space between X and Y (fig. 2).

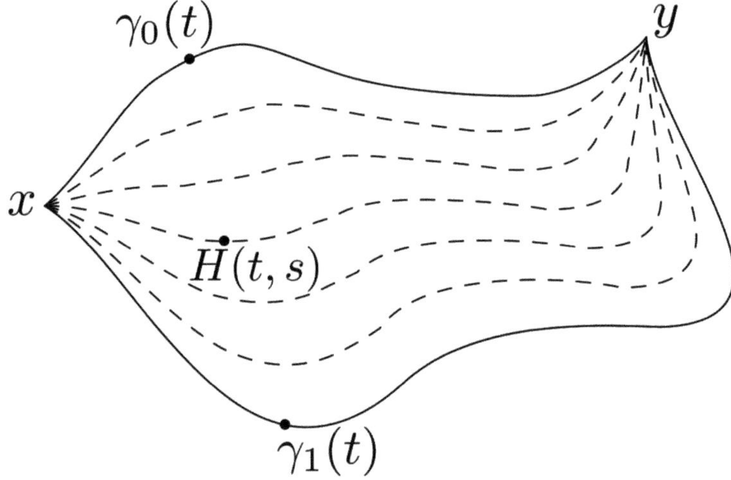

[Figure 2] Homotopy of two paths y: [0,1] → X, Credits: Archibald, Wikipedia, https://commons.wikimedia.org/wiki/File:Homotopy_curves.svg

Thus, in the case of human–robot collaboration, the model is implemented to compute the robot's desired joint positions after sensing the haptic cues of its human partner. Through the continuous deformation of one space into another, the robot's and the human's inputs are programmed as a homotopy between two impedance controllers—or in other words, the internal forces of the agent's haptic cues (Evrard 2013, 35). In this sense, the encoding of the homotopy model entails the transformation of social codes into a "haptic language." Intuition becomes a modus operandi in which "the robot can be shaped between the extreme leader and follower roles" (Evrard 2013, 35). As the engineers write, the robot cannot differentiate between the intention of its partner or a "misunderstanding" of the human's intentions. What the robotic agent senses as internal forces and what it computes as an adequate answer for being *in between* the role of a follower or leader is only materialized by the position of the table. Hence, intuition as the modus operandi defines technics as making the bodily and social routines of postures and haptics explicit and transforming the so-called tacit knowledge into a field of computerized models for robotic controllers. From this point of view, intuition cannot be exhausted by a technological euphoria of robots facilitating or taking away the job of the human employee. It addresses a sensible domain of socio-technological entanglements that are displayed on three levels—the modeling of the interaction as "homotopy switching," the computer simulation of the models, and the materialization of the robot.[3]

The transformation of social values into programming language and then mechanical executions are phenomena that have been neglected so far in social studies on robotics. Concerning the question of the social in robotics, ethnomethodological approaches in Science and Technology Studies describe how bodies are shaped through the maintenance of inter-actions between heterogenous agents (Alač 2016a; 2016b). Also, increasing numbers of theorists of the Actor–Network Theory (ANT) will include a dialogical and psychological dimension in their concept of communication, which refers not only to actions but to the challenge of a narration of the mechanical self (Jones 2017).[4] However, the imaginations of the social are also interwoven with the engineer's models and their chosen collaborative tasks. The aforementioned ambiguous situations of indecisive or misinter-preted haptic cues call for the mediation of factors like trust, autonomy, and the creation of an addressable self in the partner's actions. So, here the question arises—How to extract these factors from the data of the agent's movements?

3   The materialization and design of the robot are not explicated here further with regard to the collaboration. For a wider discourse on the engineering of anthropomorphic robots in the laboratory, see Suchman 2011.

4   In her article "What makes a robot 'social'?", Rashad Jones criticizes the ethnometh-odological approaches for being too restrictive in only focusing on the interactions observed by the researcher. Therefore, the thesis of anthropomorphic relations is maintained through a one-dimensional focus on the interactions between technical objects and humans. Jones formulates this as a critique of the STS approaches to social robotics and pleads for an ANT concept of the "social" that embraces non-human, non-anthropomorphic entities and the modes of creating a kind of general acceptance of them, which also includes new ways of attributing personality to technical agents (2017, 568–70).

Today, the challenge of predicting upcoming states with incomplete datasets is often solved with so-called Nearest Neighbor algorithms. One such algorithm is the estimation-maximization (EM) algorithm taken from stochastics. Since the robot's perception of bodies is always incomplete due to the complexity of changing movements and the noise and range limitations of sensor technologies, a procedure is needed to automatically complete the data until something like a body posture has been "recognized." At the same time, the robot must remain aware of its own location in space. This problem of mapping several sensorial inputs within a certain time frame, while it remains uncertain what will be sensed and where, is called the "data association problem" (Thrun 2002, 56). Thus, the EM algorithm calculates an expectation based on the associations of sets of sensed data. If the datasets are incomplete, as in the case of haptic communication during a collaborative task, the algorithm does not and cannot wait until the data are complete but calculates new expectations of incoming data iteratively. After this step, the algorithm generates so-called posterior sequences with an increasing likelihood of them happening.

As for the question of an operative intuition in human–robot collaboration, this leads to several more questions. First, the importance of the social aspect of collaborations, the weighting of one's own intentions with that of your partner's, depends on mapping and training algorithms. Whether the robot suggests movements like a leader or stays passive as a follower depends on the calculated expectations and the mapping of a contingent environment. The algorithm is part of the internal state estimation, which turns into a social factor that becomes observable through the interface of the carried table. On the one hand, the notion of intuition embraces still the meaning of a non-discursive, effortless but effective way of formulating a phrase or executing a movement.

> Intuitively, when the trajectories are the same, it is likely that no conflicting situation occurs; on the contrary, different desired trajectories induce a situation of conflict that needs to be negotiated and resolved. (Evrard and Kheddar 2009, 47)

On the other hand, intuition refers to a complex procedure of modeling and simulating the tacit knowledge of bodily communications between two agents. Negotiating a desired trajectory does not only mean designing a solution and programming its conversion through the robot. It also embraces a conglomerate of media like models, programs, algorithms and— not least—the material for the construction itself to articulate the social bond between the mechanical and human agents. This complex can be illustrated with Bruno Latour's concept of "delegation." Delegation, from the human point of view, contains both the expectation and the trust that the other agent will meet one's own intentions, as well as the new, passive status of the human in the network of non-human agencies. Latour takes his example from the traditional practice of a shepherd who guides his flock:

> As a common shepherd all I have to do is delegate to a wooden fence the task of containing my flock—then I can just go to sleep with my dog beside me. Who is acting while I am asleep? Me, the carpenters, and the fence. Am I expressed in this fence as if I had actualized outside of myself a competence that I possessed in potential form? Not in the slightest. The fence doesn't look at all like me. It is not an extension of my arms or of my dog. It is completely beyond me. It is an actant in its own right. (Latour 1996, 239)

Although, seemingly, the gap between Latour's shepherd laying in the countryside and the collaborating robots could hardly be wider, the means by which the fence becomes an agent "in its own right" takes up the withdrawal of the human subject and the opening up of a new space of expected and executed delegations. This is a space of intuition as operation. In opposition to Latour, the time of negotiation here is infinitely more critical, as is the impact of sensing each other's bodies. That's why the homotopic model represents both—the ideal of a collaborative task with agents leading and being led as well as the model to program controllers who manage flexible and fast force changes. The result is an en- and re-coding of proximity in man–robot collaborations that not only program bodily movements but also new ways of computationally dealing with social affects. Therefore, instead of maintaining its magical role of an unmediated immediacy, intuition is here the term for a transformation of knowledge—from body postures over haptic communications to the standardized ways of carrying a table.

Conclusion

The human "gut instinct" of intuition does not only belong to the depths of human thinking anymore. The concept of intuition has undergone, as I argued, an important semantic shift that relates it today to affective media technologies like human–robot collaborations. Due to our embodied media habits and screen environments, intuitive gestures belong meanwhile to a tacit user knowledge. Hence, on the one hand, this knowledge entails finger movements, body postures, screen-gaze couplings—all those little acts that don't have to be demonstrated because they are performed every day. On the other hand, intuition turns also into an operative mode that constitutes new interfaces as in-between spaces—like the carried table as a task modeled after the mathematical model of "homotopy switching." Thus, the notion of intuition refers to this twofold meaning: a tacit knowledge in interaction with media and an operation that constitutes new interfaces between man and technology through the formalization and simulation of this tacit knowledge.

In this sense, the table becomes the materialization of an algorithmic proximity. This does not lead to another turn of hybridized embodiments, but to human–robot practices that involve the formalization of gestures, the encoding of a semantics of routine bodily practices, and of haptic codes for social questions of leading and being led as well as the numerous indefinite states of transition. It is here where intuition becomes a modus operandi for the computerization of affects.

Therefore, to describe the phenomena of human–robot collaborations as an example of a posthuman society to come would be shortsighted (Gladden 2016). This overlooks the importance of the messiness of the transformation of our bodily tacit knowledge through models, simulations, and constructions. Instead, the formalization of tacit bodily knowledge retroacts on the social space—in other words, to sense and read human bodies presupposes to model the human as a part of the robot's environment. Drilling down to the level of routine bodily practices, the encoding of proximity becomes a research object for new ways of describing human-centered concepts like autonomy and free will. This shift then triggers also the question of how these new companions should address us in order to be understood as easily as products like ElliQ promise to be.

References

Archibald. 2009. "Homotopy Curves." *Wikipedia*. Accessed October 10, 2020. https://commons.wikimedia.org/wiki/File:Homotopy_curves.svg.

Akinci, Cinla, and Eugene Sadler-Smith. 2012. "Intuition in Management Research: A Historical Review." *International Journal of Management Reviews* 14 (1): 104–22.

Alač, Morana. 2016a. "Social Robots: Things or Agents?" *AI & Society* 31 (4): 519–35.

———. 2016b. "'Points to and Shakes the Robot's Hand:' Intimacy as Situated Interactional Maintenance of Humanoid Technology." *Zeitschrift für Medienwissenschaft* 15 (2). Accessed April 29, 2018. https://www.zfmedienwissenschaft.de/online/points-and-shakes-robots-hand.

Bergson, Henri. (1934) 1946. *The Creative Mind*. Translated by Mabelle L. Andison. New York: Philosophical Library.

Evrard, Paul. 2013. *Control of Humanoid Robots to Realize Haptic Tasks in Collaboration with a Human Collaborator.* Dissertation: Université Montpellier. Accessed March 28, 2018. https://tel.archivesouvertes.fr/tel-00807094.

Evrard, Paul, and Abderrahmane Kheddar. 2009. "Homotopy Switching Model for Dyad Haptic Interactions in Physical Collaborative Tasks." In *World Haptics – 3rd Joint EuroHaptics conference and Symposium on Haptic Interfaces for Virtual Environment and Teleoperator Systems*, edited by IEEE Technical Committee on Haptics, 45–50. Salt Lake City: IEEE Digital Library. doi: 10.1109/WHC.2009.4810879

Freud, Sigmund. (1919) 2003. *The Uncanny.* London: Penguin Classics.

Gladden, Matthew E. 2016. *Posthuman Management: Creating Effective Organizations in an Age of Social Robotics, Ubiquitous AI, Human Augmentation, and Virtual Worlds.* 2nd Ed. Indianapolis: Synthypnion Press.

Gleeson, Brian, et al. 2013. "Gestures for Industry: Intuitive Human–Robot Communication from Human Observation." *Proceedings of the 8th ACM/IEEE International Conference on Human–Robot Interaction (HRI).* 3–6 March 2013, 349–56. doi: 10.1109/HRI.2013.6483609

Husserl, Edmund. (1929) 1977. *Cartesian Meditations: An Introduction to Phenomenology.* Translated by Dorian Cairns. The Hague: Martinus Nijhoff.

Jones, Raya A. 2017. "What Makes a Robot 'Social'?" *Social Studies of Science* 47 (4): 556–79.

Kahneman, Daniel, and Amos Tversky. 1981. *On the Study of Statistical Intuitions.* Technical Report, Engineering Psychology Programs, Office of Naval Research. Arlington, VA.

Kant, Immanuel. (1791) 1998. *Critique of Pure Reason.* Translated and edited by Paul Guyer and Allen W. Wood. Cambridge: Cambridge University Press.

Kasprowicz, Dawid. [in preparation]. "New Labor, Old Question: Practices of Collaboration with Robots." In *Connect and Divide: The Practice Turn in Media Studies.* Edited by Ulrike Bergermann, Monika Dommann, Erhard Schüttpelz, and Jeremy Stolow. Berlin: Diaphanes.

Latour, Bruno. 1996. "On Interobjectivity." *Mind, Culture and Activity* 3 (4): 228–45.

Luhmann, Niklas. 1995. *Social Systems.* Translated by John Bednarz and Dirk Baecker. Stanford: Stanford University Press.

Merriam-Webster.com Dictionary, s.v. "intuition (*n.*)." Accessed November 29, 2019, https://www.merriam-webster.com/dictionary/intuition.

N.N. 2017. "Elli-Q, Part I: Name and Face." *Blog Intuition Robotics*, July 6. Accessed October 10, 2020. https://elliq.com/blogs/elliq-blog/designing-elliq-part-i-name-and-face.

Norman, Donald. 1998. *The Invisible Computer: Why Good Products Fail, the Personal Computer Is so Complex, and Information Appliances Are the Solution.* Cambridge, MA: MIT Press.

———. 2011. *Living with Complexity.* Cambridge, MA: MIT Press.

Polanyi, Michael. (1966) 2009. *The Tacit Dimension.* Chicago: Chicago University Press.

Simon, Herbert A. 1947. *Administrative Behavior.* New York: Free Press.

———. 1987. "Making Management Decisions: The Role of Intuition and Emotion." *Academy of Management Executive* 1 (1): 57–64.

Suchman, Lucy. 2011. "Subject Objects." *Feminist Theory* 12 (2): 119–45.

Thrun, Sebastian. 2002. "Probabilistic Robotics." *Communications of the ACM* 45 (3): 52–57.

Williams, Bernard. 1996. "Introductory Essay." In *René Descartes: Meditations on First Philosophy. With Selections from the Objections and Replies.* Edited by John Cottingham, vii–xxxviii. Cambridge: Cambridge University Press.

SMART HOME

CARE SERVICES

HABITS

AUTONOMY

CARE

8

Autonomous Dwelling: Smart Homes and Care IT

Irina Kaldrack

In the context of eHealth, the development of smart homes aims to enable older and ill people to live in their own home environment. This paper focuses on the relationship between dwelling, autonomy and care, approaching it from three perspectives: from the perspective (and interests) of the vendors, from the experience and perspective of the people living in the smart home, and from the view of care providers and services.

The introduction and implementation of smart and autonomous technologies in private households is frequently accompanied by three arguments: the new technology will improve convenience for its user, enhance security, and help to sustain or increase individual independence. According to the "Smart Home Monitor 2017," a representative survey of Germany, this holds for smart home technologies as well: prospective buyers of networked household appliances and central controls for home automation wish for comfort (63.9%) and security (39.1%). The actual utilization of smart home technologies covers energy management (59.7%), entertainment and communication (56.1%), home automation (36.4%), surveillance/security (32.5%) and health (15.5%) (see Splendid Research 2017).

Although smart home technologies may not seem to be used primarily for health reasons, they feature as a field of research and teaching in informatics, medical informatics, and eHealth. Additionally "Ambient assisted living" and "assistive technologies" are subjects of different funding programs on a national as well as on a European level.[1]

Two main arguments stress the imperative of the development and implementation of smart home technologies: the first points to increasing costs and the growing need for personnel and nursing facilities in times of ageing societies. The second makes the point that people want to live at home as long as possible. Following these arguments, smart homes fulfill the desires of the individual and solve the upcoming societal problems of the near future (see Neven 2015; Domínguez-Rué and Nierling 2016b).

In the following I want to demonstrate how smart homes for medicine (re-)configure dwellings in a specific way. My focus lies on the relationship between dwelling, autonomy, and care. I describe this relation from three different perspectives. First, the perspective (and interests) of the vendors—developers of technologies, and providers of housing and care services —which could also be seen as a "backend" perspective or as an external view on the smart home, and second, the experience and perspective of the people living in the smart home, thus being-in the smart home. In comparing these perspectives, their similarities and divergences become apparent. Finally I consider the view of care persons and service providers, whose positions regarding the smart home and its agency change and develop, entering the smart home from the "outside" and leaving it from the "inside."

1. Perspective: Development

I will continually refer to one specific example: the so-called smart home for medicine, developed and researched at the Peter L. Reichertz Institute for Medical Informatics at Technische Universität Braunschweig. The Institute runs the research apartment Halberstadtstraße in Braunschweig, which is equipped with all sorts of sensors to track activity and deduce behavior.

---

1   For the EU program "Active and Assisted Living Research and Development Programme (AAL)," see: http://www.aal-europe.eu/, accessed May 7th 2019. In Germany, AAL is part of the High-Tech Strategy of the Bundesregierung as well as of the Digitale Agenda 2014–2017.

It is a kind of testbed to collect data, evaluate methods, and develop algorithmic analyses. "The goal of the 'research apartment Halberstadt-straße' (HSS) is to establish the home as a site for diagnostics and therapy for medical care" (Mielke, Voss, and Haux 2017, 93).

The research apartment aims to detect mental illnesses such as depression, dementia or bipolar disorder at a very early stage of the disease. The collected data are used to deduce behavioral patterns and the habits of the resident. On the basis of such analyses the flat is then supposed to decide whether its inhabitant is healthy or ill. The vision of the developer is that in the future the flat will be able to intervene at a very early stage of an illness.[2]

1.1   Sensors and Data Collection

Crucial for the survey of behavior patterns and habits of the inhabitant of a smart home are several factors: the sensors, the collected data, their computation, and the interpretation of their results. In the research apartment every room is equipped with presence and brightness detectors installed in the ceiling, and temperature and humidity sensors in the walls (see Mielke, Voss, and Haux 2017, 94).

The presence detector contains three passive infrared sensors (PIR) that detect temperature changes (changes in thermal radiation) in their respective reception area. A brightness sensor uses a photodiode to measure the intensity of light in a room. Every window and the front door is equipped with (magnetic) contact sensors to indicate whether they are open or closed. Finally, there are sensors monitoring all taps, measuring when and for how long cold or warm water is running. These sensors record values either in short intervals or, if a particular condition is detected, send them (via a bus) to a MiniPc, where they are stored as time series.[3]

Essentially, the data can tell us *when*, *where*, and *what*: where a heat-emitting object (maybe a person) is, and where and when which devices are used. To then deduce behavioral patterns and habits from these data, the data have to be merged, analyzed, and interpreted.

---

2   Interestingly, Rosalind W. Picard uses the same argument as early as 1997 to underline the use of computer-based recognition in her book *Affective Computing* (Picard, 1997).

3   For more detailed descriptions regarding the sensors, see Cook and Krishnan (2015, 11ff.).

1.2   Analysis and Interpretation of Stored Data

There are different stages of data analysis and interpretation: the first two weeks of data storage are set as a reference phase—the measured data are considered to represent the normal everyday life of the subject. Based on this, the monitoring/surveillance is supposed to recognize differences and deviations from that norm.

Regarding these stages of data processing, statistical methods are used to calculate characteristic parameters like maxima, minima, means, deviations, variations, and the like. These numbers summarize and characterize the time series output of one sensor in a chosen time interval. As such, they characterize first of all the activity of a specific sensor.

Regarding the detection and interpretation of the behavior and habits of a person, it is reasonable to relate the data from a number of different sensors.

> For example, in a smart home setting, multiple sensors such as motion, temperature, and pressure sensors gather complementary data about a Cooking activity. Motion sensors can provide data about a human presence in the kitchen area, temperature sensors provide clues to whether the stove is on and pressure or vibration sensors can indicate whether any kitchen objects are being used. While these three sensor classes may independently be weak at characterizing the Cooking activity, fusing them together leads to a stronger model. (Cook and Krishnan 2015, 34–35)

In order to relate measurements made by different sensors data mining methods are used. Statistical analyses of the single sensor measurements show patterns—what sensor events occur when and how often. With methods like correlation it becomes obvious which of the sensors are most likely to simultaneously measure activity.

The interpretation of the data follows the framework of the so-called ADLs, or "activities of daily living." There are a couple of ADL indexes, depending on national traditions and on the contexts in which they are used, but they all provide a categorization of activities of self-care. They include tasks like bathing, dressing, toileting, transferring, continence, and feeding. The ADL indexes define (to a certain extent) standard specifications of self-care and provide a kind of test or rating of how self-care has to happen. They are used in health care of elderly people, where their ability to perform certain ADL tasks can be a crucial factor in deciding whether they can be discharged from hospital. In this perspective, ADL indexes allow the assessment of the degree of a person's autonomy.

1.3 The Relation Between Dwelling, Autonomy, and Care

From my perspective, the smart home for medicine considers dwelling as daily routines—what do people usually do in their apartment? The "doing" itself is mainly being in and moving through the space and using its facilities and devices. The "usually" is determined by two aspects: *firstly* by the data collection of the reference phase, in which the data are set as "normal" and used to recognize differences and deviations in the data. *Secondly* the "usually" is determined through the definition or categorization of ADL. Then dwelling is performing daily routines, which includes performing enough ADL and taking sufficient time or duration for each of them.

Care is understood initially as self-care with regard to physical or personal hygiene. The smart home for medicine incorporates a diagnostic view or perspective of elderly care in its monitoring. In this view self-care activity and self-care ability are references for normal behavior and autonomy.

In the context of the smart home and its diagnostic view, autonomy predominantly means the ability to live alone without health service intervention. Thinking about autonomy as a concept, it has a double structure of independence and self-determination (the latter in the sense of self-legislation—giving oneself aims and performing them with discipline).[4]

The smart home evaluates whether the behavior of its resident with regard of performing independent and self-determined actions guarantees the preservation and care of the body and its vital functions. Thus autonomy somehow equals self-care or, to be more precise, autonomy shows itself in self-care; self-care is a feature of autonomy. Which means that one's autonomy is proven, because one is performing sufficient self-care in using the facilities in the home. Conversely, that means not performing sufficient self-care is the indicator that one's autonomy is somehow broken. The envisioned health services and interventions do cure the symptoms:

---

4   There is a vital debate in philosophy and social science as well as in media studies around the term and concept of autonomy. The crucial points are, if anybody might be seen as isolated from others, or if everybody is embedded in (social) relations and every self is influenced by cultural and governmental issues. I do take up the discussion with a focus on relational autonomy later. Another question is, how (media) technologies enter in the formation of self-conception (Selbst-Verständnis), self-relation (Selbst-Verhältnis), and technologies of the self (Selbst-Technologien)— which are crucial for autonomy.

the smart home would call for support or assistance, to get its data back to normality. With this analysis, I do end up in a bio-cybernetic vision of organism-and-environment (see e.g., Morin [1981] 2015). Care IT would then provide a form of self-regulation for this composite of organism and environment, which materializes as self-regulation of the data streams representing it.

In a way, this diagnosis is unsatisfactory: the relationship between living and autonomy is not limited to personal hygiene—it includes categories of personal space, having control and feeling at home, which includes aspects of affect regulation as well. Following up, I would like to consider the questions: What does dwelling mean in the experience of the living human? And how does this relate to autonomy and care?

2. Dwelling as Experience and Perception— Inhabitants' Perspective

What is dwelling? As a part of an adequate standard of living "the right of housing" is recognized in the Universal Declaration of Human Rights (1948). It has been regarded as a freestanding right in International Human Rights Law since 1991. As such it demands that there is sufficient living space (including necessary infrastructure such as electricity and water) and that the housing is protected against state and private interference (see Krennerich 2018).

> [H]aving a home is undoubtedly one of the most basic of human needs: the right to adequate housing is founded and recognised under international law. Described under article 25(1) of the Universal Declaration of Human Rights, the right to adequate housing is one that has also been identified within other major international human rights treaties. Referring to much more than the robustness of a building, 'adequate housing' encompasses also the intangible, but no less essential elements of what makes a dwelling into a home. This includes creating a private space that is secure and safe, which encloses and facilitates the formation and maintenance of human relationships and personal bonds. (Guihen 2016, 141–42)

In these terms of human and political rights, housing serves to protect against the forces of nature and society and is the condition that enables physical well-being and emotional relations. Dwelling or living—*wohnen* in German—is more than housing: it refers to being or feeling at home.

Thus on a basic level dwelling comprises a demarcation and thus a distinction between outside and inside. At the same time, dwelling is emotional or affective: the inside becomes a living place in subjective experiences and the affective inhabitation of the space. This understanding of dwelling is grounded in the experience of the subject, and resonates with approaches of (phenomenological) philosophy at the beginning of the 20th century.[5]

Around 1900, the traditional notion of a preceding, empty, homogeneous (Euclidean) space extending into infinity became problematic. In different disciplines space is no longer thought of as an independent and given container, but as something becoming, something evolving in relations and in perceptions. In the early phenomenological thinking of Edmund Husserl the corporality is the origin of perception and experience, and it is in the intentional experience that space is constituted. Thus the "here" of the own body is the zero point of orientation in the space. Equally the space arranges itself in relation to my "here" in top/bottom, front/back, right/left, and near/far (see Hebert, 2012, 56ff.).

Even though Ernst Cassirer was not a phenomenologist in a strict sense, he has contributed important considerations to the relationship between space (constitution), experience, and affect. Following Bösel's reconstruction, Cassirer shows that the mythical relation to space is bound to physiological differentiations such as top/bottom, front/back, and right/left. More importantly, these differentiations are structured by emotional or affective values:

> The principle of differentiation occurs as an affectability that allows to distinguish sites, districts or areas that are perceived as particularly powerful from the rather inconspicuous places in space. (Bösel 2018, 144 [translation by author])[6]

Bösel emphasizes that already in protoreligious and cultic practices—as examined in Cassirer's "Mythical Thought"—the demarcation, the act of limitation, is accomplished as a kind of space-modulating activity. The separation of interior and exterior space "... does not only have the

5   I do refer here mainly to two expositions/explanations. Firstly I follow Saskia Hebert's reconstructions of phenomenological notions of space for the context of architecture (see Hebert 2012, 53–112). Secondly I am referring to Bernd Bösel's habilitation thesis *Die Plastizität der Gefühle: Eine genealogische Kritik der Affektverfügung* (Bösel 2018).

6   "Als Differenzierungsprinzip tritt dabei eine Affizierbarkeit auf, die es erlaubt, als besonders machtvoll empfundene Stätten, Bezirke oder Gegenden von den eher unauffälligen Stellen im Raum abzusetzen."

power of space division, but also of highlighting, if not constituting, a special atmosphere" (Bösel 2018, 145 [translation by author]). That means: limitation is an affective differentiation of space, which is actively created. This applies to sacred rooms, but Bösel extends this double operation with Heidegger to inhabited/residential rooms. Accordingly, both Cassirer and Heidegger share the assumption of a "foundation of the inhabited space in the basic act of enclosure" (Bösel 2018, 146 [translation by author]).

In the paper "Building, Dwelling, Thinking" (Heidegger 1971) Heidegger expatiates on the intertwining of building (as the act of actively creating a place) and dwelling. Accordingly, building as construction is what makes living possible in the first place. Furthermore, according to Heidegger, the etymology of the word Bauen/building refers to staying as well as to cultivating and sparing as in the sense of agriculture.[7]

> The old word *bauen*, which says that man *is* insofar as he *dwells*, this word *bauen* however *also* means at the same time to cherish and protect, to preserve and care for, specifically to till the soil, to cultivate the vine. Such building only takes care—it tends the growth that ripens into its fruit of its own accord. Building in the sense of preserving and nurturing is not making anything. (Heidegger 1971, 145 [italics i.o.])

Building and dwelling coincide, whereby the Gothic word for dwelling/ Wohnen emphasizes the experience associated with it:

> *Wunian* means: to be at peace, to be brought to peace, to remain in peace. The word for peace, *Friede*, means the free, das *Frye*, and *fry* means: preserved from harm and danger, preserved from something, safeguarded. (147 [italics i.o.])

Conversely Heidegger's concept of dwelling is linked to his concept of being-in or being-in-the-world (as a mode of Dasein): "To be a human being means to be on the Earth as a mortal. It means to dwell" (145). In this sense, being-in-the-world means to inhabit the world, to make the world habituated and to experience equally protection and freedom. In turn "… dwelling itself is always a staying with things" (149). In this way it is based, as Hebert argues, equally in the unconscious, pre-reflective, active handling of things (see Hebert 2012, 63–64). Thus dwelling might be characterized as

---

7   On the etymological interconnections between building, living, being and cultivating, see also the entries on "bauen," "Frieden," "frei" and "wohnen" in Kluge (2011).

a performative act grounded in an action context.[8] It is strongly related to everyday activities, bodily routines, and habits.

Thus the condition of dwelling is the limitation as an active and affective space division, differentiating between an inside and outside space. The inside space becomes an inhabited space, a "living room" and a home through performative acts and routines grounded in actions, making the space familiar/habituated.

The reference to the context of action opens up another aspect of what constitutes home, dwelling, and living. Getting back to International Human Rights Law, the inside is not only a familiar place, but a protected place— it is supposed to be protected against state interference. This protection against interference opens up a space of freedom and self-determination. Saskia Hebert argues with reference to Bernhard Waldenfels:

> The apartment as an own space is separated from the surroundings as a foreign space. Within the boundary that separates the outside from the inside, the protected private space is created: "My" apartment (a way of speaking that I also use when I am not the owner but rather "inhabitant") is the place, where, within certain limits, I am free to do whatever I like. (Hebert 2012, 68 [translation by author])

Thus the inhabitant has control over the space, allowing them a certain freedom of action. One's own home is therefore a familiar place, and a self-determined place, a place that one can have at one's disposal by acting.

This means that a home—and the experience of being-at-home from a phenomenological point of view—modulates dwelling as a creation of an "own" space grounded in action contexts—these encompass habits and daily routines as well as the freedom to do what one wants, which necessitates a certain self-determination in acting. The repeated performative acts of dwelling resonate with caring in the sense of cultivating, sparing, and preserving. The aspect of self-determination resonates with a "classical" understanding of autonomy. In such a "classical" approach, autonomy is characterized as self-determination or self-government that is based on the rational mind and free will of a "self" or subject—which includes it being independent of external forces or coercions. Although the freedom to do whatever one wants does not equal rational driven

---

8   "Das Einräumen der Orte, bei Heidegger durch Um- und Wegräumen der Dinge ergänzt, ist ein *performativer* Akt, der das Wohnen wesentlich in einem *Handlungs-zusammenhang* gründet" (Hebert 2012, 64 [italics i.o.])

self-government in all aspects, both forms of self-determination include the aspect of not being surveilled.

To put it very pointedly: the autonomous rational universal (male) subject is—since Descartes—formed as an interior almost independent of the outside world. In and through its thinking, it processes and evaluates the impressions that enter from the outside to its inside. In addition, and this is crucial, it has a reflective relationship to itself, it can think about itself. At the same time, the Descartes subject has far-reaching control over what steps from inside to outside, be it as statement or expression. Similarly, the private sphere associated with housing is conceptualized as an interior independent of external powers, in which the responsible citizen processes impressions and information about the external world and internalizes them in opinions about or attitudes towards the world. What is decisive, especially for the formation of political will, is that this space is largely protected from state intervention. The (politically) mature citizen has control over what moves outside.

Of course, the notion of the self-contained autonomous subject is not tenable in this way, and even Descartes' philosophy includes aspects of being interwoven with and affected by the outside world. Historically, a different understanding of the connected, and thus affected and relational, subject can be drawn from Leibniz via Spinoza, Bergson, and Merleau-Ponty to Deleuze. More recent concepts of relational autonomy also emphasize that the rational, universal subject does not exist.

> The critiques emphasize that an analysis of the characteristics and capacities of the self cannot be adequately undertaken without attention to the rich and complex social and historical contexts in which agents are embedded; they point to the need to think of autonomy as a characteristic of agents who are emotional, embodied, desiring, creative, and feeling, as well as rational, creatures; and they highlight the ways in which agents are both psychically internally differentiated and socially differentiated from others. (Mackenzie and Stoljar 2000, 21)

Accordingly, the self-relationship is not to be thought of as autonomous and isolated from others.

> One's relationship to oneself, then, is not a matter of a solitary ego reflecting on itself, but is the result of an ongoing intersubjective process, in which one's attitude toward oneself emerges in one's

encounter with another's attitude toward oneself. (Anderson and Honneth 2005, 130–31)

In more recent media studies on what can be described as the infrastructure of living, it has become apparent that the inside space is by no means closed off from the outside space. On the contrary, exchanges have long been taking place between the inside and the outside: sewage/water, gas and electricity lines, radio and telephone break through the separation. In contemporary discourses, the intrusion of the "new" media such as radio and telephone was addressed particularly under the aspect of surveillance and intrusion into the private sphere (see Kammerer 2014).

An early example of the outside–inside connection is the electrified doorbell, as Florian Sprenger demonstrates in the essay "Elektrifizierte Schwellen. Zur Kulturtechnik der Klingel" (Sprenger 2015). He refers to the signal technology possibilities in households described by the Kaiserliche Telegraphen-Inspektor (Imperial Telegraph Inspector) Oskar Canter and locates these in the context of logistical control:

> According to Canter, electrical alarm systems occupy the thresholds of a house to report their crossing, door locks can be locked remotely, and thermometers in control systems indicate the temperature of remote rooms. Contacts are activated and circuits are opened or closed so that the desired event of ringing, chiming or lighting occurs. ... All these processes serve to regulate the flows of invited and uninvited guests, of energies and objects—or at least to suggest measures for this purpose. Entering the house by passing the threshold becomes an act monitored from a distance; the intruder can be stopped at the threshold, controlled or even let in automatically. (Sprenger 2015, 208–9 [translation by author])

However, and this is crucial, control over the intrusion into homes with telephones "around 1900" is greatly reduced. Following on from Walter Benjamin's *A Berlin Childhood around 1900* (Benjamin 2006), written in the 1930s, Sprenger describes:

> According to Benjamin, no one can escape the ringing of the bell, which disturbs a world-historical epoch during the midday sleep, no wall, no door stops it. In the era of the domestication[9] of electricity, the

---

9   With domestication, Sprenger refers to Silverstone's concept of "domestication," which describes how "new technologies" are incorporated into the everyday lives of users, especially through their utilization in the domestic environment (see Silverstone and Hirsch, 1992).

> thresholds and the transmission of electricity modulating space and time also change the status of the house as the "other" of the world—as the place where the world is turned into its opposite, because inside and outside are redefined and intertwined here. (Sprenger 2015, 215 [translation by author])

With regard to my thoughts on the relationship between dwelling and autonomy, as it is modulated in the "infrastructure" of the smart home for medicine, it can be said that the smart home seems to reverse external–internal relationships. The relationship between dwelling as experience and being-in the world is shaped by the fact that the living person has control over the interior. On the one hand, s/he obtains this in a pre-reflexive action context, handling the domestic environment and dwelling in the rooms. On the other hand, the protected interior also gives the residents a certain freedom in their actions and decisions. This goes hand in hand with the fact that control over the interior consists of (or is imagined as) determining what enters or leaves the living space.

With the smart home and its monitoring, this is inverted: it is not so much a question of whether and what enters from the outside to the inside. Rather, the interior moves outwards, in the form of the measured representation of living-as-a-habit. Autonomy is equated with the ability to live alone, i.e., to care for oneself (and the home). The aspect of autonomy, which is connected with decision and freedom of action (and which is bound to privacy), is suspended.

3. Care Services—Entering the Inside

From the perspective of the developers of the smart home for medicine, this suspension may not be so decisive, since it applies to people affected by depression or dementia in old age.

> Where our mind is often considered the core of our existence as independent, self-directing individuals, dementia tends to be portrayed as involving a loss of self. This depiction effectively makes people with dementia invisible as persons and easily leads to a "malignant social psychology" (Kitwood 1997, 4) that further undermines their personhood by stigmatization, infantilization and objectification. (Kamphof 2016, 164)

Kamphof's research is interesting for my purposes because she has undertaken qualitative ethnographic research of situated practices in the context of telecare. In the Dutch pilot project, apartments of elderly dementia patients were equipped with smart technologies that are very similar to the technologies and evaluation principles described above.

Kamphof accompanied the work of the caregivers ethnographically and examined how the handling of technologies affects care relation-ships. Following Kitwood Kamphof understands "dementia care as 'person work' " (Kamphof 2016, 165) and emphazises the close connection of "perceptive attention to the needs of frail elderly people with ethical respect for their unique personhood" (166). Following on from the meaning of the word respect as seeing again, Kamphof examines

> how processes of technologically mediated *seeing again* and of care's tinkering take shape in a specific compound in Dutch homecare, and how respect—or disregard—for clients as persons is part of emerging care practices. (166)

Kamphof describes the conditions of success for monitoring-supported care: first of all, patients must accept that their home and their behavior are measured:

> Clients have to refrain from meddling with the sensors, they have to entrust themselves to the system and the observation of caregivers, and allow these to bring up issues. The system asks them to be, at the same time, generally aware of the security provided, but to forget its presence on a daily basis. (174)

The caregivers, in turn, must become engaged in monitoring and read into the data patterns:

> Caregivers mentioned being struck by the observed consistency of patterns displayed by their clients. Habits, in this view, are not dull con-formity to norms, but an expression of being able to live in-the-world and a vital part of our embodied identity.

> Lifestyle monitoring thus operates in a field of tension between the inherited and normative and individual being-in-place. Seeing rhythms connects the quantitative where and when, detected by sensors and algorithms, with qualitative aspects of bodies living in space. Detecting rhythms is not computing averages; it requires observers to open their body to the resonance of emerging patterns ... . Within the monitoring compound, the observing body open to rhythms ... is a composite of technology and the sensibility of human caregivers. (169)

Ideally, the data streams or data patterns mediate between the people in charge and the people being looked after. People with dementia can hardly name what they have done and only partly express what their needs and desires are. With reference to the data streams, however, their behavior can be named and it is possible to derive their needs or wishes from the data.

> Increasing familiarity, both with the system and their client, makes them recognize specific patterns as typical for their client. When discussing data displays, they often referred immediately to particular situations. Hermeneutic perception, with the help of contextual knowledge and imagination, thus turns into an embodied feeling of clients through the system. (177)

The crucial point is that this technology is embedded in a structure of care relations in which the results of monitoring are the basis for "negotiations." The carers read the results, allowing themselves to be affected by the everyday life of their care recipients on a rhythmic level, so to speak. In this way, caregivers can also strengthen the freedom of action for an "autonomous dwelling," which threatens to disappear through the orientation of data processing to the norm of habit. Ideally, they allow a reflective access to the behavior of the resident, thus empowering him or her to work on their own personhood and opening up opportunities for intersubjective negotiation.

Regarding the affective transformations taking place in this form of computer-aided autonomous dwelling, I would like to offer the following conclusions: the technical-medial infrastructure of the smart home relates to dwelling, autonomy and care (services) in a specific way. In particular, their non-conscious registers are addressed: here living is considered as a habit, which also includes practices of self-care and autonomy as living-by-oneself in the lanes of regular and "normal" activities.

The domestication of surveillance and monitoring is being justified by economic-liberal arguments—elderly people want to be able to live by themselves and this wish can only be realized through care IT in an afford-able way. The technical-normalizing access (see Angerer and Bösel 2016) to autonomous living occurs in turn on a level of non-conscious processes, on the level of habits, pre-reflective contexts of action, and affective qualities. In this approach, aspects that have to do with autonomy as self-made deci-sions in an unsupervised space are particularly neglected.

Within this regime, carers are able to create leeway because they can inter-pret the deviations from the normal and the habitual—which are regarded as markers for a loss of autonomy in technical monitoring. However, this interpretation mainly takes place at the level of empathy with data patterns, as an aesthetic affirmation, so to speak.

It remains to be asked whether such shifts to the level of the affective really are reservoirs of resistance. Maybe it is time to open up new registers.

References

Anderson, Joel, and Axel Honneth. 2005. "Autonomy, Vulnerability, Recognition, and Justice." In *Autonomy and the Challenges to Liberalism: New Essays,* edited by John Christman and Joel Anderson, 127–49. New York: Cambridge University Press.

Angerer, Marie-Luise, and Bernd Bösel. 2016. "Total Affect Control: Or: Who's Afraid of a Pleasing Little Sister?" *Digital Culture & Society* 2 (1): 41–52.

Benjamin, Walter. 2006. *A Berlin Childhood Around 1900.* Cambridge, MA: Harvard University Press.

Bösel, Bernd. 2018. *Die Plastizität der Gefühle: Eine genealogische Kritik der Affektverfügung.* Unpublished habilitation thesis, submitted to the Faculty of Philosophy of the University of Potsdam.

Cook, Diane J., and Narayanan C. Krishnan. 2015. *Activity Learning: Discovering, Recognizing, and Predicting Human Behavior from Sensor Data.* Hoboken, NJ: Wiley.

Domínguez-Rué, Emma, and Linda Nierling, eds. 2016a. *Ageing and Technology: Perspectives from the Social Sciences.* Bielefeld: transcript. http://www.jstor.org/stable/ j.ctv1xxrwd.

Domínguez-Rué, Emma, and Linda Nierling. 2016b. "All that Glitters is not Silver: Technologies for the Elderly in Context. Introduction." In *Ageing and Technology: Perspectives from the Social Sciences*, edited by Emma Domínguez-Rué and Linda Nierling, 9–23. Bielefeld: transcript. https://www.jstor.org/stable/j.ctv1xxrwd.

Guihen, Barry. 2016. "Making Space for Ageing: Embedding Social and Psychological Needs of Older People into Smart Home Technology." In *Ageing and Technology: Perspectives from the Social Sciences*, edited by Emma Domínguez-Rué and Linda Nierling, 141–61. Bielefeld: transcript. https://www.jstor.org/stable/j.ctv1xxrwd.

Hebert, Saskia. 2012. *Gebaute Welt | Gelebter Raum.* Berlin: jovis.

Heidegger, Martin. 1971. "Building Dwelling Thinking." In *Poetry, Language, Thought.* New York: Harper & Row.

Kammerer, Dietmar. 2014. "Die Enden des Privaten: Geschichten eines Diskurses." In *Medien und Privatheit*, edited by Simon Gartnett, Stefan Halft, and Matthias Herz, 243–58. Passau: Karl Stutz.

Kamphof, Ike. 2016. "Seeing Again. Dementia, Personhood and Technology." In *Ageing and Technology: Perspectives from the Social Sciences*, edited by Emma Domínguez-Rué and Linda Nierling, 163–81. Bielefeld: transcript. https://www.jstor.org/stable/j.ctv1xxrwd.

Kitwood, Tom. 1997. *Dementia Reconsidered: The Person Comes First.* Buckingham: Open University Press.

Kluge, Friedrich. 2011. *Etymologisches Wörterbuch der deutschen Sprache.* 25., durchgesehene und erweiterte Auflage. Berlin: De Gruyter.

Krennerich, Michael. 2018. "Ein Recht auf (menschenwürdiges) Wohnen?" *APuZ—Aus Politik und Zeitgeschichte*, Zeitschrift der Bundeszentrale für politische Bildung 68 (25–26): 9–14.

Mackenzie, Catriona, and Natalie Stoljar. 2000. "Introduction: Autonomy Refigured." In *Relational Autonomy: Feminist Perspective on Autonomy, Agency, and the Social Self*, edited by Catriona Mackenzie and Natalie Stoljar, 3–31. New York: Oxford University Press.

Mielke, Corinna, Thorsten Voss, and Reinhold Haux. 2017. "Residence as a Diagnostic and Therapeutic Area: A Smart Home Approach." *Studies in Health Technology and Informatics* 238: 92–95.

Morin, Edgar. (1981) 2015. "Ist eine Wissenschaft der Autonomie denkbar?" *Trivium [En ligne]* 20. Accessed May 10, 2019. https://journals.openedition.org/trivium/5165.

Neven, Louis. 2015. "By Any Means? Questioning the Link between Gerontechnological Innovation and Older People's Wish to Live at Home." *Technological Forecasting & Social Change* 93: 32–43. doi: 10.1016/j.techfore.2014.04.016.

Picard, Rosalind W. 1997. *Affective Computing*. Cambridge, MA: MIT Press.

Silverstone, Roger, and Eric Hirsch, eds. 1992. *Consuming Technologies Media and Information in Domestic Spaces*. London: Routledge.

Splendid Research. *Smart Home Monitor 2017*. Accessed May 7, 2018. https://www.splendid-research.com/de/smarthome.html.

Sprenger, Florian. 2015. "Elektrifizierte Schwellen: Zur Kulturtechnik der Klingel." In *Architektur in transdisziplinärer Perspektive*, edited by Susanne Hauser and Julia Weber, 195–220. Bielefeld: transcript.

DISCOURSE ANALYSIS

DESIRE

MEDIA HISTORY

INDUSTRY

9

Happy, Happy, Sad, Sad: Do You Feel Me? Constellations of Desires in Affective Technologies

Serjoscha Wiemer

Affective media technologies are becoming more and more standardized, and objects of commercial interest. Based on concepts of critical discourse analysis, this contribution argues that current developments cannot be explained solely as the result of technological progress, but should be understood as the effect of a heterogeneous network of relations. A central element for the stabilization of this network lies in the characteristic "constellation of desires" (Hartmut Winkler) of affective technologies. What are the relevant promises and expectations that drive the ongoing "industrialization of emotions"?

> *… affective computing is not just the science*
> *fiction of tomorrow; it is being used today not*
> *only as a marketing tool but also in medicine*
> *and a number of other fields.*
> Tara J. Brigham (2017, 400)

Affect technologies have recently been met with a previously unknown interest. This is not only true for theories of affect in cultural and media studies.[1] For some years now, there has been a growing number of applications for technologies that are optimized towards the recording, processing, and influencing of affects. In addition to robotics, security research and psychotherapy ("augmented mental health"), such fields of application also include gaming and health applications, and various types of recommendation systems. Individual affect technologies are part of everyday smartphone apps. Automotive technology (e.g., EVA[2]), marketing and consumer registration ("affdex for market research") are commercial hotspots for affective media.

The company Affectiva, which can point out that Rosalind Picard, one of the well-known protagonists of so-called affective computing, was one of its co-founders, promotes its services by claiming one quarter "of the Fortune Global 500, including 1,400 brands like Mars, Kellogg's and CBS" would use its "emotion database" for advertising and media analysis.

Affective technologies are also being used, or scenarios for their implementation being developed, in the fields of education, training and human resources management as well as employee training and workplace

1   With the "affective turn" an increased attention to affects was already observed in the 1990s. However, as Clough (2008) states correctly, this "turn" was connected with debates in cultural studies since the 1990s, and could in part be attributed to a movement against structuralist and poststructuralist theoretical approaches (cf. Gregg and Seigworth 2010). In addition, the affective turn showed an interest in the body and the temporality of movements that could escape regulation and measurement or could not be fully controlled. The new interest in affects, which has been emerging since the 2010s, differs from the previous affective turn in that, among other things, technical and biomedial constellations are now given, which are accompanied by a fundamental media-technical reconfiguration of affects. The field of affective computing is exemplary here, in that it is now precisely the measurement and technical regulation of affects and affective constellations that are at stake.

2   EVA is the acronym for a research agenda on Emotion-Awareness for Intelligent Vehicle Assistants (Vögel et al. 2018).

design.[3] A survey a few years ago already counted more than 100 publications that deal with applications of "affective computing in education" (Wu, Huang, and Hwang 2016).

Despite all the differences in detail, the core of each of these publications deals with the developments in and applications of human–machine systems that are optimized for affect detection and production. In view of the breadth of possible applications, it is not surprising that affect technologies are discussed in economic and technical discourses.[4] In order to find out what expectations, hopes, and promises characterize affect technologies or are associated with their introduction, I have examined a collection of discourse fragments.[5]

The material I have examined has been selected to bring together affirmative positions in the field of application-oriented discourses. In particular, I have looked at those strands of discourse that are related to the development and dissemination of affect technologies and those that include management aspects. Texts, videos, software and databases from the fields of affective computing, management, computer science and information economics were selected as sources. In addition, I looked at different cloud services offering the recognition or processing of emotion and affective data in a standardized form.[6]

Most of the corpus comes from the field itself:
– One source, for example, is taken from the journal *IEEE Transactions on Affective Computing*. The author Björn Schuller is co-founder and Editor in Chief of the journal and is himself a computer scientist, university

---

3   Mental health, audience research, and marketing or advertising are the leading "success stories" on affective computing company Affectiva's website: www.affectiva. com/success-story.

4   This is quite a remarkable development considering that only a few decades ago the preoccupation with affects could be located primarily in the fields of art, psychoanalysis, or cultural theory. Now, in addition to artists, psychologists and cultural theorists, programmers, engineers, economists and managers are increasingly concerned with affects.

5   In the terminology of discourse analysis, a discourse fragment is a materially present utterance that deals with a specific topic. A "strand of discourse" consists of discourse fragments on the same topic. An important question in discourse analysis is how discourse fragments are combined to form strands of discourse and how different strands can "intertwine." This is relevant for the effectiveness of discourses. It can be assumed that effects of discourses depend on how they can intertwine, i.e., how they can influence and support each other (Jäger 2004, 159f.).

6   The blog rapidapi presents more than 20 providers of such services and gives a comparative market overview (RapidAPI Staff 2018).

professor for artificial intelligence, and entrepreneur. Among other things, he was involved in an EU research project dealing with "Social Semantic Emotion Analysis for Innovative Markets," which aims to combine big data analysis with emotion recognition.[7]

– An EU-funded research project named the "Mixed Emotion Toolkit": The project publishes reports on its approach to developing an open-source software infrastructure that combines all popular forms of emotion monitoring in one package in a generally accessible way.

– Other discourse fragments are taken from the growing cloud business of standardized emotion recognition services. Websites are promoting their services of cloud-based application and data exchange interfaces. Among them are the large companies in the IT industry such as Microsoft, Google, Amazon and IBM, followed by YouTube tutorials for these services or other third-party offerings.

This brief list is intended to illustrate what is meant by the notion of industry-related or affirmative discourse fragments. As "fragments" they may represent certain positions within the affirmative discourse with exemplary and explicative value.

The heterogeneous discourse fragments refer to affective technologies in quite different ways. What they have in common is that they participate in processes that I suggest understanding as the movement of the "industrialization" of affect technologies. By this I refer to efforts to institutionalize and standardize technologies and practices that work towards the broadest and most effective dissemination, application, and economic exploitation of affect technologies or affirmatively accompany such developments.

Methodological Orientation: Structures of Desires, Affect Technologies, and Discourses

For the fundamental question of the promises, hopes and expectations associated with media transformations, Hartmut Winkler's approach of the "constellation of desires" contains an elaborated theoretical concept. Winkler developed the idea that media history "pursues describable sets of implicit utopias" (1997, 17). For the study of media history it is not sufficient to describe the state of the technological tools and to hold it responsible for media development. Rather, Winkler claims, the implementation of certain

---

7   "MixedEmotions = Big Linked Data Platform for Emotional Analysis" as described on
     the project's website (Buitelaar n.d.).

technologies in media history is based on a "precisely describable structure of desires" (17). In his investigation into discourses of digitalization and the computer, he shows that it is possible to identify certain desires through affirmative enunciations, which are important for a media constellation and for the interrelation of politics, society, technology and economy, also in the sense of an invocation and evocative practice. A constellation of desires is presented by Winkler as a "terrain" on which different exposed points can be identified (51).

What is interesting about Winkler's concept of desire is that a characteristic of desire is seen in its "impossibility." It is not clear whether this applies to all desires in Winkler's sense, but it is certain that one of their important functional principles is seen in the fact that, "despite a real impossibility, they have very real effects" (40). The desire can thus also become effective in terms of media history, without the desire itself having to be fulfilled. Here, "desires" are not bound to persons and individual subjectivities. The term does not directly belong to a "psychological" theory, but rather designates certain structural elements of discourse dynamics. Constellations of desires are related to deficits and contradictions in existing media–technological formations. They gain their relevance because they reject them or promise the dissolution of existing contradictions. In Winkler's concept, desires are not only mirroring certain media developments or making them describable, but can, more broadly speaking, function as "a driving force" in the development of new media (40).

The question of structures of desire in the current development of affect technologies concerns the relationship between media technology and discourses. I use the term "discourse" here in reference to approaches to critical discourse analysis, following Foucault, and with regard to a discourse-analytical concept of media, as a part of German media theory (cf. Conradi 2015, 65–90; Winkler 2004; Stauff 2005). A characteristic feature of the theory of critical discourse analysis is that discourses are seen as relevant power factors. Discourses exercise power, for example, as "'carriers' of respectively valid 'knowledge'" (Jäger 2004, 149). And they contribute to the "structuring of power relations in a society" (149). If the dynamics of the development of affect technologies in media history depend on the fact that technical, economic and managerial strands of discourse can overlap, influence and support each other, then constellations of desires can be seen as an element of the interweaving of these strands of discourse.

According to discourse-analytical concepts of media formations, discourses are not external to technologies or media formations. Structures of desires and discourses are not a kind of affirmative accompaniment of affective media technologies or a side effect of technical developments, but are involved in the very production of these technologies and in their social, political, economic, and infrastructural shaping. In critical discourse analysis, the strategic as well as legitimizing function of discourses is particularly emphasized in order to underline their operative and productive effectiveness (cf. Jäger 2004; Link 2008).

For a contemporary concept of media that describes the constitution of media as the concatenation and formation of practices, discourses, and technology, the function of discourses is even further amplified. Markus Stauff, for example, understands media as a temporarily stabilized "heterogeneous network of relationships" (2005, 200). Such a concept of media not only takes into account the changing dynamics and instability of digital media (formations), but also draws attention to the fact that discourses and practices are included in the development of media from the outset. Discourses "enable and stabilize the technical functioning" (192). This applies in particular to the realization of new technologies, which in their emergence are dependent on the interplay, the increasing interlocking—and thus on the intertwining—of different fields of knowledge and spheres of action. If one considers affect technologies in this sense as media-in-the-making or as media formation, then the constitution and productivity of affective media technologies must be analyzed as a concatenation and temporarily stabilized formation of heterogeneous practices, discourses, and techniques.[8]

A decisive hurdle for the media function appears in the problem of concatenation. How does a discourse organize its own continuity and the interaction of heterogeneous practices and discourses? It is important to understand how the operativity of discourse stabilizes the heterogeneous elements, the "heterogeneous network of relationships" (Stauff), and how the continuity of a formation is established in the first place.

The assumption that constellations of desires and the expression of hopes and expectations play an important function is supported by the fact

8   The distinction between discourses, practices and technology is anything but strict. In materialist traditions of discourse theories, the term "discourse" does not designate specifically a totality of *symbolic* practices, but can refer to practices as well as utterances. Similarly there is no strict ontological difference between technology and practices as technology emerges from continued practices (cf. "the model," Winkler 2004, 116–30).

that—as will be shown later—an intensification of the parallelism of discourses of technical application and of the articulation of wishes can be observed in the field of affective media technologies.

Algorithmic Affective Technologies—Steps towards the Industrialization of Emotions

The fact that the IEEE (the Institute of Electrical and Electronics Engineers) has been publishing *Transactions on Affective Computing* since 2010 can be seen as a sign of a flourishing scientific and commercial interest in affective technologies. The IEEE describes itself as the "world's largest technical professional organization for the advancement of technology." It is influential as a scientific community and a relevant institution when it comes to technical standardization. The regular volumes of the *Transactions on Affective Computing* follow the aim of "disseminating results of research on the design of systems that can recognize, interpret, and simulate human emotions and related affective phenomena."

In the introduction to the first issue, Rosalind Picard emphasized the shift of affective computing from an experimental theoretical field to a widely received and "serious" undertaking (2010). She claims that "insights about emotions" have become a necessary part of the "engineering dreams to build intelligent machines." In 2017 Björn Schuller took up the rhetoric of this "engineering dream" in an editorial for the journal, to merge these "dreams to build" with the rise of artificial intelligence to form a new dream of commercial success that should come when the technology conquers broad consumer markets:

> In its eight years, the *IEEE Transactions on Affective Computing* (TAC) has witnessed a time of great opportunities for the field: Artificial Intelligence (AI) and Machine Learning have recently made great progress increasing the distribution and usage of intelligent solutions in the greater public and commercial world. This progress bears many great chances for Affective Computing, as with increasing intelligence of machines, one may increasingly desire according intelligent systems to also possess emotional intelligence as the "next big thing" in commercial exploitation of AI—the Artificial Emotional Intelligence or AEI for short. To give but a few examples, with the advent of spoken language assistants in our homes, and the day-by-day rising usage of such assistants on smart phones and personal computers, it seems more than timely to also lend these assistants the ability to

> understand their users' emotions and react appropriately to them. Similarly, there is a huge trend in measuring oneself in many ways to track activity, steps, heart rate, sleep time, and whatnots 24/7—one may easily expect emotion tracking to become of broad interest soon, as well, which certainly also bears high promises for serious medical applications. As a last example, with gradually smart retrieval of multimedia, the emotional aspect will likely soon play a much more important role, when—for example—asking your retrieval agent for some funny pictures, bluesy music, or a movie loaded with tension and surprises. Obviously, this also bears a huge challenge for robustness, as the expectancy will be nothing but high once Affective Computing finds its way into the broad consumer market where severe real-world conditions need to be faced. (Schuller 2017, 1)

This quote is given in such extensive detail to convey the way in which a rhetoric of desire or "dream" is unfolded here, which provides an understanding about the direction in which affect technology is developing in the phase of its industrialization. Or more precisely: how different strands of discourse are intertwined in order to continue the discourse and create a "future." One striking feature, for example, is the formula of "next big thing": the rhetoric used raises expectations and sketches future prospects in a way that makes it difficult to distinguish between the description of possibilities and the call to actively bring about a certain future.

An entanglement of scientific, economic and institutional strands of discourse becomes apparent. As the rhetoric of Schuller and Picard reveals, these different fields of action and discourse are strategically linked with each other, which, following Stauff's discourse-analytical concept of "media," can be understood as a discursive practice to stabilize a heterogeneous "network of relations" and to secure a (future) technical functioning (aiming at the realization or market-driven implementation of partially new technologies compatible for broad consumer markets).

Parallel to this type of discursive practice, transformations take place at the level of tools and techniques, which are characterized by tendencies towards the standardization and automation of procedures and processes. There is a trend towards a standardization of modules or building blocks that can be used to produce more effectively and uniformly what is "manufactured" in the course of an "industrialization of emotions." This happens in order to identify, excite, reproduce or simulate and process emotions on a mass scale and at low cost.

This development is based in particular on the algorithmically rationalized side of affect technology. It is precisely through the use of software that the scalability of applications (for growing markets) and thus ubiquitous mass compatibility is expected. The production of software itself, however, is often dependent on services that cannot be completely standardized: programming can be characterized as a highly individual, creative, and manual process. Software can be understood as a "mosaic of algorithms, protocols, infrastructures, and programming conventions" (Mackenzie 2006). Nevertheless, software development also operates with levels of standardization in order to achieve uniformity, effectiveness, or cost savings. Basic examples are the use of standardized development environments (IDEs), quasi-standardized tools (such as certain editors for writing code), and unifying interoperability interfaces (APIs), shared databases, or standardized code libraries.

An example of these standardization tendencies is the approach of the Mixed Emotion Toolbox, an open-source toolbox for multimodal emotion analysis.[9] This programming toolbox is a plug-and-play platform that combines functionalities for the "multimodal" analysis of text, audio, video and data structure links in one package. This includes functions for sentiment and emotion analysis from texts, for the recognition of emotion, age and gender from audio processing, and functions for face detection and emotion tracking with video processing, which also includes estimation of head and body postures, and the integration of linked data as knowledge graphs (Buitelaar et al. 2018, 2455).

Another example of the state of development towards the commercialized mass application of affect technologies and associated standardization are the numerous cloud services that offer emotion recognition as a technical service. Among the market leaders in this area are the market leaders in the IT industry such as Microsoft, Google, Amazon, and IBM. All these companies offer cloud-based application and data exchange interfaces. They provide an infrastructure that allows virtually any user or programmer to perform algorithmic identification and processing of "emotion" according to pre-defined schemes without the need to invest in individual infrastructure or deep knowledge of affective computing. The number of providers of such services is so large that there are guidebooks and online

---

9   It should be noted that the Mixed Emotion Toolbox can be seen as an example of standardization efforts. However, its actual function could not be verified. Questions to the authors of the Mixed Emotions Toolbox, via the official e-mail-address, on the status of the projects remained unanswered.

comparisons that offer "customers" orientation in a growing market of cloud-based emotion recognition services.[10]

At Google, the emotion-recognition application interface is part of Google Cloud Vision. The "Cloud Vision API" provides face recognition based on different characteristics; emotion identification is simply one of several modules integrated into the face recognition infrastructure. Microsoft, with the "Oxford" project, has offered an application interface for the recognition of emotions since 2015. Emotion recognition is part of the "Microsoft Azure" cloud computing platform. The company points to the fact that since 2019, emotion recognition has been generally integrated into its face recognition services: "Try the emotion recognition capabilities of Face API now." The offer is addressed to the potential customers who build "personalized apps." The associated pricing model includes a free service to get started ("Emotion API—Free: 30,000 image transactions free per month") and prices between $0.10 and $0.25 per 1,000 transactions (Azure 2018).

These and other offerings are complemented by a variety of available databases on the internet that provide access to photos or videos of facial expressions either free of charge or for a small fee (e.g., to train neural networks), or databases with text segments that are already pre-categorized according to emotional values to perform language analysis as sentiment analysis.[11] In addition, there are—no surprise—numerous YouTube tutorials that explain how to use the offerings and how to program your own apps, e.g., for smartphones.

Discourses and Great Promises

As the examples show, the technology is on the market and ready for widespread use. This supports the hypothesis that affective media technologies are in a phase of industrialization and standardization. And it helps to illustrate the change in media history that is taking place with regard to affective media. The relevant function of the constellation of desires that supports and drives such a change becomes more apparent against the background of the actual breadth and intensity of this development. So what are the related promises and desires? And what are the existing contradictions that they are positioned against?

---

10   For example, more than 20 vendors are compared in Kairos and Rapid API (RapidAPI Staff 2018; Virdee-Chapman 2018).

11   A selection of such databases is presented on https://www.face-rec.org/databases (Grgic n.d.).

In her essay "Merging Technology and Emotion," Tara Brigham (2017) refers to the unavoidable and ubiquitous "interactions between humans and computers" that permeate everyday life and the work environments as the basis for one of the fundamental promises of affective computing, which, according to Brigham, consists of optimizing interaction and understanding in the handling of computer-based technologies. Technical systems could be improved if they would respond to subtle or subliminal traces of emotional expressions in their interaction with users, in order to increase the "effectiveness and satisfaction" of human–machine interactions.

What Brigham describes is a common trope in the discourse of affective computing. It is often that this idea of an optimized human–machine inter-action is accompanied by the promise of a more "natural" interaction. The prospect of optimized machines is also mutually connected with the concept of an optimization of human users, for example in the idea of aug-menting human emotional abilities. An example for this position can be found on the blog of "ventureradar":

> While great advances are being made in the analytical capabilities of computer systems there are also impressive developments being made in *making computers more emotionally intelligent*. This field is known as Affective Computing, and is defined as the study and development of systems and devices that can recognize, interpret, process, and simulate human emotions (or affects). These developments are being *driven by a need for more natural human–computer interactions*, but there are also many examples where affective computing technology is augmenting our own abilities, and *enabling us to become more emotionally intelligent*. (Thomson 2016, emph. SW)

Another position in the affirmative discourse aims at an increase in knowledge and cognition. Machines that process emotions are imagined as being useful "in order to understand humans better" (Brigham 2017, 400). However, the idea of an increase in knowledge is not limited to philo-sophical self-knowledge, but can repeatedly be found linked with business thinking or the desire for commercial exploitation. In the magazine article "Empathy—the killer app for artificial intelligence," the hope for a new man–machine relationship is expressed, in order to "help businesses peer into our inner feelings" and to "make customers and employees happier" (Noga et al. 2017).

A technologically enhanced, controllable and digitally expandable "emotion awareness" could benefit companies, customers and employees alike and help them achieve greater "happiness." These and similar topoi can be found in many places, albeit with different accents. For example, in an article in the business-oriented online magazine D!GITALIST, which explains "How Emotionally Aware Computing Can Bring Happiness to Your Organization," the promise of increased attention to feelings is associated with happier employees (heading: "Do You Feel Me?"). Employers could observe the feelings of their employees and thus change work processes in such a way that productivity, effectiveness, and job satisfaction increase. The happiness promised or longed for here is not only "satisfaction" at work for employees, but, combined with it, an economic benefit—as if it would belong together: "increase in productivity, effectiveness, and satisfaction" (D!GITALIST 2017).

To achieve these promises, it is seen as necessary (and desirable) for employers to be able to monitor the mood of employees at any time and in any place by means of "mood recognition technology": "through the application of machine learning, Big Data inputs, image recognition, sensors, and in some cases robotics, artificially intelligent systems hunt for affective clues: widened eyes, quickened speech, and crossed arms, as well as heart rate or skin changes" (D!GITALIST 2017). The monitoring of feelings could help to identify and classify negative moods at an early stage in order to counteract them with appropriate measures. Through "positive feedback," motivation and satisfaction should be increased.

Maricel Cabahug, the "Chief Design Officer responsible for SAP's overall design strategy and product design," describes the future of a "more emotional" work environment through the emotional responsiveness of machines in a euphoric manner and optimistic terms: affect technologies would create "room for more natural kinds of dealings with machines" and the interaction between man and machine would become more emotional and thus more personal (Cabahug 2018).

Affect technologies, Cabahug claims, would make dealing with machines less abstract, and instead more natural, intuitive, and therefore more human. An "emotional connection" with the digital tools would be created in a mutual fashion. This could be achieved in particular through digital assistants equipped with "personality." Affect technologies, in this perspective, are a means of overcoming the separation between man and machine and enabling more "intimacy" and connectedness.

> Our expectations for intelligent systems to understand us, help us, and connect with us on an emotional level will increase exponentially in the coming years. We will be conversing and interacting more and

more with machines, expecting them to sound and react in a way that is convincingly human. (Cabahug 2018)

The company itself is thought to be transformed into an "emotional enterprise." The transformation of the work environment that Cabahug envisions is staged as a radical "disruption" with a new "immersive experience" on the horizon: "Being transported visually and acoustically in time and space gets under your skin and goes directly to primitive centers of the brain … work is about to get much more human and much more rewarding" (Cabahug 2018).

Constellations of Desires and "Natural" Machinic Intimacy

Looking at the briefly outlined positions, it is striking that it is not only about the topic of "emotion," but many different motives are addressed: human self-awareness, the relationship with machines, the hope for more happiness, more efficiency, more satisfaction at work, more control over employees, more knowledge (and power) over customers, success in business, etc. Many of these topics are—considered separately—quite trivial. They are formulas that one might associate with product advertising—life should become more beautiful, better, happier. According to the theoretical concept of a constellation of desires, however, it is not the superficial advertising messages and clichés that are remarkable, but rather the characteristic *constellation* of heterogeneous and partially contradictory structures, which in sum contribute to the result of the stabilization and continuity of the discourse.

Concurrently the discourse fragments show that a bundle of statements directly addresses problems of *technological mediation*, such as user interfaces, man–machine communication and, in general, the mediality and relationality between man and machine. In conjunction with the turn towards affect technologies, the desire for overcoming abstraction and for a more "natural," humane and personal technology is articulated. In addition, the desire for a dissolution of boundaries and resistances between human sensory realities and machine "others" is emerging. An example of this can be seen in the vision of an immersive emotional connection (Cabahug 2018), which is to be created from "natural kinds of dealings with machines." The affirmation of affective technologies poses itself thus, at least in part, in opposition to the characteristics of modern, technology-dependent society or is connected with the (paradoxical) desire to overcome alienation, abstraction and a-human technology by an intensification of human–machine interactions.

At this point, it should be recalled once again that the "impossibility" of their fulfillment in Winkler's concept can almost be considered a characteristic of desires. At least in so far as it is one of their (discursive) functional principles, "despite a real impossibility, the more real effects they have" (Winkler 1997, 40).

"Natural" interaction, intimacy, immediacy and emotional connectedness as characteristics of human–machine communication are virtually opposed to the complex technicity of communication through digital mediation. The discourse on affective media technologies is resonating with the desire for a-mediality and immediacy. This desire for immediacy is diametrically opposed to the factual logic of computational quantification and the hyper-medial machinic coding and re-location of emotions in complex media networks, databases, and human-algorithmic-sensory assemblages. A further analysis could take this contradiction as a subject for further investigation into the discursive dynamics of affective media technologies.

References

Affectiva. 2020. "Affectiva Media Analytics." *Affectiva*. Accessed March 7, 2020. https://www.affectiva.com/product/affdex-for-market-research.

Azure. 2018. "Azure Cognitive Services Pricing." Accessed October 17, 2020. https://azure.microsoft.com/en-us/pricing/details/cognitive-services/.

Brigham, Tara J. 2017. "Merging Technology and Emotions: Introduction to Affective Computing." *Medical Reference Services Quarterly* 36 (4): 399–407. https://doi.org/10.1080/02763869.2017.1369289.

Buitelaar, Paul. n.d. "The MixedEmotions Project." Accessed April 20, 2020. https://mixedemotions-project.eu/about/emotionanalysis.

Buitelaar, Paul, I. D. Wood, S. Negi, M. Arcan, J. P. McCrae, A. Abele, et al. 2018. "MixedEmotions: An Open-Source Toolbox for Multimodal Emotion Analysis." *IEEE Transactions on Multimedia* 20 (9): 2454–65. https://doi.org/10.1109/TMM.2018.2798287.

Cabahug, Maricel. 2018. "The 'Emotional' Enterprise." *The Digitalist*. Accessed April 27, 2020. https://www.digitalistmag.com/future-of-work/2018/05/22/emotional-enterprise-06168832.

Clough, Patricia T. 2008. "The Affective Turn: Political Economy, Biomedia and Bodies." *Theory, Culture & Society* 25 (1): 1–22. https://doi.org/10.1177/0263276407085156.

Conradi, Tobias. 2015. *Breaking News: Automatismen in der Repräsentation von Krisen- und Katastrophenereignissen*. Schriftenreihe des Graduiertenkollegs "Automatismen." Paderborn: Wilhelm Fink.

Digitalistmag. 2017. "How Emotionally Aware Computing Can Bring Happiness to Your Organization." Accessed April 27, 2020. https://www.digitalistmag.com/executive-research/how-emotionally-aware-computing-bring-happiness-to-your-organization.

Gregg, Melissa, and Gregory J. Seigworth, eds. 2010. *The Affect Theory Reader.* Durham, NC: Duke University Press.

Grgic, Mislav. n.d. "Face Recognition Homepage—Databases." Accessed April 27, 2020. https://www.face-rec.org/databases.

Jäger, Siegfried. 2004. *Kritische Diskursanalyse: Eine Einführung.* 6th ed. Edition DISS 3. Münster: Unrast.

Link, Jürgen. 2008. "Sprache, Diskurs, Interdiskurs und Literatur (mit einem Blick auf Kafkas Schloß)". In *Sprache—Kognition—Kultur,* edited by Heidrun Kämper and Ludwig Eichinger, 115–34. Berlin, Boston: de Gruyter.

Mackenzie, Adrian. 2006. *Cutting Code: Software and Sociality.* New York: Peter Lang.

Noga, Markus, Chandran Saravana, and Stephanie Overby. 2017. "Empathy: The Killer App for Artificial Intelligence." *The Digitalist.* Accessed April 27, 2020. https://www.digitalist-mag.com/executive-research/empathy-the-killer-app-for-artificial-intelligence.

Picard, Rosalind W. 2010. "Affective Computing: From Laughter to IEEE." *IEEE Transactions on Affective Computing* 1 (1): 11–17. Accessed April 27, 2020. https://doi.org/10.1109/T-AFFC.2010.10.

RapidAPI Staff. 2018. "Top 26+ Emotion & Sentiment Analysis APIs (2018) | RapidAPI." *Last Call—RapidAPI Blog* (blog). July 24, 2018. Accessed April 27, 2020. https://blog.rapidapi.com/top-emotion-sentiment-analysis-apis.

Schuller, Bjorn W. 2017. "Editorial: IEEE Transactions on Affective Computing—Challenges and Chances." *IEEE Transactions on Affective Computing* 8 (1): 1–2. https://doi.org/10.1109/TAFFC.2017.2662858.

Stauff, Markus. 2005. *Das neue Fernsehen: Machtanalyse, Gouvernementalität und digitale Medien.* Münster: LIT.

Thomson, Andrew. 2016. "15 Leading Affective Computing Companies You Should Know." *VentureRadar* (blog). September 21, 2016. Accessed April 27, 2020. https://blog.ventureradar.com/2016/09/21/15-leading-affective-computing-companies-you-should-know.

Virdee-Chapman, Ben. 2018. "Face Recognition: Kairos vs Microsoft vs Google vs Amazon vs OpenCV." *Kairos* (blog). Accessed September 25, 2018. https://www.kairos.com/blog/face-recognition-kairos-vs-microsoft-vs-google-vs-amazon-vs-opencv.

Vögel, Hans-Jörg, Christian Süß, Thomas Hubregtsen, Elisabeth André, Björn Schuller, Jérôme Härri, et al. 2018. "Emotion-Awareness for Intelligent Vehicle Assistants: A Research Agenda." In *2018 IEEE/ACM 1st International Workshop on Software Engineering for AI in Autonomous Systems (SEFAIAS),* 11–15. Gothenburg: IEEE.

Winkler, Hartmut. 1997. *Docuverse: Zur Medientheorie der Computer.* München: Boer.

———. 2004. *Diskursökonomie: Versuch über die innere Ökonomie der Medien.* Frankfurt/M.: Suhrkamp.

Wu, Chih-Hung, Yueh-Min Huang, and Jan-Pan Hwang. 2016. "Review of Affective Computing in Education/Learning: Trends and Challenges." *British Journal of Educational Technology* 47 (6): 1304–23. https://doi.org/10.1111/bjet.12324.

HUMANITARIAN AFFECT

VIDEO ACTIVISM

SOCIAL MEDIA

HUMAN RIGHTS

[1 0]
Mediated Humanitarian Affect

Andrew A. G. Ross

This contribution reflects on the cultural politics of affective media in the field of global humanitarianism. Liberal advocates of internet connectivity continue to celebrate mobile and other digital networking technologies as vehicles for global dialogue and transnational justice. A key conceit of this tradition is an ontological linkage between the scale of mediated communication, the sensorial range of human experience, and the capaciousness of moral attention. In reference to recent developments in digital humanitarian advocacy, this chapter disrupts these linkages and tells a more complex story about the politics of mediated humanitarian affect. Digital humanitarian campaigns enhance moral sensitivities but also engender new forms of digital labor, data gathering, and political control. Crisis mapping technologies

expand opportunities for liberal institutions to manage distant populations according to specific rationalities of governance. And the algorithms that circulate video advocacy campaigns are translating distant conflicts into new sites for enjoyment and moral urgency. The case of mediated humanitarian affect reveals the extent to which human affective energies are being captured by the technologies and regimes of power characteristic of neoliberal societies.

In a January 2010 address on the topic of internet freedom, then-United States Secretary of State Hillary Clinton celebrated online and text messaging efforts that had raised massive funds for victims of a devastating earthquake in Haiti. She reported that the Text HAITI campaign had already generated more than $25 million and described it as "a showcase for the generosity of the American people" (Clinton 2010). This success story revealed the great democratic potential of the digital age, as information technologies create what she, recalling Marshall McLuhan (1994), described as "a new nervous system for our planet." The idea that communications technologies might encourage global sensitivity and thereby increase humanitarian responsiveness has deep roots in liberal internationalism. And, as evidenced by commentators who invoke the potential for internet connectivity to sustain democratic openness on a global scale (MacKinnon 2012; Shirky 2011; Slaughter 2016), the notion of a "global village" continues to inform the liberal imagination (Srinivasan 2017). The central conceit of this tradition is an ontological linkage between the scale of mediated communication, the sensorial range of human experience, and the capaciousness of moral attention.

In reference to recent developments in digital humanitarian advocacy, this chapter disrupts these linkages to tell a more complex story about the politics of mediated affect.[1] Dispensing with narratives focused on

---

1   I assume that, despite the availability of many compelling philosophical critiques
     of human rights (Arendt 1973; Rancière 2004), Western humanitarian advocacy
     continues apace and needs to be understood as a force unto itself in cultural politics.

geographic scale, I argue that viral expressions circulated through social media are reconfiguring the landscape of cultural authority and power in ways that confound liberal aspirations toward a generalized empathy. The visual images and expressive acts associated with campaigns to save child soldiers in Uganda, to free the so-called Chibok girls of Northern Nigeria, and to help refugees in Syria are laying channels of sensitivity selectively attuned to particular events, beneficiaries, and problems. Through these sensitivities, practices of digital humanitarianism are creating affect-generating outlets for cultural expression, sites of entertainment, and opportunities for enjoyment. To explore such processes, here I will focus not on individual participants, campaigns, and movements but instead on non-subjective affective energies I call "mediated humanitarian affect."

While humanitarian campaigns and networks are engaged in moral advocacy, mediated humanitarian affect bears no necessary, normative, or political valence. Mediated flows of humanitarian affect cannot be reduced to the generalized compassion or empathy of Fassin's "humanitarian reason," and nor do they conform to the ironic gestures associated with Chouliaraki's "post-humanitarianism" (Fassin 2012; Chouliaraki 2010). And yet, because they enable specific, politically significant forms of cultural authority, they call for the critical ethos that these authors invoke. Digital humanitarian practices comprise part of a larger cultural political economy of distributed agency, with humanitarian affect serving to direct attention, instantiate sites of cultural authority, and sustain new forms of political control. These social and political consequences of mediated humanitarian affect remain concealed as long as we accept the tight linkage between the scale of communication, the possibility of human sensory enlargement, and the capaciousness of moral imagination. I thus begin with a critical genealogy of these associations.

1. **Feeling Global**

When Clinton and other liberal observers attribute a global scale to media technologies, they give expression to the latter's historical identification as instruments of communication. The concept of communication evokes the idea of sharing or making common (Peters 1999, 7), but the idea of achieving such a shared exchange across geographic distance only emerges historically as technologies facilitate wider spheres of transmission and engagement (Thompson 1995). Technologies such as railway-enhanced postal delivery, telegraphy, and radio broadcasting created an association between communication and the transmission of informational content across geographic space (Guillory 2010; Headrick 2000; Peters 1999, 7–9). During the modern period, mediated experience thus becomes associated with communication—understood, through "a metaphor of geography or transportation" (Carey 1989, 15), as the sending of informational data.

As opportunities for mediated communication proliferated during the nineteenth century, they became implicated in the political economies of liberal internationalism. Figures such as David Livingstone, Leonard Woolf, and Norman Angell held up transportation and communication technologies as opportunities for achieving cross-national understanding and peace (Rosenberg 2012). These claims echoed the utopian ideas of Saint-Simon and Michel Chevalier, both of whom saw communication as the key to fostering transnational solidarity (Mattelart 2000, 15–16). Networks of travel and communication together held the potential to promote unity and imperialist conceptions of civilization, important antidotes to the nationalist and racial fragmentations characteristic of nineteenth-century politics. Such theories laid the groundwork for an explicit connection between the sociology of communication and the politics of liberal internationalism.

The normative value of communication was further enhanced during the twentieth century, as new technologies permitted both faster transmission and worries about a corollary loss of authenticity. The proliferation of channels facilitating communication thus served to underscore its value for promoting democratic sociability. The American sociologist Charles Horton Cooley embraced these potentials and approached communication as a liberation from geography—even regarding communication technologies as facilitating a kind of unconscious spiritual connection across distances (Peters 1999, 187). But, as Peters notes, Cooley's reflections are indicative of a broader cultural anxiety over the impact of new technologies. The advent of everyday opportunities for long-distance communication only placed a greater premium on face-to-face—and other forms of social and spiritual— connection regarded as possessing greater authenticity. In this vein, Dewey (1946) and others expressed a characteristically twentieth-century effort to recover authentic forms of deliberative communication, and social and political threats such as fascism and commodification only augmented that endeavor (Habermas 1989; Horkheimer and Adorno 2002).

While Dewey, Habermas, and other democratic theorists focused on public deliberation at a national level, the moral potential of communication found its logical realization in discussions of a "global public sphere" (Fraser 2007; Fraser et al. 2014; Volkmer 2014). Such late-century theories of global dialogue are staged against the backdrop of post-WWII institutional experiments aimed at peace, education, and scientific cooperation. The *Constitution of the United Nations Educational, Scientific, and Cultural Organization* (UNESCO) thus declared in its preamble the intention to leverage communications practices and technologies "for the purposes of mutual understanding and a truer and more perfect knowledge of each other's lives." And, while UNESCO accepted the United Nations' fundamental commitment to state sovereignty, it nevertheless pursued a global mandate: the "sacred duty" to support "the wide diffusion of culture, and the education of humanity." Through the work of this institution, the idea of "one world" successfully displaced cultural pluralism as the basis for liberal internationalism (Duedahl 2011, 103). Protecting the "free flow of information" through mass media became a key preoccupation in the service of those objectives and is now reflected in UNESCO efforts to protect internet freedom (Duedahl 2016, 27; Peters 1999, 26; Dutton et al. 2011, 8). Clinton's efforts to align global-scale communication with moral solicitude and democratic values resonate with these multilateral projects.

But recent developments in humanitarian practice suggest that the digital technologies Clinton celebrates are being used in ways that confound mid-century visions of "one world." McLuhan was surely correct in his claim that media technologies alter the sensory capabilities of the human beings that use them. But, in the early twenty-first century, his attribution of global scale to that sensory realignment seems remarkable for the holism it presumes. The contention that our "global village" is a "resonating whole" allowing for "totality and inclusiveness" or "world consciousness" (McLuhan and Powers 1989, 91, 95, 103) does not adequately reflect the manner in which processes of mediation are sustaining more localized and differentiated affects. The "planetary nervous system" is not one unified organism but a multitude of selective sensitivities fueled by specific repertoires of digital practice.

2. Humanitarian Affect

Enthusiasm for digital humanitarianism is a chapter in this narrative of global holism. Various digital technologies—including social media platforms, video sharing sites, serious video games, and crowdsourced crisis mapping—are now routinely used for humanitarian advocacy by governments and various non-governmental organizations. And, while both scholars and practitioners have begun to assess the effectiveness of these practices on an operational level, the advent of digital humanitarianism has yet to be contextualized in relation to the broader history of communication, its capacity to augment sensory and affective experience, and its connections with the project of liberal internationalism. Taking steps in this direction, I suggest that these digital humanitarian practices are producing localized flows of humanitarian affect induced by specific events, campaigns, and issues, rather than generating global awareness or sensitivity.

Advocacy for human rights has long been associated with augmentations of human sensory experience. Since human rights violations are often concealed by the state actors who perpetrate them, and since humanitarian crises often occur at a distance from the outside actors who respond to them, the task of humanitarianism is inherently dependent upon public awareness and witnessing. Human rights is, at its core, "a visibility project" (Gearty 2006, 4). Organizations such as Amnesty International were founded on the practice of witnessing, employing techniques such as letter-writing and prisoner adoption as the conduit for extra-local public involvement and advocacy (Hopgood 2006; Scarry 1985). Beginning in the 1980s, images circulating via newspapers, magazines, and direct mail campaigns helped to bring outside attention to famines and other humanitarian crises in the Global South (Moeller 1999). During the 1990s, real-time news coverage was seen as playing an important role in not only securing public attention (Robinson 1999), but also in the inauguration of a new sensory regime of visual simulation (Baudrillard 1995). Because human rights claims have historically involved geographical and cultural distance, we can understand them only by excavating the mechanisms of visibility and simulation connecting and constituting willing humanitarians and would-be beneficiaries.

Social networks and the algorithms behind them have qualitatively transformed mediated access to human suffering. As mobile computing and social networking technologies afford opportunities for ordinary users to co-produce media content, broadcasting networks and centralized organizational structures are no longer integral to mediatized humanitarianism. Indeed, much attention has been paid to such "user-driven" capabilities, which Castells (2009) associates with the phenomenon of "mass self-communication" and Bennett and Segerberg (2013) with the "personalization" of social movement organizing. But these accounts reposition agency onto the individual user without calling into question the ontology of intentionality that privileges communication as the primary aspect of mediated experience. What makes social networking and mobile computing practices distinctive is not only their reliance on user-generated content but also the manner in which they distribute opportunities for cultural expression and agency. Here the suffering human is more than an external object triggering action; they are part of an assemblage of technical, sensory, and affective processes involved in channeling human activity and directing attention.

Humanitarian campaigns built around hashtags, viral videos, and iconic images therefore do more than merely communicate information to a user: they distribute inducements to affective expression. Human rights organizations are increasingly seeking to capitalize on the power of crowd-sourcing through innovative use of digital media tools (Cornell, Keisch, and Palasz 2004; Joyce 2010). Viral video and hashtag campaigns such as KONY 2012 and #BringBackOurGirls showcase the potential for new forms of participation (Berents 2016; Carter Olson 2016; Loken 2014): the latter generated over four million retweets during the second half of 2014 (Carter Olson 2016, 773), while the Kony video attracted more than 100 million views in just six days (Brysk 2013, 158). The significance of this participatory element can be seen in both the content generated by users and the affective energies produced by the curatorial practices of clicking, for-warding, liking, and posting. Crisis maps and other forms of digital crowd-sourcing generate data for the purposes of witnessing and coordination among relief agencies (Ziemke 2012), but they also distribute the experi-ence of solidarity and moral confidence within an emergent assemblage of mediated participation. What results are "circulations of affect" (Ross 2014) that coalesce around the catastrophic events, celebrity activists, and iconic images that most acutely direct attention to human suffering.

These humanitarian affects do not pre-exist the mediations that induce them: they are socioculturally constituted and contextually specific responses rather than generic emotions. The emotionality of human rights advocacy has been widely recognized by various cultural histories of humanitarianism, with many accounts pointing to the importance of compassion and empathy in motivating and defining the scope of human rights consciousness and advocacy (Crawford 2014; Hunt 2007; Ure and Frost 2014). And yet, as I have suggested elsewhere (Ross 2018), these stereotyped emotions do not capture the various emotions and moods—including anger and guilt—that can arise in response to human suffering. Moreover, as Hutchison (2016), Käpylä and Kennedy (2014), and others have demonstrated, even seemingly commonplace emotions such as compas-sion are shaped and disciplined by the images and campaigns that elicit them. Humanitarian practices such as celebrity activism and its attendant technologies, moreover, have enhanced certain styles of affective expression, such as the intimacy of "confession" (Mitchell 2016, 295). These affects are generated through the social processes, cultural values, and technical media that sustain contemporary humanitarianism.

Humanitarian affect does not pre-exist its expression because human affectivity is so deeply constituted by media technologies. Contemporary media theory suggests that mediation needs to be understood not as human actors using instruments of communication but as human and material elements co-evolving within composite systems, or assemblages (Clark 2003; Clough 2000; Galloway, Thacker, and Wark 2014; Hayles 2012; Massumi 2002). Mediated practices of humanitarianism have become important nodes in this co-constitution of technological and human capability. Research in neuroscience shows that affective responses are predicated on patterns of embodied sensitivity, such that exposure to an emotionally significant object activates responses in the brain. But the class of images, objects, and experiences that qualify as "emotionally competent stimuli" (Damasio 2003) changes with experience. The brain's capacity for plasticity (Angerer 2017; Malabou 2008; Wexler 2006) ensures that affective capabilities are continually channeled and directed according to repeated patterns of exposure and stimulation. What at first seems to be a quintessentially human endeavor—pooling the capabilities of some human beings to attend to the needs of others—is also the interface between cultural representations of suffering, the algorithms and other technical processes that distribute them to human sensory receptors, and the styles of affective response that both help to normalize.

Studies of humanitarian practice provide some indications of these new styles of affect. One shift has been toward enhanced opportunities for pursuing enjoyment through helping others. Critical commentaries point to the danger of "narcissism" as a generation of social media users becomes absorbed in self-expression and public performances of generosity (Papacharissi 2009; Rifkin 2009). Even without fully endorsing such worries, however, we can accept that digital humanitarian practices are providing opportunities for experiencing pleasure through small acts of perceived generosity. Helping, giving, and saving involve distinct exchanges of affect, and, as Bornstein suggests, we need to understand "the subtle shades of humanitarian efforts—differentiated by varied imperatives, impulses, and systems of obligation and assistance" (2012, 11). The digital labor associated with navigating and curating humanitarian content builds new styles of affect around distributed forms of action. Research in moral psychology suggests that moral judgment and altruistic actions generate feelings of pleasure and pride (Haidt 2003; Prinz 2007, 81). Contemporary forms of mediated humanitarianism are multiplying opportunities for these joys of moral action (Chouliaraki 2010).

Ethnographic research also points to the growing salience of urgency within contemporary humanitarianism. Whereas older forms of human rights advocacy tolerated incremental change, the accelerated forms of communication afforded by digital technologies are amplifying moods of urgency within humanitarian networks (Mitchell 2016, 290; Pandolfi 2010). The Rwandan genocide was a key catalyst for this specific temporality, which helped to fuel international support for the "Responsibility to Protect" doctrine. It is in this cultural context that the Invisible Children organization invested their KONY 2012 campaign with such a distinctive impatience. The short film at the heart of that campaign relates the story of American students on a church mission trip who, after witnessing the plight of child soldiers in Uganda, are eager to expose the injustice and catalyze American intervention. As the film's narrator pivots into an explanation of the campaign, he states "we can change the course of human history but time is running out" (Russell and Invisible Children 2012). The imperative to "do something!" has more authority in an environment in which readily accessible forms of digital engagement give the impression that its sole alternative is to "do nothing." As many critics have suggested in the aftermath of the KONY 2012 case, the rapid responses enabled by digital humanitarian campaigns disempower local actors, mis-represent the structural causes of suffering, and promote misguided remedies as a consequence (Brysk 2013, 156–60; Finnegan 2013; Mamdani 2012).

Urgency, enjoyment, and other forms of mediated humanitarian affect are not well understood as manifestations of a uniform expansion of sensory range or a global enhancement of empathy. Human rights advocates continue to embrace new media as opportunities to realize the ambitions of liberal internationalism. In this vein, Michael Ignatieff asserts that new media technologies are facilitating "the steady enlargement of the audiences before which we feel we much justify ourselves" (2017, 15). Indeed, as tools of communication, digital media have the potential to reach globally distant users—but as sites of affective mediation, their impact is both more differentiated and more mutable. Iconic images and signal events hold the potential to forge specific sensitivities that direct attention in a selective manner and generate styles of affectivity within specific media milieus. Generalized assertions of global empathy and moral concern obscure such affective processes.

3. Capturing Humanitarian Affect

Political assessments of digital media and social movements often alternate between celebration and suspicion. On one side are those who regard digital tools as affording new mechanisms for enhancing civil society and organizing and facilitating collective action without a strong organizational center (Bennett and Segerberg 2013; Castells 2012). The emphasis here lies on the mechanics of organizing, especially the potential for user-driven contributions to achieve an outsized impact through digital networking and aggregation. On the other side are those who worry that online activities such as social media networking are producing a deficit of authentic political commitment (Joyce 2011; Morozov 2013; Rifkin 2009). In this vein, Gladwell (2010) argues that social media-driven movements lack the personal sacrifices and "strong ties" that underpinned the US civil rights movement. He and other skeptics argue that clicking, liking, and posting amount to a form of "slacktivism" that cannot produce real change.

While not without their merits, both views are quick to apply metrics of effectiveness that leave the broader political economy of digital humanitarianism unexamined. The last three decades have seen human rights advocacy subsumed within the market rationalities of neoliberalism (Goodale 2009; Hopgood 2013; Moyn 2010). Organizations and networks operate within a competitive marketplace wherein media, donors, and celebrities play an integral role in securing attention among would-be sympathizers (Bob 2005; Chouliaraki 2013; Vestergaard 2010). Moreover, use of social media and other digital tools is creating a growing imperative for actors in the humanitarian sector to tailor their publicity to social media algorithms and other data analytic tools. That supporters are often motivated by genuine concern for human suffering does not insulate the enterprise of humanitarianism from capture by the processes, technologies, and cultural authorities that comprise neoliberalism.

Humanitarian affect helps to secure human participation in those broader neoliberal assemblages. The joy and urgency associated with representations of human suffering fuels the circulation of digital content within global economies of giving and receiving. In this context, messages, posts, and appeals become significant not only for their content, but also for the role they play within a larger system that Jodi Dean calls "communicative capitalism"; they are, to use her words, "mere contributions to the circulation of images, opinion, and information, to the billions of nuggets of information and affect trying to catch and hold attention" (2009, 24). Campaigns seek to leverage evocative images and alluring celebrities in order to accumulate "caring acts" within a distributed pool of "audience labor" (Wilson 2014, 114).[2] Affect thus creates the basis for distributed agency in the absence of geographic proximity, cultural identity, or ideological coherence. The resulting social formations consist of both constellations of individual users and circulations of pre-individual affects that direct attention and inspire action even before the emergence of networks of "mass self-communication" becomes visible.

The moral and political motivations behind digital humanitarian labor tell us little about the regimes of power into which they are drawn. When digital media create opportunities for crowdsourcing and the co-production of content, they serve as engines of participation but do so according to specific terms of intelligibility. Flows of humanitarian affect direct attention to those kinds of human suffering for which moral sensitivities are most acute. Research on transnational social movements notes that issues involving bodily harm receive special attention (Keck and Sikkink 1998); others point to media representations that treat children as privileged objects of moral concern (Moeller 2002) or non-Western populations as needing benevolent Western assistance (Hutchison 2016). These selections are visible expressions of humanitarian sensitivity associated with certain privileged issues, beneficiaries, and cases. Genocide, child soldiers, sex trafficking—each of these high-profile issues provokes such sensitivities and, as a result, presents different potentials to engender flows of humanitarian affect.

This capacity for selectivity means that humanitarian affect enters politics in ways that empower and legitimize certain kinds of norms and institutions. The urgency and enthusiasm generated by the KONY 2012 campaign, for example, became integrated into institutional responses associated with outside military and juridical intervention (in this instance, by the United States military and the International Criminal Court). Moreover, digital tools used to crowdsource the practice of human rights witnessing creates affective channels of authority and dependency between helpers and beneficiaries.[3] For example, a study by Kamari Clarke examines user-driven crisis tracking platforms and smart phone-based capabilities for video capture that are being used by international criminal justice institutions. She argues that these "capture technologies" are

---

2   On the idea of "digital labor," see, for example, work by Thrift (2008), as well as
     Clough (2013) and other contributions to Scholz (2013).
3   Grove (2015), for example, points to the way in which crowdsourced contributions
     to digital crisis maps can help to reproduce specific forms of power within "human
     security governance."

leveraging the affective potential of the "victimized body" and investing digitally equipped helpers with surveillance capacity and political authority once held by the state (2017, 365). Mediated flows of affect thus serve as mechanisms for eliciting and sustaining local human involvement in the institutional sites of neoliberal world politics.

4. Conclusion

The field of humanitarian practice affords insight into the "affective media transformations" of the twenty-first century. In making creative use of social media networking and various forms of mobile computing, humanitarian movements are crowdsourcing the work of witnessing, fundraising, and cultural awareness. But these technical capabilities are not creating the "planetary nervous system" that McLuhan once predicted and that liberal internationalists associate with internet freedom and global connectivity. Instead, contemporary humanitarian practice is producing a more differentiated and mutable field of affective sensitivities and flows. In this context, generalized accounts of empathy cannot capture the channels of enhanced sensitivity that direct attention to specific issues, popula-tions, and campaigns. Humanitarian affect needs to be understood in the particular.

The phenomenon of humanitarian affect offers further indications about how human elements function within contemporary media assemblages. To begin with, the willful intentions and subjective experiences of individual users comprise some but not all of those human elements. As human beings inhabit humanitarian media environments, affective sensitivities co-evolve with the demands placed upon them to contribute specific kinds of digital labor. That such effects are less visible than the communicative and networking functions of digital media does not make them any less significant for the field of cultural politics. Moreover, the moral motivations behind humanitarian practice bear no fixed imprint on the normative and political valence of humanitarian affect. Images and representations of human suffering engender flows of affect, but that humanitarian genesis offers an unreliable indicator of the institutions and regimes of cultural authority with which they later align.

References

Angerer, Marie-Luise. 2017. *Ecology of Affect: Intensive Milieus and Contingent Encounters*. Translated by Gerrit Jackson. Lüneburg: Meson Press.

Arendt, Hannah. 1973. *The Origins of Totalitarianism*. New ed. New York: Harcourt Brace Jovanovich.

Baudrillard, Jean. 1995. *The Gulf War Did Not Take Place*. Translated by Paul Patton. Bloomington: Indiana University Press.

Bennett, W. Lance, and Alexandra Segerberg. 2013. *The Logic of Connective Action: Digital Media and the Personalization of Contentious Politics*. New York: Cambridge University Press.

Berents, Helen. 2016. "Hashtagging Girlhood: #IAmMalala, #BringBackOurGirls and Gendering Representations of Global Politics." *International Feminist Journal of Politics* 18 (4): 513–27. doi: 10.1080/14616742.2016.1207463.

Bob, Clifford. 2005. *The Marketing of Rebellion: Insurgents, Media, and International Activism*. New York: Cambridge University Press.

Bornstein, Erica. 2012. *Disquieting Gifts: Humanitarianism in New Delhi*. Stanford: Stanford University Press.

Brysk, Alison. 2013. *Speaking Rights to Power: Constructing Political Will*. New York: Oxford University Press.

Carey, James W. 1989. *Communication as Culture: Essays on Media and Society, Media and Popular Culture*. Boston: Unwin Hyman.

Carter Olson, Candi. 2016. "#BringBackOurGirls: Digital Communities Supporting Real-world Change and Influencing Mainstream Media Agendas." *Feminist Media Studies* 16 (5): 772–87. doi: 10.1080/14680777.2016.1154887.

Castells, Manuel. 2009. *Communication Power*. New York: Oxford University Press.

———. 2012. *Networks of Outrage and Hope: Social Movements in the Internet Age*. Malden, MA: Polity Press.

Chouliaraki, Lilie. 2010. "Post-Humanitarianism: Humanitarian Communication beyond a Politics of Pity." *International Journal of Cultural Studies* 13 (2): 107–26.

———. 2013. *The Ironic Spectator: Solidarity in the Age of Post-humanitarianism*. Malden, MA: Polity Press.

Clark, Andy. 2003. *Natural-born Cyborgs: Minds, Technologies, and the Future of Human Intelligence*. New York: Oxford University Press.

Clarke, Kamari Maxine. 2017. "Rethinking Sovereignty Through Hashtag Publics: The New Body Politic." *Cultural Anthropology* 32 (3): 359–66. doi: 10.14506/CA32.3.05.

Clinton, Hillary. 2010. "Remarks on Internet Freedom." Newseum, Washington, DC, 21 January.

Clough, Patricia Ticineto. 2000. *Autoaffection: Unconscious Thought in the Age of Tele-technology*. Minneapolis: University of Minnesota Press.

———. 2013. "The Digital, Labor, and Measure beyond Biopolitics." In *Digital Labor: The Internet as Playground and Factory*, edited by Trebor Scholz, 112–26. New York: Routledge.

Cornell, Tricia, Kate Keisch, and Nicole Palasz. 2004. *New Tactics in Human Rights: A Resource for Practitioners*. Minneapolis: Center for Victims of Torture.

Crawford, Neta C. 2014. "Institutionalizing Passion in World Politics: Fear and Empathy." *International Theory* 6 (3): 535–57.

Damasio, Antonio R. 2003. *Looking for Spinoza: Joy, Sorrow, and the Feeling Brain*. New York: Harcourt.

Dean, Jodi. 2009. *Democracy and Other Neoliberal Fantasies: Communicative Capitalism and Left Politics*. Durham, NC: Duke University Press.

Dewey, John. 1946. *The Public and its Problems, an Essay in Political Inquiry*. Chicago: Gateway Books.

Duedahl, Poul. 2011. "Selling Mankind: UNESCO and the Invention of Global History, 1945–1976." *Journal of World History* 22 (1): 101–33.

Duedahl, Poul, ed. 2016. *A History of UNESCO: Global Actions and Impacts*. New York: Palgrave Macmillan.

Dutton, William H., Anna Dopatka, Michael Hills, Ginette Law, and Victoria Nash. 2011. *Freedom of Connection, Freedom of Expression: The Changing Legal and Regulatory Ecology Shaping the Internet*. Paris: UNESCO.

Fassin, Didier. 2012. *Humanitarian Reason: A Moral History of the Present Times*. Berkeley: University of California Press.

Finnegan, Amy C. 2013. "Beneath Kony 2012: Americans Aligning with Arms and Aiding Others." *Africa Today* 59 (3): 137–62. doi: 10.2979/africatoday.59.3.137.

Fraser, Nancy. 2007. "Transnationalizing the Public Sphere: On the Legitimacy and Efficacy of Public Opinion in a Post-Westphalian World." *Theory, Culture & Society* 24 (4): 7–30.

Fraser, Nancy et al. 2014. *Transnationalizing the Public Sphere*. Edited by Kate Nash. Malden, MA: Polity.

Galloway, Alexander R., Eugene Thacker, and McKenzie Wark, eds. 2014. *Excommunication: Three Inquiries in Media and Mediation*. Chicago: The University of Chicago Press.

Gearty, Conor. 2006. *Can Human Rights Survive?* New York: Cambridge University Press.

Gladwell, Malcolm. 2010. "Small Change: Why the Revolution Will Not Be Tweeted." *The New Yorker*.

Goodale, Mark. 2009. *Surrendering to Utopia: An Anthropology of Human Rights*. Stanford: Stanford University Press.

Grove, Nicole Sunday. 2015. "The Cartographic Ambiguities of HarassMap: Crowd-mapping Security and Sexual Violence in Egypt." *Security Dialogue* 46 (4): 345–64. doi: 10.1177/0967010615583039.

Guillory, John. 2010. "Genesis of the Media Concept." *Critical Inquiry* 36 (2): 321–62.

Habermas, Jürgen. 1989. *The Structural Transformation of the Public Sphere: An Inquiry into a Category of Bourgeois Society*. Cambridge, MA: MIT Press.

Haidt, Jonathan. 2003. "Elevation and the Positive Psychology of Morality." In *Flourishing: Positive Psychology and the Life Well-lived*, edited by Corey Keyes, L. M. and Jonathan Haidt, 275–89. Washington, DC: American Psychological Association.

Hayles, Katherine. 2012. *How We Think: Digital Media and Contemporary Technogenesis*. Chicago: The University of Chicago Press.

Headrick, Daniel R. 2000. *When Information Came of Age: Technologies of Knowledge in The Age of Reason and Revolution, 1700–1850*. New York: Oxford University Press.

Hopgood, Stephen. 2006. *Keepers of the Flame: Understanding Amnesty International*. Ithaca, NY: Cornell University Press.

———. 2013. *The Endtimes of Human Rights*. Ithaca, NY: Cornell University Press.

Horkheimer, Max, and Theodor W. Adorno. 2002. "The Culture Industry: Enlightenment as Mass Deception." In *Dialectic of Enlightenment: Philosophical Fragments*, edited by Gunzelin Schmid Noerr, 94–136. Stanford: Stanford University Press.

Hunt, Lynn. 2007. *Inventing Human Rights: A History*. New York: W.W. Norton & Co.

Hutchison, Emma. 2016. *Affective Communities in World Politics: Collective Emotions after Trauma*. New York: Cambridge University Press.

Ignatieff, Michael. 2017. "Human Rights, Global Ethics, and the Ordinary Virtues." *Ethics & International Affairs* 31 (1): 3–16. doi: 10.1017/S0892679416000629.

Joyce, Daniel. 2011. "New Media Witnessing and Human Rights." *Human Rights Defender* 20 (1): 23–26.

Joyce, Mary, ed. 2010. *Digital Activism Decoded: The New Mechanics of Change*. New York: International Debate Education Association.

Käpylä, Juha, and Denis Kennedy. 2014. "Cruel to Care? Investigating the Governance of Compassion in the Humanitarian Imaginary." *International Theory* 6 (2): 255–92.

Keck, Margaret E., and Kathryn Sikkink. 1998. *Activists beyond Borders: Advocacy Networks in International Politics*. Ithaca, NY: Cornell University Press.

Loken, Meredith. 2014. "#BringBackOurGirls and the Invisibility of Imperialism." *Feminist Media Studies* 14 (6): 1100–01. doi: 10.1080/14680777.2014.975442.

MacKinnon, Rebecca. 2012. *Consent of The Networked: The World-wide Struggle for Internet Freedom*. New York: Basic Books.

Malabou, Catherine. 2008. *What Should We Do with Our Brain?* New York: Fordham University Press.

Mamdani, Mahmood. 2012. "What Jason Didn't Tell Gavin and His Army of Invisible Children." *The Daily Monitor*.

Massumi, Brian. 2002. *Parables for the Virtual: Movement, Affect, Sensation*. Durham, NC: Duke University Press.

Mattelart, Armand. 2000. *Networking the World, 1794–2000*. Minneapolis: University of Minnesota Press.

McLuhan, Marshall. 1994. *Understanding Media: The Extensions of Man*. Cambridge, MA: MIT Press.

McLuhan, Marshall, and Bruce R. Powers. 1989. *The Global Village: Transformations in World Life and Media in the 21st Century*. New York: Oxford University Press.

Mitchell, Katharyne. 2016. "Celebrity Humanitarianism, Transnational Emotion and the Rise of Neoliberal Citizenship." *Global Networks* 16 (3): 288–306. doi: 10.1111/glob.12114.

Moeller, Susan D. 1999. *Compassion Fatigue: How the Media Sell Disease, Famine, War, and Death*. New York: Routledge.

———. 2002. "A Hierarchy of Innocence: The Media's Use of Children in the Telling of International New." *The Harvard International Journal of Press/Politics* 7 (1): 36–56. doi: 10.1177/1081180X02007001004.

Morozov, Evgeny. 2013. *To Save Everything, Click Here: The Folly of Technological Solutionism*. New York: PublicAffairs.

Moyn, Samuel. 2010. *The Last Utopia: Human Rights in History*. Cambridge, MA: Harvard University Press.

Pandolfi, Mariella. 2010. "Humanitarianism and Its Discontents." In *Forces of Compassion: Humanitarianism between Ethics and Politics*, edited by Erica Bornstein and Peter Redfield, 227–48. Santa Fe, NM: School for Advanced Research Press.

Papacharissi, Zizi. 2009. "The Virtual Sphere 2.0: The Internet, the Public Sphere, and beyond." In *Routledge Handbook of Internet Politics*, edited by Andrew Chadwick and Philip N. Howard, 230–45. New York: Routledge.

Peters, John Durham. 1999. *Speaking into the Air: A History of the Idea of Communication*. Chicago: University of Chicago Press.

Prinz, Jesse J. 2007. *The Emotional Construction of Morals*. New York: Oxford University Press.

Rancière, Jacques. 2004. "Who Is the Subject of the Rights of Man?" *The South Atlantic Quarterly* 103 (2): 297–310.

Rifkin, Jeremy. 2009. *The Empathic Civilization: The Race to Global Consciousness in a World in Crisis*. New York: J.P. Tarcher/Penguin.

Robinson, Piers. 1999. "The CNN Effect: Can the News Media Drive Foreign Policy?" *Review of International Studies* 25 (2): 301–09.

Rosenberg, Emily S. 2012. "Transnational Currents in a Sinking World." In *A World Connecting, 1870–1945*, edited by Emily S. Rosenberg, 815–997. Cambridge, MA: Belknap Press of Harvard University Press.

Ross, Andrew A. G. 2014. *Mixed Emotions: Beyond Fear and Hatred in International Conflict*. Chicago: University of Chicago Press.

———. 2018. "Beyond Empathy and Compassion: Genocide and the Emotional Complexities of Humanitarian Politics." In *Emotions and Mass Atrocity: Philosophical and Theoretical Explorations*, edited by Thomas Brudholm and Johannes Lang, 185–208. New York: Cambridge University Press.

Russell, Jason, and Invisible Children. 2012. KONY 2012. [San Diego]. Accessed October 16, 2020. https://invisiblechildren.com/kony-2012/.

Scarry, Elaine. 1985. *The Body in Pain: The Making and Unmaking of the World*. New York: Oxford University Press.

Scholz, Trebor. 2013. *Digital Labor: The Internet as Playground and Factory*. New York: Routledge.

Shirky, Clay. 2011. "The Political Power of Social Media." *Foreign Affairs* 90 (1): 28–41.

Slaughter, Anne-Marie. 2016. "How to Succeed in the Networked World." *Foreign Affairs* 95 (6): 76–89.

Srinivasan, Ramesh. 2017. *Whose Global Village? Rethinking How Technology Shapes Our World*. New York: New York University Press.

Thompson, John B. 1995. *The Media and Modernity: A Social Theory of The Media*. Cambridge: Polity Press.

Thrift, Nigel. 2008. *Non-representational Theory: Space, Politics, Affect*. New York: Routledge.

Ure, Michael, and Mervyn Frost. 2014. *The Politics of Compassion*. New York: Routledge.

Vestergaard, Anne. 2010. "Identity and Appeal in the Humanitarian Brand." In *Media, Organizations and Identity*, edited by Lilie Chouliaraki and Mette Morsing, 168–83. London: Palgrave Macmillan.

Volkmer, Ingrid. 2014. *The Global Public Sphere: Public Communication in the Age of Reflective Interdependence*. Malden, MA: Polity.

Wexler, Bruce E. 2006. *Brain and Culture: Neurobiology, Ideology, and Social Change*. Cambridge, MA: MIT Press.

Wilson, Julie A. 2014. "Cosmopolitan Stars, Interactive Audience Labor, and the Digital Economy of Global Care." *Television & New Media* 15 (2): 104–20. doi: 10.1177/1527476412448469.

Ziemke, Jen. 2012. "Crisis Mapping: The Construction of a New Interdisciplinary Field?" *Journal of Map & Geography Libraries* 8 (2): 101–17. doi: 10.1080/15420353.2012.662471.

AFFECTION

DIVIDUATION

BIO- AND SOCIO(TECHNOLOGY)

POLITICAL AESTHETICS

AFROPOLITANISM

AFRICAN FILM AND ART

Affection and Dividuation

Michaela Ott

In order to counter the monolithic understanding
of "affect," coined by Brian Massumi in a specific
reading of Gilles Deleuze's concept, I want to unfold
a more epistemologically demanding understanding
of affective processes through a historical recon-
sideration of the philosophically differentiated
term "affection," meaning "doing with" or "doing
by" in its literal sense. In Maurice Merleau-Ponty's
phenomenology it is conceived as a self-contracting
temporal process able to catalyze and synthesize
interactions and inter-passivities between different
entities. Because of its inevitable participation in
and with others, I want to highlight its "dividual"
character. "Dividual" is a term coined by Deleuze
for the aesthetics of film and music, which, due
to their temporal character, cannot be identified
as individual, undivided expressions. Extending

on this, I consider dividual affections as stimuli and participants of bio- and socio(techno)logical processes where they can be intentionally reinforced for political aims. Finally I present aesthetic-political affections in a (post)colonial perspective, with regard to Achille Mbembe's concept of "Afropolitanism" as to different art works of "African" artists.

Around ten years ago, when I began my study on the concept of affection, I did so with the intention of countering the undifferentiated, block-like understanding of affect that has become widespread in academic discourses (as a consequence of certain post-structuralist statements). I wanted to introduce a historically differentiated concept that would set the discourse of affect in motion once more, and would also make cultural theory analyses available to it. In this, I saw a genuine task of philosophy: to replace the term affect with the more processual one of affection, both in its historical genesis and systematically, as the effect of certain ontological constructions and their conceptual codings—which, admittedly, are confined to the West—and thus to contribute to the development of a differentiated way of thinking about affect.

Ever since Gilles Deleuze's emphatic, Spinoza-echoing interpretation of affect, which unites physical and media affection processes with demands for their intensification and multiplication, affect has become overstrained in academic discourse itself, leading to a de-differentiation of discourse. It is not only that insufficient distinction is made between affects and emotions, affection processes and affect expression, including in terms of language—the term affection is not considered in its historicity and its different connotations in the English, French or German languages. In the very same way as the affective is used in the electronic media for advertising and manipulation purposes, so too is it deployed in the manner of a buzzword in academic discourses, in a spirit of self-advertising. Resorting to the concept of affect appears in itself to be attractive and timely; it is amalgamated with other discourse parameters and is composed of set pieces from various theory traditions, from anthropology, cybernetics, and poststructuralism to biology, technology, and political science, so that ultimately it can no longer be used as a self-evident term.

In my critical reconstruction of the affective I proceeded on the conviction that it should not be understood as an automatic given value, as it was by Aristotle (1926), who listed 11 affects (*pathei*) in his *Nicomachean Ethics* and passed this down as a doctrine so that up to the 16th century Latin scholars, mainly Albertus Magnus (1951) and Thomas Aquinas (1937, 1955) wrote commentaries on it. Thus, they perpetuated an understanding of human affects that is still largely accepted today. In order to counter this ahistorical and schematic understanding of human subjectivation, I have attempted, with the aid of Maurice Merleau-Ponty's *Phenomenology of Perception* (1945), to base affect in temporally occasioned micro-processes of affection, and to develop affect expression as a time, culture, and media-dependent value. Affections, as I learned to understand with him, are autogenetic synthesis and differentiation processes that, in union with the relevant set of cultural codes, are indispensable for the constitution and cohesion of the most widely diverse range of phenomena, from the smallest organisms to persons and social constructs, cultures, religions, and artworks. The way in which they unite with aesthetic qualities in order to become perceptible and to achieve expression is part of what interests me in my work as an aesthetic theorist.

So, in my book *Affizierung: Zu einer ästhetisch-epistemischen Figur* (Ott 2010) I tried to reconstruct the processual and philosophically changing term of affection in its specific historical situatedness and its Western understanding. By unfolding its changing epistemological application I am calling for a disaffection of the affect discourse and for as sober as possible an analysis of affection processes that, in our present day, feed into biological, cultural, and sociological sciences research. In order to counterbalance the political-media affection strategies that influence our societal life in a problematic way, I tried to highlight the deviations from affective stereotypes in philosophical theories and artistic, mainly cinematic, practices.

Affection and Dividual Expression

In order to explain my understanding of affection more precisely, let us once again revisit its foundations in Merleau-Ponty's phenomenology (1945)[1]: according to him, the potential of affection processes lies in their autogenetic character, insofar as they, identified with temporality, are supposed to bring themselves about by repeating their antecedent infinity, and to coalesce in temporal syntheses that are different in each case, as a condition of the possibility of anything whatsoever emerging. They open up

1   For a more thorough analysis of his philosophy, see Ott (2010, 438–41).

a microstructural field that makes affect understandable as an ephemeral value that is in interaction and inter-passivity with others and brings itself to expression and transforms through media coding. The interesting thing about affective articulations is that, because they are the result of micro-processes, they can offer unknown ways of expression. The precondition for this is that they are not immediately categorized under the known taxonomy. In this sense, those neurobiological sciences that uncritically presuppose emotions—the English term often used for non-culturalized psychic expressions similar to the German understanding of affect—as a given should be contradicted: for instance, when they reveal the area of the brain whose blood supply is boosted during a specific emotion's articulation. In this scenario, one is told nothing about the complex psycho-physical and culturalized affection processes, only about the possibility of visualization of movements in the brain, which are then coupled with names that appear to stand for something self-evident.

And yet, in epistemological, political, and aesthetic terms, it is of relevance to the affection processes that they often bring together that which was hitherto not related and place it in a tension-rich relationship, thereby revealing cross-discipline interferences and generating unknown expressions. They also compel one to the insight that affections are to be thought of as non-individual processes, manifesting as sub-surface powers in many agents simultaneously. Thereby, they cross between self-contained entities and connect these multidirectionally, producing affective associations and participation problems, which I have begun to negotiate under the heading of de-individuation or "dividuations" (Ott 2018). The term dividuations places the accent on the various types of participation, of the simultaneous distribution and captures of capacities with which we struggle to learn how to live; it eliminates the "in" of individuation, thus contesting the assumption of undividedness—of anything at all—because an undivided entity is encountered only where some sort of violence is deployed, in the realm of identified beings, things, cultures, and so forth. Thanks to refined technologies, we can recognize today that the assumption of indivisible elements is a fallacy, and that everything exists within relationships of interference and affection, even if they possess coherence and their own affect quality.

By so doing, I am building on specific assumptions and terminologies invented by Gilles Deleuze, primarily those used in his text on the philosophy of film, *Cinema 1: The Movement-Image* (1986). Here he defines affect expression as on the one hand indivisible, and on the other hand as continuously aesthetically subdividing. As he relates in the subchapter "The

Affection Image," filmic affect expression—precisely because of the time-based character of the filmic medium—does not represent an unchangeable and fixable value; it displaces the visual and auditive in relation to one another, continuously undertakes other dividuations of the visual elements, constructs intensity sequences between different aesthetic markers, and creates intervals: Deleuze calls this aesthetic procedure, which undermines the opposition of the individual and collective, "dividual" (14). He is particularly interested in the producing of ambiguous affect articulations and, plainly, in those that cannot be easily recognized or reapplied on known ones. It is no accident that, like Guattari, he adopts a program of ethics—the so-called three virtues—intended to amount to inconspicuousness, impersonality, and indistinguishability of expression. Thus, both are united by the hope that, through the deconstructing of the individual-named features, a kind of re-embedding in the societal field and the unconscious affections will become possible, and thus an articulation with unknown others, a way of speaking that is dividual and politically relevant, because it brings to expression unconscious sensations, wishes, enunciations, and fantasies.

In his late text, *Postscript on the Societies of Control,* Deleuze (1992) acknowledges the tendency brought on by digital media to numerically put everything into relation with everything, for instance, human subjectivations with non-human values such as currency fluctuations and data streams. Against this background, he warns against the becoming-dividual of the human as the expression of the tendency to adapt affectively to all social demands and to obey the imperative of enhancing performance and monetizing one's own abilities. In an era in which every product and also academic discourse seeks media praise and wants to keep itself in view in as high-profile and recognizable a manner as possible, the ethical imperative to re-embed oneself back into the social structure through minimalization and aesthetic subtraction, and to help as many others as possible to articulation, has forfeited much of its attractiveness. At the same time, it is precisely the question of affection that makes it clear that those who are excluded as non-affiliated may also co-affect us, for which reason we are dividuated by them, even if we resist it. Even if they are kept on the other side of the geopolitical or cultural boundary drawn by us, they belong to our economy of affection simply by virtue of their wish to reach us.

By expanding on Deleuze's explanations of the dividual I started to argue in my next book, *Dividuations: Theories of Participation* (Ott 2018), that media affections and the resulting dividuations of the human are observable in the bio- and socio(techno)logical, the cultural and political realms, and should now be considered in more detail; they demand that we question the existing drawing of boundaries, and compel a considered self-monitoring. Thanks to the refined technologies of today we are in a position to deploy these for targeted affection, appropriation, and surveillance purposes. They can contribute to a more complex understanding of the person in that they recognize the person as both voluntarily and involuntarily gripped and entangled, with the person's many-layered affections having to be balanced out in relation to each other. More than a few people are today fleeing to wifi-free zones, where they do not risk being captured by digital affection, as people are already becoming aware that their powers of concentration are significantly impaired by constant enforcements of affection.

As can be seen from this, my understanding of the affective has nothing in common with the related terms of emotion or feeling, as these are located on different constitutional levels. Whilst affections are quasi-primary constitutional processes, which possibly recall phylogenetic and inherited information, feelings in my understanding are culturally specific reworkings of the affective material. When this is mixed, the special quality of inconspicuous affections, which betray that there are non-human and non-technologically occasioned effects upon well-being, is not experienced. In order to emphasize the many-layered nature of affection processes, I shall now briefly outline the bio(techno)logical level, before going on to discuss the socio(techno)logical and aesthetic-political affections and their media-occasioned transformations, which are of greater interest in this context.

The Bio(techno)logical Level

In the realm of micro- and molecular biology, affective interferences and coalescences of micro-organisms are researched today primarily with regard to biodiversity and ecological contexts. How precisely individual affections proceed is of less consequence than the assumption that their effects are decisive in the multiplying of life, its dynamic, its exchange processes, and the question of species demarcations. Evolutionary biology, microbiology, molecular biology, and genetics teach us today that the epistemological proximities between the species must be rethought and re-evaluated, since we are presumably aware of only one percent of the life forms existing in the microscopic realm.[2] Thanks to increased differentiation in investigation and surveying methods, and to optical

---

2   Here I do not want to refer to the discourses on companion species by Donna
     Haraway and others, but to the unconscious and widely unnoticed cohabitation with

instruments that are penetrating into ever-smaller microscopic realms, these microbiomes are being opened up in all their multifarious and highly mobile forms.

As is discussed by Paul-Michael Agapow, a London-based researcher in bioinformatics, the shifts in molecular genetics incorporate other temporal, material, and epistemological levels and bring about "populations that are more finely grained" (2005, 60). Bio(techno)logical de-individuation grows exponentially with the more differential investigative methods, as genetic analysis makes it clear that a larger number of affective intersections, splittings, variations, and hybrid formations exist than can be seen in the phenotype. It reveals polymorphisms that are not visible morphologically. Agapow therefore demands the putting in place of research criteria not geared towards the specification of individuals, economic advantage, or evolution information. His criticism is directed toward a biologically under-stood philosophy of nature protection that fights for the preservation of macroscopically visible species at the expense of others that are inac-cessible to the human eye. Agapow's very justifiable criticism is that the important thing is not to save individual populations, or to preserve individualized species regardless of issues of ecological interplay and the promotion of biodiversity. Agapow himself focuses attention on "super-specific" groups that co-exist and co-evolve with many species. He strongly advocates for the inclusion of micro-organisms—bacteria, archaea and lower eukaryotes—and their affective interferences and co-constitutions with respect to biodiversity. Such a level of observation inevitably leads to the adoption of minimal dividuations in the realm of living things, as observation shows that the majority of plants and animals

> [live] in obligate symbiotic contact with one or with several bacteria species. Frequently, one finds the phenomenon of cospeciation, which ... would mean that there are at least as many species of micro-organisms as there are plants and animals, that is, over a million. (Roselló-Amann 2001, 161–80)

However, since most life is microstructural, both in biomass and in bio-diversity, what is needed is a shift in the focus of attention in order to actually integrate micro-affective relationships into the discussion of life.

non-human entities on a microbiological level, such as bacteria and viruses that influence even the unfolding of our genome.

The Socio(techno)logical Level

In parallel to the bio(techno)logical level, the field of socio(techno)logical research has also expanded, structuring itself laterally to conventional criteria and differentiating itself through media affection processes. Recent sociological theories outline the new phenomenon of upcoming world societies and the new affective relations by which they are brought about on a globalized scale. Ultimately, the German sociologist Ulrich Beck describes the bringing together of different institutions and initiatives to form a world society as an irreversible development of today that forces agents to participate as undetermined affective multitudes, all the more so since no identity formation of nation-state, cultural society, or individual is now possible:

> The unity of state, society, and individual presumed by the first modernity is being dissolved. World society does *not* mean world *state* society or world *economy* society, but a *non*-state society, that is, an aggregate condition of society, for which state-territory guarantees of order, but also the rules of publically legitimate politics, lose their binding character. (Beck 1997, 174)

The world society of which Beck speaks appears as an action space of different organizations and single persons, not tied to territories, but tied together by shared affections and interests. World society's "aggregate state" as he outlines it is inevitably not "one" but a dividual structure of single and group initiatives, transnational and transcultural connections, boundary-breaking power and affect relationships.

Beck's description of "multiple-location, transnational, glocal biographies of the contact and crossing points of human beings" (178) expanding and propagating in the growing world society is no longer applicable only to the Western world. Interconnected single agents or organizations log themselves into various function systems and take part in variously rational medial processes. A non-governmental organization (NGO) or a so-called terrorist group can simultaneously cooperate with different institutions in different locations in different affective and medial expressions, and can intervene in or bring about various sensitive points. Organizations of this type cannot be described as units or purely as the sum of their single agents; they are temporary allies, with distributed interests, their solidarity with others dependant on phase, deciding jointly on their modes of participation and their willingness to engage, dividing competencies and modes of action among themselves, affectively concentrating themselves in articulations, and engaging in joint risks. "With no alternative to cooperation and thus mutually obliged to take account of one another's interests" (185) they extend—partially replacing classical interest representatives such as trade unions—into the decisions of states and, in their transverse network operations, form new affective socialities. Not only transnationally operating NGOs but also militant groups such as Islamic State (IS) can be considered to be world societies of this type, all the more so since IS aimed to reconstruct an empire and rejuvenate the Eastern Roman empire of Ottoman times.

For this purpose, the IS fighters developed a media affect policy along several lines: they used the internet and their portal "Global Islamic Media Front" (Engelhardt 2014, 66) to advertize their state ideology poster fashion, and to win youthful and even child recruits for its propagation, but they also deployed "Western" video aesthetics and the US horror film in order to spread fascination and to connect with the perception patterns of young people, especially through familiar aesthetic formats such as *Game of Thrones*. This fantasy world, in which men are massacred, women raped, and children abused, was implemented in reality and documented on video. Additionally, they showed a consciousness of history, popularizing their planned caliphate under the online magazine title "Rumiyah," meaning "Rome," also referencing the identity of Constantinople/Istanbul as a "second Rome" and as a successor to the Roman and Ottoman Empires.

Under the impression produced by destructive transnational initiatives of this type, but also in light of globally organized social inequality, Ulrich Beck draws attention, in a late text, to "the sudden alienness of society" (2010, 176). He emphasizes vehemently that

> after all, the experience of "globality" asks for recognition of cross-border distributions of social inequality not registered by a nation-state perspective. The place of territorial, political, economic, and socially established space has been replaced by the *"ambivalence* of co- and multinational action spaces and life circumstances" and a *"contingency* of non-congruent boundary constructions." (24)

He even accentuates the fact that an expanded perspective results in the insight that "the ability and possibility of crossing boundaries has become a significant resource for social inequality in the globalised world," (25) thanks to the unequal distribution of access to state welfare institutions, to general security, and to a better standard of life with freedom from violence. Beck wishes to take more into account those processes "that penetrate the boundaries of nation states" (26) and affect their inhabitants with "transnational currents and forces," such as climate change, but also "the incalculability of transnational terrorism and the unilateralism of the world's greatest military power." Involuntary affections arise as a consequence of those political decisions that have implications across nation-state boundaries:

> Often it is the case that one exports the danger, either spatially—to countries whose elites see it as an opportunity—or temporally: to the future of unborn generations. One spares money by transporting the risk to somewhere where the security standards are low and the arm of the law does not reach … This applies to the export of torture as it does to the export of waste. (28)

Here, Beck outlines significant and temporally far-reaching political and economic affections of world populations. They result from the interplay of social need, acceptance of danger, and economic greed for profits and from the fact that "active" and "passive transnationalization" (32) are distributed to different global regions. For Beck, this does not mean that poor societies are not part of and not affected by world societies: "Rather, the reverse is true: they are the worst affected owing to the scant resource of silence that they can offer: a fateful magnetism prevails between poverty, social vulnerability, corruption, and accumulation of danger" (28). He thus draws the conclusion (which once again undermines the belief in the possibility of leading an individual life) that "the resource and capacity of 'boundary profit,' that is, of crossing nation-state boundaries or instrumentalizing them for the accumulation of life opportunities, has become a key variable of social inequality in the globalized world" (31). In his description of the "average migrant" Beck recognizes the consummate contemporary embodiment of boundary profit. As "artist of the border," this figure explores a form of existence that, in its multiple economic, political, and cultural affections, can by no means be called individual: "In these forms of life that are tested in border-crossing opportunities, *different national-state spaces of social inequality* intersect and interpenetrate" (32).

In view of this development, Etienne Balibar sees a new/old affect gaining in strength:

> With … globalization, fear is displaced anew, and in a certain way, it switches sides: it is no longer capitalists who fear revolution, but workers who fear competition from immigrants. Thus the relation of forces that underlay the exterior of the constitution of the national-social state is destabilized the moment the limits of its universalism also appear from within. (Balibar 2014, 17).

The Aesthetic-Political Level

I shall conclude by briefly characterizing some contemporary aspects of the aesthetic-political realm—which concerns me professionally—in its contrary affection movements: on the one hand, artistic practice is praised for its possibilities of affective and conceptual deviation and heterogeneity, its possibilities recognized for creating ambiguity in affect expression, and its potential to take them to the edge of human expression and to connect with things hitherto not symbolized. On the other hand, today it sees itself increasingly threatened by globalized art market forces and aesthetic standardizations. Even art biennials that promote local and regional art and wish to enhance the value of specific art languages are engaged in an affection contest with biennials worldwide. And yet it is precisely the authors from the southern hemisphere such as Achille Mbembe (2010) who praise the global decentralization of art events, because it opens up to African artists the possibility of liberating themselves from the Africa niche to which they had been assigned by the art market, to practice cross-cultural affection and sampling processes, and to lend themselves a post-ethnic mode of appearance. The Afropolitan aesthetic that he presents as timely is precisely concerned with accentuating spatiotemporal intertwinings and, all in all, the interwovenness of different art languages. To Mbembe, it appears unquestionable that culturally composite forms of expression are the only articulation form appropriate to contemporary circumstances. Numerous authors from the non-Western world argue—in the same spirit—for the de-individuation of the understanding of the sub-ject and art. For instance, the Senegalese philosopher Souleymane Bashir Diagne (2017) hails the terminology of dividuations because it indicates that the term "individual," or "the undivided," expresses a negation, the negation of participation and dividuatedness by others, which appears to be no longer appropriate in times of worldwide exchanges and mutual influences of all sorts.

When one looks at globalized art and discourse events such as Documenta or the Venice Art Biennial, we see that today a distinction is made between refugees from African countries who are violently rejected as of no concern to our more and more nationalized affection readiness, and academic or art-oriented speakers from non-Western contexts who are welcome as new voices invigorating the cultural self-reflections of Europe, the art market, and its need for change. We have started to pay attention to voices from other cultural contexts, to perceive different affective articulations, and to perceive ourselves more critically. Unfortunately this does not mean that we face and modify the unequal division of labor that also exists in the scientific realm. Gayatri Spivak criticizes this division of labor and raises the question of why theoretical affection is still directed toward the old centers of science, and of prestige (2008, 40).

Today, Afropolitan theorists and artists respond to this with a provocative self-confidence: no longer do they deplore their "extraversion," their inevitable orientation to Western knowledges and globalized aesthetic formats, but instead try to take them over advantageously, to subvert them, and to parody them. As an example of this, I would like to mention the film *Aristotle's Plot* (1995) by the Cameroonian filmmaker Jean-Pierre Bekolo, who created this commissioned piece of work for the British Film Institute as the "African" contribution to the centenary of cinema in 1995. This film develops a hilarious play with the question of what an African cinema could be, with the cineaste's affection for an art cinema à la francaise and the oppositional love of African movie goers for American action movies. The film parodies the image of Africa stereotypically produced by the West in its standardized Aristotelian-Hollywood film dramaturgy, its conception of narrative patterns, and of the affective reactions of pity and fear that paradoxically are best stimulated by documentary images of Africa.

In one of its significant achievements, Documenta 14 in Kassel and Athens opposed stereotypical cultural attributions. The African is no longer exhibited as a dancing curiosity: instead, paintings, bronze sculptures, and sound installations by African artists were displayed. Oghbo has the current stock market prices performed by a choir; the curator Bonaventure Ndikung, who had particular responsibility for the acoustic side of the Documenta, talked about the need for a new "deep listening," and included the radio program, as a direct affection medium, into the overall plan. In this, he was concerned with artistic offers of an alternative hearing, with unconventional sound compositions that do indeed broadcast indeterminate affect expressions and are intended to once again reconnect with oral culture. The concentration on the auditive contains an implied criticism of the commodification of art works, but also an affection offer through neglected cultural techniques. Achille Mbembe signals in his book *Critique de la Raison Nègre* (2013) that the Africans of today should no longer be associated with physicality and emotionality. "Black reason" is attributed not to a specific ethnic group, but explicitly to all of those who, regardless of their origin, are excluded from the value creation chain and are victims of the striations of the world according to economic (non)participation criteria. It offers itself as a disaffected capacity for the negotiation of affective, symbolic, and economic dividuation possibilities.

References

Agapow, Paul-Michael. 2005. "Demarcation and Diversity." In *Phylogeny and Conservation,* edited by Andy Purvis and John L. Gittlema, 57–75. Cambridge: Thomas Books.

Albertus Magnus. 1951. *De passionibus.* Münster: Aschendorff.

Amann, Rudolf, and Ramón Roselló-Mora. 2001. "Mikrobiologische Aspekte der Biodiversität." In *Wissenschaftstheorie der Biologie: Methodische Wissenschaftstheorie und die Begründung der Wissenschaften,* edited by Peter Janich and Michael Weingarten, 161–80. München: Fink Verlag.

Aristotle. 1926. *The Nicomachean Ethics.* Translated by H. Rackham, II. v. 2. London: William Heinemann/Cambridge, MA: Harvard University Press.

Balibar, Etienne. 2014. *Equaliberty: Political Essays.* Durham: Duke University Press.

Beck, Ulrich. 1997. *Was ist Globalisierung? Irrtümer des Globalismus – Antworten auf Globalisierung.* Frankfurt/M: Suhrkamp Verlag.

———. 2010. *Große Armut, großer Reichtum: Zur Transnationalisierung sozialer Ungleichheit.* Berlin: Suhrkamp Verlag.

Bekolo, Jean-Pierre. 1995. *Aristotle's Plot.* London: BFI.

Deleuze, Gilles. 1986. *Cinema 1: The Movement-Image.* Minnesota: University of Minnesota Press.

———.1992. "Postscript on the Societies of Control." *October* 59 (Winter): 3–7.

Diagne, Souleymane Bashir. 2017. "Translation and the Universal," interview with Michaela Ott and Sophie Lembcke. *Lerchenfeld* 39 (July): 34–40.

Engelhardt, Marc. 2014. *Heiliger Krieg – Heiliger Profit: Afrika als neues Schlachtfeld des Internationalen Terrorismus.* Berlin: Christoph Links Verlag.

Mbembe, Achille. 2010. *Sortir de la grande nuit: Essai sur l'Afrique décolonisée.* Paris: La Découverte.

———. 2013. *Critique de la raison nègre.* Paris: La Découverte.

Merleau-Ponty, Maurice. 1945. *La Phénomenologie de la perception.* Paris: Gallimard.

Ott, Michaela. 2010. *Affizierung: Zu einer ästhetisch-epistemischen Figur.* München: edition text und kritik.

———. 2018. *Dividuations: Theories of Participation.* New York: Palgrave Macmillan.

Spivak, Gayatri. 2008. *Can the Subaltern Speak?* Wien: Turia + Kant.

Thomas von Aquin. 1937. "Wesen und Ausstattung des Menschen." In *Die Deutsche Thomas-Ausgabe.* Bd. 6. Leipzig: Verlag Anton Pustet.

———. 1955. "Die menschlichen Leidenschaften." In *Die Deutsche Thomas-Ausgabe.* Bd. 10. Köln: Styria Verlag.

ATTUNEMENT

AESTHETICIZATION

POLITICS

EMISSARIES OF THE DIVINE LIGHT

AFFECTIVE ALTER-POLITICS

Attuning to What? The Uncanny Revival of the Aestheticization of Politics

Mathias Fuchs

One of the key notions posited in Brian Massumi's "Keywords for Affect," a supplement to *The Power at the End of the Economy,* is "affective politics." Massumi establishes a close connection between affect, aesthetics, politics and the body, stating: "Aesthetic politics brings the collectivity of shared events to the fore" and he continues to say that this is a "multiple bodily, potential for what might come." The problem German readers will encounter with these lines is that whenever "body," "community," and "future" (Körper, Gemeinschaft, Zukunft) are mentioned in one sentence, they'll immediately be reminded of what Leni Riefenstahl demonstrated with her film *Triumph des Willens* (1935), the infamous propaganda film of the 1934 Nazi Party rally in Nuremberg, Germany. Memories of the dark side of an aestheticization of political

phenomena are roused. Many 1930s German directors, writers and painters were in line with Riefenstahl in being apologetic of the regime, often not explicitly, but via an atmospheric side by side with the ones in power. The underlying ideology of Riefenstahl's films, related texts, paintings and movies was what Walter Benjamin warned us of when he said: "Such is the aestheticizing of politics, as practiced by fascism. Communism replies by politicizing art." This article tries to relate Massumi's concept of attunement and affective politics to earlier speculations about "affective attunement" and to put into a historic context the attempts to replace rationality with bodily intensities.

Political thought flourishes with noncognitive primary consciousness.
Brian Massumi (2014, 40)

The discourse on affective transformations is not only a debate about the psychology of precognitive consciousness. It is also a debate about perception and aesthetics, and it is a discourse touching the very sensitive matter of the politics of affect. Far from an enlightened perspective of politics as rational decision-making or from a Habermasian *Theory of Communicative Action* (1981) there are authors suggesting that politics might be triggered, influenced and shaped primarily by affects, and not by critical reason and communicative action. The notion of "attunement" is crucial for an understanding of affect-based politics. I will therefore try to trace back the concept of "attunement" to philosophical, psychological and esoteric proposals of the 1940s and 1950s.

It comes as a surprise that a school of philosophical thinking—comprising Massumi, Erin Manning and some of Massumi's students—vehemently points out that affects have to be distinguished from conscious thought or emotions and that affect precedes psychology and the social in the formation of politics. These authors deliver quite a few hints—often vague and ambiguous—suggesting that in some undisclosed and mysterious way, affect might be accountable as the key driver for politics and the social. This is surprising against the background of an understanding of politics as a rational process and the hope that society is malleable and can be improved via enlightened thinking—or alternatively via communicative action (Habermas 1981). In his *Keywords* Brian Massumi talks about "affective politics" (2015b, 110), appropriates Alfred North Whitehead's formula of "intensity of contrasts," and interprets his own creation of "affective alter-politics" (111) as an affect-led form of politics. Massumi seems surprised by his own reasoning. How could the very same types of affect that William James assigned to "the neural machinery," and that the latter held responsible for various emotions (1884, 190), now take the role of a driving force of politics? We can follow Massumi, when he muses: "This does not sound very political" (Massumi 2015b, 111). He continues: "at least not in the sense of what we usually take as political." There is no doubting that Massumi is right again. We understand politics as collective action in the field of social relations, of power and ownership, and of access to the means of production. We are not always conscious of these relationships and ownerships, but we can try to think about them. Politics are different to belief systems or incomprehensible ventings. Politics can be talked about. Massumi's texts are valid proof of that. But then Massumi arrives at a conclusion that hardly anyone since the days of Leni Riefenstahl would have dared to propose. "Aesthetic politics brings the collectivity of shared events to the fore ... a multiple, bodily potential for what might come" (111). Who would not be reminded of and alarmed by the proximity to manipulative propaganda and filmmaking in the style of *Olympia—Fest der Völker* (Riefenstahl 1938) or *La Nave Bianca* (Rosselini 1941)? Massumi promotes what Walter Benjamin warned us of almost a century ago. For Benjamin "the aestheticization of politics" was a key ingredient of fascism, and "the politicization of aesthetics" would rather have to be looked for. Massumi displays an interest in—and a lack of critical distance to—processes that have been used for propaganda and manipulation when he says: "Bodies can be inducted into, or attuned to, certain regions of tendency, futurity, and potential" (Massumi 2015b, 108). Petteri Pietikainen comments on this under-complex understanding of the body when he assesses what the consequence for politics would be if bodies were that simple: "Politics is reduced to a tweaking of the *selection fitness function* and nothing more" (Pietikainen 2017, 20).

I guess Massumi writes with the best of intentions, and when he mentions former-President Barack Obama's success in using affective politics he does not hide his sympathies for the latter. It is worrying, however, that after the publication of Massumi's *Keywords,* another US President used affective politics for less desirable goals than the ones the Obama administration had. Massumi's positive assessment of "the Obama campaign's recueing of fear toward hope" (2015b, 109) would need a corrective statement today, pointing out that the recueing of fear into hope can under certain circumstances be closely followed by a recueing of hope into horror. His statement about the "reservoir of political potential" would now require more thought and a warning about the reservoir of political destructiveness of affective attunement of the collective bodies.

Affect Attunement—Divine Light

The *Keywords'* considerations of attunement refer to Daniel Stern directly, and to Deleuze/Guattari indirectly, via the concept of "microperceptions" (Massumi 2015b, 107). The notion of "attunement" has roots in experimental psychoanalysis and in French philosophy. Guattari followed Stern's observation of children at an early age experiencing their environment via an empathic contact with a caregiver before they are able to use language; he calls this mode of perception "affect attunement" (Stern 1985, 138–61). The term is most often associated with said philosophers, but it has deeper roots in less prominent esoteric schooling and dubious doctrines. If we follow the line of influences that the notion of "affect attunement" has been built upon we will not only find Gilles Deleuze, Félix Guattari and Daniel Stern, but also healer-gurus like Lloyd Arthur Meeker and the contested pseudo-scientist Albert Ackerley.

In his para-scientific writings, Meeker (1907–1954), who called himself "Uranda," proposed that affective attunement would be the core mechanism for energetic medicine (1988). Meeker and his spiritualistic group of the *Emissaries of the Divine Light* taught a healing practice based on bodily and ethereal energies. In the training-school classes at the cult's Sunrise Ranch, potential healers had to recognize their skills of moving the invisible forces within the triangle of God–Patient–Chiropracter. The *G-P-C* method was hoped to be an effective tool to compensate for misalignments and suppress pain. Originally based on physical patient–therapist contact, the esoteric healers soon reached out for further possibilities. Ackerley, who first worked as an assistant and marketing manager for Meeker, started experimenting with a tele-therapeutic approach. Originally claiming that he could establish the *G-P-C* triangle without touching the patient, he extended the effective radius of his alleged healing rays to a few meters and then to transcontinental distances.

The intellectual climate of the USA in the 1940s and '50s privileged theories based on energetic flow, touch-free transmission, and remote effects. This added to the Emissaries' chance to establish their cult as a scientific business. In the fifth decade of the twentieth century, tele-healing groups, ham radio communities, the Manhattan project and cybernetics research flourished, received widespread attention, and were nourished by hopes and fears that there is "something up there in the air." For a collective phantasm, it does not matter whether the remote actors up there are German airplanes, radio transmission stations, or Divine energy beams.

Teleological Society—Travelling by Telegraph

One should add that the 1942 "Cerebral Inhibition Meeting" in New York City, an important predecessor conference to the series of *Macy* conferences, introduced hypnosis as a central topic and discussed it extensively. Hypnotic communication was examined as a teleological process for a non-material, long-distance control technique. A year after the "Cerebral Inhibition Meeting" Ross Ashby and Norbert Wiener named the group, consisting of the formerly mentioned and Gregory Bateson, Margaret Mead, Warren McCulloch, Frank Fremont-Smith and others, as the "Teleological Society" (Masani 1997, 490).

Wiener's fantasy of teleporting an architect through space is characteristic of the obsession with non-corporeal travel. In *The Human Use of Human Beings* (1950) Wiener suggests a thought experiment: if we can code the structure of human design decisions as a message, then the work of an architect who is occupied with planning a building in a far-away land can be sent through telegraph lines. In some way this would be equivalent to reconstructing the human architect at the remote location. In Wiener's words: "… the idea that one might conceivably travel by telegraph, in addition to travelling by train or airplane, is not intrinsically absurd" (Wiener 1967, 139–40).

Hearing Voices

The possibility of intercorporeal communication was a challenge and a tempting thought for scientists Ashby and Wiener and for esoteric healers Meeker and Ackerley. It was—and still is—the core to paranormal experiences. Lisa Blackman (2010) points out that the spiritualist practice of hearing voices is based on the possibility of telepathic transfer.

> One example that perplexed me at the time … was the particular affective workings of practices within the UK Spiritualist Church, which enacted voices as modes of telepathic transfer; that is, the understanding that voices can be heard and transferred between members of the group and even between the living and the dead. (Blackman 2010, 164)

In the case of hearing voices, an inaudible voice has to be made perceptible by the spiritualist community members and it therefore has to be made physical. The process is a materialization of an imagination or an expectation. This materialization stunt can only be performed with a method at hand called "attunement," as Blackman explains:

> The voice-hearer would subtly shift their attention and focus to feelings, sensations, rhythms and movements which would allow them to attune to the more pre-verbal and intensive dimensions of the voices. This attunement might take place within an associated milieu known as the 'development circle', which connects the group members such that they might experience a flow of energy within the room or particular setting. … The voices … become shared rather than isolated singular experiences. This is a mode of 'being-with' that mediates the voices such that they might be considered intercorporeal and plural where distinct boundaries between the self and other, inside and outside, and material and immaterial dissolve. (164)

In the 1940s the idea of immediate transmission had become a popular trope. It was in the very same decade that Wiener proposed to teleport architects and that the *Emissaries* healed over distances. In addition, during the 1940s, secret services from both the West and the East experimented with telematic technologies. We cannot but be bewildered when we remember that *KGB* agents cut rabbit throats in Leningrad to scientifically measure the delay of a reaction of the twin rabbit in Vladivostok. The idea was that some information might travel faster than light and that an immediate transmission could pave the way to powerful Cold War weapons. US military research played with science fiction scenarios as well. Experts in wireless communication, telematic control and nuclear ray technologies played at the border of what we consider scientific today. It is therefore also comprehensible that the *Emissaries of the Divine Light* suspected that the *CIA* tried to hijack and then shot down the airplane of their leader Lloyd Arthur Meeker in an attempt to better understand the secrets of attunement.

In university research during the 1950s, army facility projects and secret investigations in top-level labs run by the *CIA* and *KGB* converged with esoteric experiments of long-distance attunement. This idea seems to have been prevalent then: killing, healing, economic operations, urban planning, and technical networking can happen without physical contact and possibly without delay. These processes might be executed ubiquitously and regardless of the material conditions of communication.

In the 1970s and 80s these ideas seemed to lose their attraction, but a revival of remote technology conceptions can be observed at the end of the 20th century. Massumi uses a vocabulary that picks up the technological terminology from what was cutting edge in the 1950s. Immediation, he explains, "has more to do with complex field effects, and their wave-like amplification and propagation, than with point-to-point transmissions," and he continues "'[a]ttunement' refers to the direct capture of attention and energies by the event" (Massumi 2015a, 115). Waves and energy are no longer considered paradigmatic categories when we think about con-nectivity today. The electrical engineers' vocabulary has been superseded by notions from computer science: the cloud, ubiquitous computing, the World Wide Web, telemedicine, and Virtual Reality. These are the structural backbone of a connectivity without limits. On the material level, drones, surveillance cameras and mobile phones complement the setting well. Popular quasi-scientific fairy tales like the one about the butterfly who flaps his wings and instantly causes a hurricane on the other side of the planet are taken out of context and prepare a paradigmatic basis for seeing "connectivity" (Ascott 2000) or "superconnectivity" (Ascott 1988) almost everywhere.

Affective Politics as Aestheticization of Politics

Of course, Massumi's theoretical approach, his carefully chosen wording and his political ethos make him stand apart from the *Emissaries of the Divine Light.* In many ways Massumi's theory is quite different from Meeker's. The former is wise enough to insist on "actual differentiation" and he points out that "thinking-feeling" is never a homogenous phenomenon (Massumi 2015b, 111), as the spiritualists and the fascists would have liked it to be. Still, it is not easy to pardon Massumi for referring to Stern's and Guattari's notions of attunement without even mentioning the irrational undertones and connotations. It is one thing to dream about the possibility and foster hope in the prelingual and presocial connectivity of bodies and "masses." This might be some form of late-hippie romanticism. It is another thing to advocate attunement for politics: this can be a politically dangerous suggestion in a time when a vague notion of an "alter-politics at the collectively in-braced heart of every situation" (109) could play into the hands of political actors keenly waiting to replace solidarity, critical discourse and socio-political consciousness with collective attunement. Those who build politics upon "a collective event … distributed across those bodies" (109) promote what Walter Benjamin wisely warned us of: the aestheticization of politics.

Benjamin reverses the aestheticization in the field of politics when he says:

> The masses have a right to changed property relations; fascism seeks to give them expression in keeping these relations unchanged. The logical outcome of fascism is an aestheticizing of political life. … Such is the aestheticizing of politics, as practiced by fascism. Communism replies by politicizing art. (Benjamin [1936] 2002, 122)

Do Massumi's "affective politics" focus on expression and forget about the structures of ownership Benjamin makes us aware of? It is difficult to imagine how political economy could fit into the system of an affect economy. The former makes sense if there is the possibility of studying relationships rationally. The latter is concerned with nonconscious processes. In his book *The Power at the End of the Economy* (2015c), Massumi stresses the importance of "nonconscious dimensions" and the individual's affective potential to "resonate" with others on infra-individual and trans-individual levels. In the end such a project has to arrive at a point where the aestheticization of economic and political relations replaces the analytical approach.

Kerstin Stakemeier proposes that an aestheticization of politics is based on a concept of aesthetics that is "not specifically reactionary. It is rather specifically progressive in terms of capitalist self-conception. It allows for a fusion of the aesthetic aura of immediateness with the administrative distance of the political" (Behrens 2015, n.p.). She also lays out how the evasiveness of the aesthetic smoothly combines with the post-Fordist achievements of continually growing, friction-free productivity. Following this line of thought, it would come as no surprise that "affective alter-politics" are a model for theorizing about society that is shaped exactly as society is. It lacks negativity. It is most closely aligned and assimilated with the object of investigation: capitalist society. It replaces thought with vibes. It celebrates instinct as a productive force (Massumi 2014) and places "the human on the animal continuum" (3). According to Massumi we have to move beyond "our sole proprietorship of language, thought, and creativity" (3). This might be a noble and most humble gesture, apologizing for the anthropocentric overestimation of exclusively human abilities to think and act rationally. But to conclude from this that we have to "see what the birds and the beasts have instinctively to say about this" (3) will lead to a big disappointment. The birds and the beasts will not solve our problems. When Massumi wonders *What Animals Teach Us about Politics* (2014) he might have called for bad advisors. The animals will be exploited and destroyed by the same system that exploits us. It would be better to rationally analyze this system with language, thought and creativity than to ask our fellow victims, the beasts, about their instinctive thoughts on the matter.

References

Ascott, Roy. 1988. "Superconnectivity in Deep Dataspace." In *European Media Art Festival* (catalogue), 332–36. Osnabrück: Medienkunst Festival.

———. 2000. *Art Technology Consciousness*. Portland: Intellect Books.

Behrens, Roger. 2015. "Interviews: Die Ästhetisierung der Politik." *Mein digitales Wohnzimmer.* Accessed November 15, 2019. http://rogerbehrens.net/die-aesthetisierung-der-politik.

Benjamin, Walter. (1936) 2002. "The Work of Art in the Age of its Technological Reproducability." In *Benjamin, Selected Writings*, Vol. 3, edited by Howard Eiland and Michael W. Jennings, 101–33. Cambridge, MA: Harvard University Press.

Blackman, Lisa. 2010. "Embodying Affect: Voice-hearing, Telepathy, Suggestion and Modelling the Non-conscious." *Body & Society* 16 (1): 163–92.

Habermas, Jürgen. (1981) 1984. *Theory of Communicative Action, Volume One: Reason and the Rationalization of Society*. Translated by Thomas A. McCarthy. Boston, MA: Beacon Press.

James, William. 1884. "What is an Emotion?" *Mind* 9 (34): 188–205.

Masani, Pesi Rustom. 1997. "Norbert Wiener and the Future of Cybernetics." In *Proceedings of the Norbert Wiener Centenary Congress, 1994*, edited by V. Mandrekar and P. R. Masani, 473–504. Providence, RI: American Mathematical Society.

Massumi, Brian. 2014. *What Animals Teach Us about Politics*. Durham, NC: Duke University Press.

———. 2015a. *Politics of Affect*. Cambridge: Polity Press.

———. 2015b. "Keywords for Affect." In *The Power at the End of the Economy*, 103–12. Durham, NC: Duke University Press.

———. 2015c. *The Power at the End of the Economy*. Durham, NC: Duke University Press.

Meeker, Lloyd A. 1988. *The Third Sacred School, Volume 8, Health, Healing and Attunements Part 2*, 475–79. Loveland, CO: Emissaries of Divine Light.

Pietikainen, Petteri. 2017: "'Neurosis Can Still Be Your Comforting Friend': Neurosis and Maladjustment in Twentieth-Century Medical and Intellectual History." In *The Neurotic Turn:*

Inter-Disciplinary Correspondence on Neurosis, edited by Charles Johns, 17–38. London: Repeater Books.

Stern, Daniel. 1985. *The Interpersonal World of the Infant: A View from Psychoanalysis & Developmental Psychology*. New York: Basic Books.

Wiener, Norbert. (1950) 1967. *The Human Use of Human Beings*. New York: Avon Books.

Films

Riefenstahl, Leni. 1938. *Olympia – Fest der Völker*. Erster Teil der zweiteiligen Propagandafilm Serie. Berlin: Olympia-Film GmbH.

Rosselini, Roberto. 1941. *La Nave Bianca*. Centro Cinematografico del Ministero della Marina.

POPULISM

DEMOCRACY

SYSTEM THEORY

PEDAGOGY

BELIEF

ALTERNATIVE FACTUALITY

Witnessing the Dismantlement of a Proven Structure of Belief: The Challenge of Populism and Alternative Facts to Liberal Democracy

Jean Clam

The crisis liberal democracy is facing today is a new challenge: the relation between alternative factuality and the unleashing of affective impulses is mediated by the transformation of the pre-existing structure of belief. There is an affective turn in the political realm—a realm structurally marked by collective sentiments and their non-relativizable nature. While the structural social and psychic setting of the functional differentiation of society remains unchanged, a crucial component of it has been strongly "affected" by a re-ordering of the function of belief within the cognitive dimension of social communication. In this crucial situation we need a new pedagogy of real-true worldliness to

develop cognitive and doxic forms immune to the fakization of any deixis of the world, be it scientific, religious, or customary.

Argument

Liberal political orders require a decisive measure of functional differentiation of society. In addition, these orders, much like the societies in which they emerge, are highly improbable realities. They both require the psychic capability of living in a constant state of cognitive and normative flux, within which no knowledge, no belief, no collective feeling can enjoy any form of stability. In order to exist in such an environment of continual and all-engulfing processuality, individuals have to learn to place trust in the creativity of high contingency, the counterintuitive benefits of complexity, and the foundational superiority of dissensus over consensus. They have to adopt and persevere with a posture of relentless cognitive openness, which is a trying psychic experience that puts extreme pressure on any sense of identity, belonging, and biographic as well as historic consistency.

The thesis I shall be defending here is that the crisis liberal democracy is facing today is a new challenge: while the structural social and psychic setting of functional differentiation of society remains unchanged, a crucial component of it has been strongly "affected" by a re-ordering of the function of belief within the cognitive dimension of social communication. It seems as if a major shift has occurred in the very same "grammar of assent"[1] that has made possible the evolution towards an ever-growing, poly-contextual, almost heterotopical differentiation of autonomous/auto-poietic spheres or fields of social meaning.

A form of diffusive narrative cognition, challenging any common knowledge and sane prime assumptions, has been invented that transforms the structure of "credibility" or the believability of contemporary reality indication (deixis of facts of the world). Such an evolution poses a challenge to any theory of liberal democracy and social differentiation: it brings to the fore the question of the dismantlement of a belief structure that has been formed under the combined action of disciplined scientific cognition and convictionally weak normation.

---

1   I am hinting at the title of Cardinal John Henry Newman's book: *An Essay in Aid of a Grammar of Assent* (1979).

The crisis of liberal democracy in our time is the crisis of an undoing of limitations that have always relied on the believability of worldly facts and the undoing of references of competence as to whom one has to refer in order to decide which worldly fact can be acknowledged as verified, i.e., factual and true. It is the crisis of the dismantlement of a structure that draws the boundaries between what is believable and what is not, in the sense that no (explicit nor implicit) consensus is holding about what is unbelievable by the very nature of its blatantly counter-evidential excessiveness, nor about the authority of institutions, individuals, subsystemically differentiated social instances or communication processes that have all along our modern collective experience[2] been recognized and empowered as the competent and authoritative instances in relation to worldly belief.

It makes it clear that if liberal democracy has to be vindicated, the most urgent task is that of the hedging of its doxological structure. Such a task is a theoretical program that has to renew the question about the conditions under which an affectively complex deixis of worldly facts can be believed, and how assent can be given to courses of action that build on such credibility potentials.

The Challenge of Populism and Its Belief Structure

Excesses of correctional regimentation of beliefs lead most observers of these facts to the conviction that liberal democracy has to be vindicated against populism by opening up to the anxieties of its "public sphere" (Öffentlichkeit). Populism, meanwhile, is a very active, dynamic, and self-confident "public sphere." It is very far from that state of dumbness that has characterized it as a mute, passive opinion basin, mobilized by occasional electoral protests. Thus, liberal democracy has to be vindicated by an effort to understand populist tendencies, bridging the gap between the enlightened, cosmopolitan, European and American elites. It has to acknowledge the plight of certain of its politics (of accelerated integration, enhanced and enforced multiculturalism, economic ideological voluntarism, etc.). It has to fulfill the promise of more democracy, less bureaucracy, and more attention to the people and their legitimate inertias. It has to favor more

2   That is: since the emancipation of the subsystem of science from the dominance of the religious system and the establishing of its pretentions to hold truth and diffuse it through all existing channels of social communication, putting in particular young intelligence to apprenticeship of its methods and contents.

pedagogy and show more restraint in the use of elite superiority of discourse and institutional power. This is neither thought nor implemented in a context in which populism has won major battles against elitism in decisive countries of the West.

The dangerousness of this development is obvious and one has to actually design a response to deflect the fatal blows European democracy is taking in the wake of such an inversion of values and power positions. The search for such a response is the urgent matter of the day, and the consciousness of the urgent nature of the quest is deepening day by day among an ever-growing number of observers. This was the conclusion of an exchange I had recently with a friend. I tell the story as it was because it is uniquely enlightening for our purpose.

The anecdote is the following story that a friend of mine told me more than a year ago, before the elections in France. Try to remember that somber period, the gloomy perspectives of a crumbling down of the European political order, with Putin *ad portas*, in Ukraine, on the borders of the Baltic states, and Islamic terrorism striking with incredible savagery in the Middle East as well as in the heart of Europe. The French elections, coming after Brexit, Trump's victory in the USA, the surge of a disquieting populism everywhere, made of France what a witty observer called "a world swing state"—that means: if these elections had led in the "second tour" (end ballot) to a confrontation between Marine Le Pen and Jean-Luc Mélanchon, the candidates of the far right and the extreme left, then an economic and political crisis of an unseen magnitude would have taken place on the old continent, leading to the implosion of the political and military order that has given this continent and the world the longest, most prosperous, and most sustainable pacific period of world history.

In this context, this friend of mine, a professor at an English university, wrote to me the following lines:

> People are summoning me to be optimistic. But all of my effort to let optimism blossom in my chest hit the wall of the following story which took place three days ago. An acquaintance of mine, with the best education, both parents university professors, living now in the US; the lady has been born in the West, today a very serious professional, leading the life of people of her cultural and professional background. At tea, which we have been taking together, I put the non-exceptional question of the day: "How do you feel today as an American?" She answers: "Well, the most important thing is that the horrible Hillary didn't succeed to become president." I thought of a long list of

supposed failures in Clinton's career. But the supplementary comment that came amazed me: "Didn't you hear of the 'pizzagate'?" I said: "No." It came out that pizzagate was the code name for a child pornography scandal which has been propagated by Hillary's adversaries—most probably the Russian disinformation apparatus—accusing her of sexually abusing children. I checked the information on my computer and was appalled. If she—to say nothing of so many other people with so much less education and ability to form their judgment in an enlightened manner—is not able to deny her assent, not to believe such stories, what are we to do to carry it off?

My friend couldn't ease his pessimism and was, until the results happily sobered him, convinced of the victory of Marine Le Pen in the French elections. To conclude his short story, he wrote: we will need a new hybrid defense against this hybrid (sort of) attack.

The conception of the problem in these terms reduces it along the scheme of a propaganda war that has to be countered. A very astute, subtle, complex and hostile propagandist is forging special tools and contents designed for the hybridity of his attack. This requires a response as astute, subtle, complex and perhaps as hostile as the former—accounting for the hybridity of the parry wished by my friend.

My thesis is that one should precisely avoid that sort of framing of the facts. One has to concentrate on the transformation of the doxological structure of social communication within our liberal societies, a transformation that is today at the very core of the risks they are making to cope with the requirements of late capitalism, post-modernity, and accelerated globalization. This means one must study the "grammar of assent" of contemporary communication, i.e., the ways in which people give their assent to indications describing what is a fact in the world (the production of factuality)—the ways they believe the current deixis of the world, which is constantly performed within the huge swarm of social communications.

To come to that point, however, we will have to state that there is a propaganda war, and that liberal democracy is under attack from multiple angles—that it has been made the target of various attempts to destabilize its fundamental views. In saying this, we acknowledge the reality of the offensive and intentional nature of what/who makes the crisis, in order to shed clarity on our contention that ultimately this strategic and agent-based aspect of the crisis is a veil inhibiting the perception of the true, intrinsic vulnerability of the target societies themselves. The advent of such vulnerability corresponds to the dismantlement of the belief structure that has governed their doxic relationship to the world for two centuries.

The Dismantled Belief Structure and the Emergence of Alternative Factuality

What must be stressed first is the necessity of doing away with any defensive thinking, and attempting to understand that the battle to be fought is an offensive, pre-adaptative proto-cognitive one, one which takes place at the elementary levels of the constitution of the knowable and the known, that is of what is held to be "out there" (a cherished expression of Donald Trump) is believed to be the fact, to be there.

The problem becomes clear when we acknowledge the perplexity of the defenders themselves, who are trying to implement their strategies to fight the propagandist on the other side of the fence. They have to recognize that all means of counter-propaganda they can mobilize to reach an undoing of dis-information are fully inefficient, simply non-operable, given the depth at which the perturbation of the credence structure is itself operating.

The defensive posture has to search for standards by which a certain type of information can be forbidden, as well as certain methods of its propagation. It should have the ability to outline an unlawful transgression, the trespassing of a normative line of liceity (of what is permissible, not prohibited). Fake news represents a deixis of an event structured/evenemential reality that integrates a high level of perceptivity into reality, which means supposedly that reality is not independent from and neutral in relation to its perception.

It is always a constructed social and medial reality that depends upon the site of observation from which its deixis is made. It is not a faking of reality, but an alternative observation of it, made from one of the other angles of sight in which an object can be seen: like a demonstration taking place on an avenue that can been seen, heard, and smelled from different places in the space surrounding it and experienced from very different mental and affective dispositions.

In the realm of factual reality there are only facts and all facts are alternative to one another. The are no factual realities that would be orthogonal, building a sole "right" angle, to all other factualities—which would be partial, incomplete representations of it. This should not be mistaken as being part of a sort of postmodern relativism in which any account of reality "goes"—be it scientific, artistic, political, moral, legal, economic, culturally estranging, magical, ceremonial, mythical, tribal, clanic, individualistic, idiosyncratic, etc. Postmodern relativism is a posture characterized by perplexity and humility, opening intersubjective exchange to (yet more) tolerance of provocative, estranging alterities. Proponents of alternative facts take their alternative version of the facts for granted, reject vehemently—aggressively—the other deixes of reality, and suppose that they are themselves faked along the interests of social groups conspiring to master reality and order it in the most profitable manner for them. They present themselves as disempowered groups whose lived version of the facts is negated and repressed by a political and medial establishment. They see the reality version of this establishment as falsely normative, legally but unlawfully binding, politically, over-empoweringly coercive (more precisely: correcting). They see that version of reality as exclusive and perpetuating the power monopoly of that establishment.

The defensive strategy is perplexed by the fact that what is acting as a massive and radical destabilization of the political order in liberal democratic societies cannot be qualified as illicit from any possible perspective. If offensive propaganda displaying foreign hostile powers nurture as a matter of fact those alternative versions of the real, those versions are not reliant on them to exist, to be disseminated, and above all to be believed by substantial numbers of people within those societies.

The thesis is that the process of the emergence, the invention, the dissemination, the credence of this alternative factuality is nowadays endemic to those societies. Alternative facts, creeds, and versions of the real are endemically, spontaneously, genuinely, internally produced within our societies. Their producers, exponents and consumers are the Trumps and their followers—and, in second place, the Putins and the Erdogans. The endemic goes beyond the typical supporters of populist preachers or politicians and reaches into the educated groups and strata of society. This is why the defensive apparatus designed to contain the "hybrid attacks" targeting our liberal orders tends to delegate the monitoring and censuring of alternative versions of factual reality to the channels through which they are conveyed to the wider public.

It is a delegation of a normative review of the contents to the medium: social media, internet providers, and discussion platforms are supposed to act as a censorial instance of reality accounts on the vague grounds of fact adequacy. They are endowed with hugely excessive competence to decide what is the real fact in the world and to deny those alternative deixes of reality any access to public notice. Our societies thus appear to be incapable of defending themselves against narrative devices/narrative viruses or viral narratives they produce from within themselves—the virus having here the structure and form of a narrative, of narrative arrangements of facts making sense of perceived reality. Their grammar of assent shows unsuspected flaws through which the viral dispositive enters the cognitive/doxological organism. The process by which assent is given to such representations of factual reality has become intrinsically problematic. *To sum it up: our liberal democratic orders are not under attack (however hybrid it may be) from an external, exogenous actor or power, but endemically by an erosion/transformation/pathology of their doxic structure.*

The Coeval Immanence of World Facts to Their Medial Production

The battle to redeem liberal democracy and the open world-society from their present predicament is akin to that fought against smallpox in the century of Rousseau. A perplexing battle given one had no idea of where or on which of its multiple fronts to engage it, and how to link those fronts to one another and thus advance the curative process. One was lacking a good understanding of the harmful processes taking place within the organism, was unable to give it clear nosographic contours, while having a precious intuition of its prophylaxes—with the idea of vaccination—but not knowing how to bundle the right information and go through it to the recognition of the emerging new structure.

In relation to the disease undermining liberal democracy, the most significant insight is that of the immanence of the pathology: it is not inflicted, propagated from the outside, but develops from the inside, with no other external causality than the occasional co-incidence of factors enhancing the endemic one. Healing the structure is a huge and improbable program—as to its conception, to say nothing of its feasibility. It has to act upon a structural setting, has to merge into the processes of its constitution and to be anchored in them, to render them less receptive to those new forms of doxic assent, which are the more efficient, the more affine they are to the most intuitive (narrative) forms of believing.

The emerging structure of belief has to do with the evolution of the world-form (Weltform) from that of the supposed autonomy of the external world to one in which the whole complex of mundane reality is produced by the media of its observation (not a philosophical-idealistic proposition, but a radical constructivist sociological one).[3] What is primarily relevant here is the insight that, from the point of view of sociology and communication theory (and not from that of an idealistic philosophy), the world is constituted in the processes of functionally differentiated subsystemic social communication and that no other world is observable than the one emerging from their operations. This major theorem is complemented by a situation in which the subsystem of mass medial communication in our societies is coming to a state of technological maturity, which makes it possible to produce world events of world observation simultaneously with their own occurrence, and not a posteriori "in relation" to them.

The media do not tell or re-tell the evential course of the human-world reality (encompassing cosmic reality) and "relate" it, that is, give an account of it, make deixis of it to subjects, individuals existing as members of society at large who receive this relation of and to the world and believe it (or don't) according to the degree of confidence they have in those media, and their possibly biased view on certain aspects of social reality. The media and the medial reality they are emitting are in themselves the evential course of the human world (anthropocosm), i.e., social communication itself.

There is no divide, no interstice, no line of distinction that can be drawn between social communication and its own medial production. This is a new foundational, ontological fact based on the technological maturity of medial transmission bringing it so close to the transmitted that no interval can be postulated between the transmitted and the transmission, the former having to occur first in order to be related to or simply, absolutely to be "related" (reported, recounted) as such. This ontological fact has not been acknowledged at this level of theoretical abstraction by the majority of individuals, nor by the strategists of disinformation and aggressive propaganda—the least one can say is that they are not interested in such abstract insights.

However, our intuition has experienced an astonishing generalization, which is that event reality (and that is human, historic, social reality) can be and is constantly fabricated by social instances, apparatuses, institutions, and organizations. Social reality is the creation of social reality along its organization to produce itself in its medial mediation/production (and not reproduction). Starting from this intuition, it is not difficult to see how the inclination of the masses as well as of the elites is to ascribe to those

---

3 I can't delve into that theme of the production of mundane reality in and by social communication, a piece of theory I developed in another context.

instances involved in the coessential, coeval production of social reality vested interests, concrete, hand-tight biases determined by those interests, manipulative intentions and techniques designed to influence public opinion and to steer it towards the acceptances and reactions useful to their plans. Such a possibility of an ascription of intentional causality is a treat to human intuitive intellection of any sort (be it popular or scientific). It neutralizes the painful demands of rational judgment building as well as the demands of building a poly-selfish subject of poly-contextual social communication. It neutralizes partially the cooling off of immediate, affective/affectual reactions to world events, a distanciation process necessitating an effective attuning to the cognitivization processes that constitute the mental and attitudinal basis for the functional differentiation of consociation.

The other aspect of the evolution is that of the empowerment of any part of social reality to vindicate its own production of its own reality. The contention here is no longer about which of the competing realities is the true and real one, which one has a greater pretention to be validated (by instances of truth validation of reality deixes); it is, so to speak, not a contention at all, but a mere factual position of reality, of its own reality by a social reality with no pretention ever of justifying, arguing, or legitimizing its own reality (which is coessential and absolutely coeval to its reality production) by way of stronger reasons or "grounds."

Reality as such has not to be justified nor legitimized by any reasons—it is the founding ground of reasons as such—: the world is what it is and reason is one fact of the world that emerges in it and can only reflect it as the ultimate ground of all grounds.

Alternative realities are in a fight for survival against one another. They do not possess any syntax of mutual tolerance, of a more or less meaningful interrelated coexistence. Hence this development is often described as a lifting of limitations put upon affects of self-assertion (Selbstbehauptung), correlating with the lifting of limitations upon affects of denying wholeheartedly any legitimacy to relativistic liberal orders. Affects of hatred, negation of the other, will to eliminate them are thus unleashed without any reserves, any consciousness that letting them play out is not consistent with the subsisting liberal political order that gives those affected by such affects paradoxically their best chance.

The Globality of Belief and the Engulfing of Science

To sum up, we have to think through:
- the structural transformation of social communication as a co-originating medial communication of itself
- the intuition of a tendency to bring the world ever nearer to a state in which it can't distinguish between reality and retold reality
- the assertion of alternative realities to other alternative realities without any privilege anchoring one of these as the reference point of all others
- and the acknowledgment that the ascription of intentionality to causal determinations of the social world revives a magical reading of the world and unleashes affects that remain uninhibited by any censorship pointing out their massive identity driven self-centeredness, their lacking of any altruistic comprehension of the constitution of alterity, their aggressiveness, and their violence in the assertion of their occupancy of space and history.

The decisive point of my argument is not however that alternative factuality is bound to an affective turn in the political realm—a realm structurally marked by collective sentiments and their non-relativizable nature. The relation between alternative factuality and the unleashing of affective impulses, which have until now been under the control of the altruistic maxim of liberal political orders, is not as simple as that. It is mediated by the transformation/dismantlement of the pre-existing structure of belief. It is because the believable has undergone a decisive extension and transformative inflexion that the conditions are ripe for such a lifting of limitations from a series of driving components of social communication.

The extension we are talking about is the process that makes believable all courses of interpretation by which social becoming can be framed as a result of a strictly immanent transformation of the social structure, fabric and course by society itself. The inflexion, on the other hand, is the apprehension of that transformation as intentional and thus ascribable to powerful instances of society, and here mainly to the subsystemic function that delivers the image of society to itself and the social groups which have the command upon that subsystem. Without that extension and inflexion of the believable no revitalization of impulsive mass affectivity within populist movements in Europe can occur;[4] without that extension

---

4   Is the same precondition required to explain the resurgence of nationalistic populism in Russia, islamo-nationalistic/sultanistic populism in Turkey? The

and inflexion the checks and controls that regulated the newly dismantled regime of believability would have reigned over it, would have neutralized it by the simple and unceasing operation of the doxically unimpeded processes of cognitivization which characterize the late modern perdifferentiation of social communication along the lines of thorough deconstruction of any starkly assertive normative stances. It would have maintained unchanged the global political, legal and doxological configuration that prevailed in the last two decades of the 20th century.

Furthermore, to explain the impact of such an extension and inflexion, we need to ascertain some of the structural traits of the dismantled regime of belief itself. Mainly the fact that our culture maintains very tenaciously a dichotomy between cognition and belief, censuring the idea that belief is an all-engulfing function that encompasses cognition, building around it the sphere of a doxic continuum, and erasing at a certain moment the highly relevant differential between science and opinion. A scientist of our day holds ultimately an opinion like any other layman and operates within the realm of the thinkable, his own combinations of thought constructing a more or less consistent image of his various environments.

Ancient philosophy thought of science (not scientific knowledge, but scientific insight) as distinct from opinion by essence and not only by means of its methods, procedures, and verificative reiterations. The difference is one of the nature of its act. Science was thought to be the operation of an intellect bestowing upon the operating intellect a union with the intellected idea. It is thus a unitive operation, which transforms the intellect into the ideally intellected. The spirit (nous, intellectus) performs acts of intellection. It is a "mind" of another nature than that which performs acts of sheer believing. There is thus a criterion given to differentiate between an intellective seizure of a thinkable and the simply doxic one.

Reflecting upon these matters from the point of view of a constructivist epistemology, that is from the only point of view we can adopt with reason under the conditions which constitute the intelligibility of the world for us today, that distinction vanishes. We thus learn to recall the scientist—he recalls himself spontaneously and without any reluctance—to reinsert himself into the mental group of all thinking and believing human beings. This comes to erase any distinction through structure or essence between science and all other forms of possible world apprehension and to

differential of modernity between these societies and the Western ones has to be taken into account when we address such a question.

de-privilege science as being in its own right of another nature than all other doxic acts.

A reminder of those ancient theories is useful at this juncture because it allows us to understand how our Weltbild (world-picture), if it is sustained by science, does not give the scientist, who is always a specialist and masters a very limited portion of world knowledge, any decisive advantage in the construction of the Weltbild. He belongs to the generality of people in respect to his doxic relationship to the world.

The democratization of knowledge deconstructs the idea that thorough, deep, ultimately foundational knowledge is the monopoly of the philosopher as an opener of epochal Weltbilder. It sociologizes science and normalizes its personnel. The only demarcation to be still set between educated (Bildungs) elites and the generality of the people is the more easily produced capacity of the former to go along with the thorough and general cognitivization of cosmic and social reality.

However, from the moment at which social reality begins to be produced alternatively by its own reflection in itself, these elites seem to unlearn their cognitivizing skills and join the majority of the minds who tend to think very intuitively. They share with them their beliefs and let themselves be guided by the affects that make for their adherence to them. Alternative factuality is, as we have seen, the immediate reflection of what one is as what one wants to believe.

A Possible Hedging of the Imperilled Structure of Belief

The Achilles heel of the society-world (Weltgesellschaft) and of its definitive pacification/hedonization has to be located today in its pistic/doxic structures. These structures are a given today, or the given of today. They cannot be eradicated.

My thesis is however that something can still be "done," which is a form of infusion of the socialization and elementary/mid-level education process into schemes of apperception and cognition, immunizing against modes of penetration and inflection of the doxic structures which have, as we have seen, undergone a very broad and (for our liberal political orders) disquieting transformation. This can be imagined as a long-term "offensive" program designed to prevent the radical destabilization that transformation carries in itself. The situation can be compared to those historical junctures at which European culture and society had to strive to ensure their viability by disarming/dismantling a certain structure of (religious or symbolic) belief.

The history of European culture and society shows us examples of the tensions that arise when simultaneous tendencies to integration and differentiation are not able to reach the end-form (telos) of sociality, which they bear as a germ within themselves, without destabilizing certain modes of belief still very deeply anchored in the psyche of most individuals.

Compared with these crises, the present one inverts in a sense the scheme and presents us with a destabilization of a doxic structure that should be saved, and not, as in the historical examples, with structures which had to be overcome and to recede in order to give room to the emergent new one. Between 1700 and 1900 deep doxic structures of religious belief had to be overcome. This could not be done without disempowering once and for all religious instances and institutions that perpetuated the framing of world perception in a mindset congruent with religious beliefs, thus instituting the autonomy and monopoly of authority of scientific truth regarding any observation, description of, or active intervention in states of the world, and its non-relevance to, its incommensurability with religious contents. The most telling and consequent achievement in this respect was the integration of evolution theory in school curricula and the definitive relegation of biblical creation narratives—i.e., an etiological narrative with total explanatory potency—into the mythological reference space. Science could not differentiate itself as an autopoietical functional subsystem without this sharp cut from the continuum of truth pretentions and plausibilities "infecting" the field of knowledge. It had to present an image of the world with absolutely self-founding justifiability and legitimacy. The question of compatibility with one another of both truths, the scientific and the religious, once central in the medieval and early modern debates, becomes absolutely irrelevant. It needs not and ought not to be put. This is the precondition for the full deployment of a scientific and technological world apprehension and its transformative impulse.

The second achievement is a more recent one. It is the introduction into school curricula of sexual education and enlightenment programs that imply the socializing generalization of access to a profane, biological and hygienic knowledge of sexuality as well as of a certain mode of coping with sexual issues. This too has been a hard-fought battle against doxic and symbolic structures whose resilience is related to their universal anthropological embedding.

What is needed is a new pedagogy of the real-true worldliness, a program grounded on Piagetian development psychology in order to help children and adolescents develop cognitive and doxic forms immune to trolling/faking of any deixis of the world, be it scientific, religious, or customary. This is quite similar to what is already the case in our reproductive and educational practices, with which we inform the faculty of judgment of our children by teaching them to cope with differentiated etiologies.

That means that while exposing them to the charms and pleasures of imagination in fairy tales, films and creative play, we also conduct them, through what we teach them discursively and non-discursively, thematically and non-thematically, by example of experiencing, feeling, thinking and acting, to construct a background reality that they do not really grasp, but which is there as a resisting and estranging prosaic reality where space is organized along transitive relationships, where time is irreversible, where both can be partitioned and counted, measured, where transversal and over-intensive sensations can be ignored in their (absent) consequences in the world, where sensorial textures can be offset by sensorial contours and object-centered thematic addresses, etc.

The new pedagogy of the real-true worldliness will have to embed itself in the flow of this already existing construction of the basis or the torso of a disenchanted reality. It lies in the continuity of the progressive inhibition of enchantment and the production of a univocized reality established on the basis of temperate, moderately intense homeostasis. It inhibits the otherwise insuperable tendency of the young mind and sensibility to very strongly adhere, affectively and doxically, to the mythological structure of world apprehension and its almost unrestrained compatibility of most narratives with most narratives.

The analogical program needed to instigate the dismantlement of the doxic regime of our liberal social and political orders could become as coessential to our culture and society as the two others. It is an urgent task because it is plausible that the whole construction of our postmodern cognitive and normative orders falls to ruin before that counter-doxology has come into operation.

The Luhmannian society-world seemed to have no other problems besides those of its peripheries and those of the inflexible societal alternative of inclusion and exclusion. Luhmannian theory ensured the recognition of that paradoxical limitation put into the dynamic of inclusiveness that is intrinsic to functional differentiation as such. However, it saw in it no inhibition for a functionally differentiated society to reach its telos. Nor was the trap of incomplete modernity at the peripheries so consequential as to offset the hyper-potent processors of the production regimes of central (i.e., European and North American) modernity.

My thesis is that the only critical vulnerability of this society-world is that of its doxic structures, which Luhmann neglected, thinking that the dynamic of differentiation was radical and powerful enough to re-appropriate those structures and to transform them *uno actu* with the accomplishment of its own operations. European and North American politics since 2016 have shown that the existing potentials to counter and inhibit differentiation are very broad and comfortable; that *no structural teleology, no immanent tendency to a functionally differentiated society can guarantee the success of differentiation*; that it is by all means possible that the other, alternative order wins the day and brushes aside the invaluable improbability of our so profoundly paradoxical liberal orders the day after.

References

Newman, John Henry. 1979. *An Essay in Aid of a Grammar of Assent*. Notre Dame: University of Notre Dame Press.

Alien Thinking: On the Return of the Sublime as an Affective Medium

Markus Rautzenberg

In recent discourse, notably concerning speculative realism and accelerationism, the sublime is rediscovered as an epistemological and aesthetic tool. This "comeback" of the sublime is deeply rooted in the attempt to think of the world in a non-anthropocentric manner and to establish a kind of *alien thinking*. Even today the notion of the sublime challenges the concept of semiomorphic knowledge. A sense of amazement interwoven with fear and terror is an integral aspect of the sublime—not only as an aesthetic but as an epistemological category. It is related to philosophical traditions of thinking the unthinkable and grasping the limits of rationality and subjectivity.

It is one of the most popular endeavors of many theoretical movements of today to amalgamate aesthetics with political theory and epistemology. This is true especially for many philosophical efforts in media theory that are concerned with notions of affect and affectivity. "Affect" seems to be the new *via regia* to understanding the challenges of globalized political movements and complex data networks alike, because it fulfills the role of a medium that is not in any way connected to "reason" or classic notions of "communication." It is all about intensities that commune or differentiate from one another.

It is here that one of the classic terms of philosophical aesthetics comes back in an unexpected way. The following will argue that current theory breathes new life into the old notion of the sublime by rediscovering its medial position between *ratio* and *emotio* or between epistemology and aesthetics, giving new perspectives to an age-old problem: How can we think the unthinkable?

In his work *After Finitude* Quentin Meillassoux states: "By 'correlation' we mean the idea according to which we only ever have access to the correlation between thinking and being, and never to either term considered apart from one another" (Meillassoux 2008, 5).

For Meillassoux—one of the main protagonists of speculative realism—the original sin of contemporary philosophy begins with Immanuel Kant, who in speculative realism takes the place that Descartes occupied for 20th century philosophy: the main antagonist. It is obvious, however, that the real target is the concept of semiomorphic knowledge, which has dominated the 20th century in the shape of the now infamous linguistic turn. In fact the notion of mediation and mediality in itself is targeted, insofar as all communication, understanding or mediation starts with a relation of some shape or form. "Generally speaking, the modern philosopher's 'two-step' consists in this belief in the primacy of the relation over the related terms; a belief in the constitutive power of reciprocal relation" (19).

We just need to remember the basic concepts of linguistics according to Ferdinand de Saussure to realize what is alluded to here: his semiology depends on the notion of semiosis as driven by arbitrariness and difference—these are the core concepts. Semiosis—and that is one of Saussure's famous innovations, which Jacques Derrida just had to emphasize later—doesn't rely on representation or mimesis of the world but exclusively on the inner systemic processes of differentiation. Saussure's semiology therefore is a theory of relations and relationality par excellence. Constructivist approaches like Niklas Luhmann's system theory have therefore—still according to Meillassoux's critique—also run into the Kantian trap, because they do not deal with reality but only with relationality. Like Kant they do not need to concern themselves with the question of what lies behind or beyond signs or social relations—they either deny that there even is something "out there" (constructivism) or argue that this outside cannot be perceived or understood in the first place (Kant). The same applies to theories of mediality as well as to the ubiquitous metaphoricity of the "net." The list is quite long.

Whether Meillassoux is right in his attempt to make Kant a scapegoat for the failure of modern philosophy or not should not concern us at this point. What matters is the thesis that for all these "constructivist" approaches an "outside" of perception, knowledge or semiosis—regardless if we call it "thing in itself" or a "transcendental signified"—is unreachable. With keeping this "outside" out of reach a marginalization takes place and it is this marginalization that speculative realism is concerned with. It is crucial to take note of this perceived insufficiency of constructivist thought that is articulated in speculative realism. For Meillassoux, for example, thinking of the "big outside" has become impossible because of this. Furthermore speculative realism has embarked on escaping this supposedly self-inflicted solipsism by promoting a kind of *alien thinking*, as I would like to call it. It is Meillassoux's declared intention to enable philosophy to think in foreign territory again, to be "entirely elsewhere":

> For it could be that contemporary philosophers have lost the great out-doors, the absolute outside of pre-critical thinkers: that outside which was not relative to us, and which was given as indifferent to its own givenness to be what it is, existing in itself regardless of whether we are thinking of it or not; that outside which thought could explore with the legitimate feeling of being on foreign territory—of being entirely elsewhere. (Meillassoux 2008, 7)

The English translation makes it sound like a trip to the countryside with a little exploring. But "the great outdoors" is not as nice as it sounds—it is a metaphor for something so alien that it cannot be understood, measured or even perceived. It is more like exploring an alien planet than a stroll among the trees. It is an echo of Schelling's absolute, something genuinely incomprehensible, and this is the reason why H.P. Lovecraft, the poet of *The Unnamable*, is so popular among speculative realists (cf. Harman [2012]; or the witty *Horror of Philosophy Trilogy* by Eugene Thacker [2011; 2015a; 2015b]). It is a form of terror that lurks here on the outskirts of our known universe. But even better than Lovecraft in this regard is John Milton:

> The other shape,
> If shape it might be call'd that shape had none
> Distinguishable, in member, joint or limb;
> Or substance might be call'd that shadow seem'd,
> For each seem'd either; black he stood as night;
> Fierce as ten furies; terrible as hell;
> And shook a deadly dart. What seem'd his head,
> The likeness of a kingly crown had on.
> (qtd. Burke 1823, 77)

Edmund Burke, still very much under the influence of his literary studies at Dublin's Trinity College, used this example of Milton's impressive talent for describing the undescribable as an ideal example to illustrate his own notion of the sublime, perhaps the most original but surely the most influential part of his early work *A Philosophical Enquiry into the Origin of our Ideas of the Sublime and the Beautiful*: "Hence arises the great power of the sublime, that, far from being produced by them, it anticipates our reasonings, and hurries us on by an irresistible force" (Burke 1823, 73–74). At the base of the sublime terror reigns supreme, a fear of getting lost, of being hurried away by irresistible forces. One of Burke's main examples is the ocean, a metaphorical realm that will remain influential from Kant to Nietzsche. Burke argues that both a vast landscape and a great ocean instill affects of awe and admiration in the mind of the onlooker because of their vastness, their spatial dimension. But only the ocean is able to induce a state of the sublime, according to Burke. This is because in addition to its vastness it can evoke a sense of terror: the ocean is amorphous and endless to the human perception, always harboring the risk of drowning even under a calm surface, an aspect that together with awe and admiration results in the sublime: "Indeed terror is in all cases whatsoever, either more openly or latently, the ruling principle of the sublime" (75).

Therefore the sublime cannot be the medium of *clara et distincta* of clear thinking. The sublime is not a realm of thought but of shock and awe— it is an affective medium, a medium of intensity. Burke alludes to the rhetorical tradition: "It is one thing to make an idea clear, and another to make it *affecting* to the imagination [emphasis added]" (78). The sublime is connected to the vague, obscure, and the fragmented; it is a realm of *affect* and not *ratio*: "It is our ignorance of things that causes all our admiration, and chiefly excites our passions. Knowledge and acquaintance make the most striking causes affect but little" (80).

This kind of amazement interwoven with fear and terror leads us away from philosophical aesthetics and into the area of religious phenomena or, to be more precise, it shows the close interrelation of both. It was the historian of religion Rudolf Otto who described the sublime regarding religion as "mysterium tremendum," which together with the "mysterium fascinans" for him lies at the core of religious experience. He explicitly refers to the sublime, however, without directly citing Burke. Otto translated "tremendum" as "schauervoll" (1920, 14–15), which in turn—one could argue—is the translation in which Burke's term "astonishment" arrived in the philosophy of Immanuel Kant. "Schauervoll" (astonishing) describes a kind of sublimity that should not be confused with fear. Considering the *tremendum* fear is more like an analogy: "it so far resembles it that the analogy of fear may be used to throw light upon its nature," but it still is "a quite specific kind of emotional response, wholly distinct from that of being afraid" (Otto 1936, 13).[1] "Schauer" (astonishment) is always connected to holiness and the sacred and refers to a form where "the soul, held speechless, trembles inwardly to the furthest fiber of its being" (17).[2] The term "numinous" (das Numinose) was invented by Otto for this occasion (7).

What is most interesting here is that this "Schauer" or astonishment is not just a petrification of all senses and intellectual capacities. It is not ratio and not affect but something equally distant from both. The feeling of holy reverence is a mode of world apprehension of being-in-and-out-of-the world that is situated between ratio and instinct, a category that is a kind of its own, alien to both of them, dissolving the dichotomy between these categories in the process.

Alien Thinking

I would like to propose that in speculative realism there is a comeback of Burke's and Otto's concept of the sublime as an epistemological and aesthetic tool to arrive at notions that not only allow us to be in foreign territory again but to transform philosophy itself into what could be called "alien thinking." Alien not only in the sense that philosophy arrives in foreign territory or the "great outdoors" like Neil Armstrong landing on the moon. This would still be a patronizing mode of perception, a kind of colonial thinking. Alien thinking would also mean a transformation of

1   Original "… zwar Ähnlichkeit hat mit der Furcht und darum durch sie analogisch angedeutet werden kann, die aber selber noch etwas ganz anderes ist als Sichfürchten" (Otto 1920, 14–15).
2   Original "… jenes tiefst innerlichen Erzitterns und Verstummens der Seele bis in ihre letzten Wurzeln hinein" (Otto 1920, 19).

thinking itself, an alienation from its own concepts, terms, and notions. Foreign territory could then be "the great inside" as opposed to "the great outside" Meillassoux was talking about, albeit again dissolving the binary notion of inside and outside that is not helpful here.

This alien thinking is of course deeply rooted in the attempt to think of the world in a non-anthropocentric manner. Here the nobilitation of the object and material cultures becomes important. However, according to Meillassoux and others the alienness of this world of things, or *nature*,—as correlationist thinking would have called it—has to be understood as absolute in the sense of Schelling, that it is absolutely incomprehensible for human thought. Every relation between subject and object is severed and it is here that terror as a part of the sublime comes back in full force—but now as an epistemological category.

It was Theodor Adorno who insisted that the sublime should be banned from the realm of politics, and today we can understand this even better when confronted with the alien thinking of speculative antirationalism and its political branch, called accelerationism.[3] This political theory, which is again very Freudian, in its love for his concept of the death-drive and with its fans like Steve Bannon and Nick Land, looks a lot like apocalyptical political theory from the Weimar Republic. At the core of accelerationism lies the belief that both socialism and capitalism have failed and will fail, and that the most "revolutionary" act left is to let capitalism (for example) run its course or even accelerate it until every natural and human resource is spent, so that something new may rise from the ashes of total annihilation. So, the sublime has devastating effects when it comes to politics, but what about philosophy?

Following Adorno again, one of the most influential theorists of the sublime in the 20th century, the answer is ambivalent. Do we need to be cautious when using the concept of the sublime? Yes. Do we need to banish and forget it as a whole? No, because Adorno's reading of the sublime does not sever the bonds between subject and object, but sees the sublime as a mode that allows the "great outside" to appear as part of subjectification itself. For him the sublime is not, as it was for Kant, a sign of human supremacy over nature, but an appearance, a showing of the self of nature within humanity, showing that the subject in its bodily existence is of course nature from the beginning.

3   The term was coined by Noys (2010); see also: Williams and Srnicek (2014).

"Outside" and "inside" finally begin to appear as false alternatives. Here aesthetic and epistemological aspects of the sublime intermingle in a way that for Adorno is of course dialectical. The point of the matter, however, is that here the interdependence of inside and outside is not relational in the sense of correlationism but recursive and integral.

> Ultimately, aesthetic comportment is to be defined as the capacity to shudder, as if goose bumps were the first aesthetic image. What later came to be called subjectivity, freeing itself from the blind anxiety of the shudder, is at the same time the shudder's own development; life in the subject is nothing but what shudders, the reaction to the total spell that transcends the spell. Consciousness without shudder is reified consciousness. That shudder in which subjectivity stirs without yet being subjectivity is the act of being touched by the other. Aesthetic comportment assimilates itself to that other rather than subordinating it. Such a constitutive relation of the subject to objectivity in aesthetic comportment joins eros and knowledge. (Adorno 1997, 331)[4]

"That shudder in which subjectivity stirs without yet being subjectivity is the act of being touched by the other." The integration of the other or the outside is the seed of subjectivity. Astonishment (shudder, Schauer) as part of the sublime is the very mode in which subjectivity stirs at the threshold of being.

References

Adorno, Theodor W. 1997. *Aesthetic Theory.* London: Bloomsbury.
———. 1970. *Gesammelte Schriften. Bd. 7: Ästhetische Theorie.* Edited by Gretel Adorno and Rolf Tiedemann. Frankfurt am Main: Suhrkamp.
Burke, Edmund. 1823. *A Philosophical Enquiry into the Origin of our Ideas of the Sublime and Beautiful.* London: Thomas M'Lean.
Harman, Graham. 2012. *Weird Realism: Lovecraft and Philosophy.* Alresford: Zero Books.

4   Original: „Am Ende wäre das ästhetische Verhalten zu definieren, als die Fähigkeit irgend zu erschauern, so als wäre die Gänsehaut das erste ästhetische Bild. Was später Subjektivität heißt, sich befreiend von der blinden Angst des Schauers, ist zugleich dessen eigene Entfaltung; nichts ist Leben am Subjekt, als daß es erschauert, Reaktion auf den totalen Bann, die ihn transzendiert. Bewußtsein ohne Schauer ist das verdinglichte. Jener, darin Subjektivität sich regt, ohne schon zu sein, ist aber das vom anderen Angerührtsein. Jenem bildet die ästhetische Verhaltensweise sich an, anstatt es sich untertan zu machen. Solche konstitutive Beziehung des Subjekts auf Objektivität in der ästhetischen Verhaltensweise vermählt Eros und Erkenntnis" (Adorno 1970, 489–90).

Meillassoux, Quentin. 2008. *After Finitude: An Essay on the Necessity of Contingency*. London: Continuum.

Noys, Benjamin. 2010. *The Persistence of the Negative: A Critique of Contemporary Continental Theory*. Edinburgh: Edinburgh University Press.

Otto, Rudolf. (1917) 1920. *Das Heilige: Über das Irrationale in der Idee des Göttlichen und sein Verhältnis zum Rationalen*. 4th ed. Breslau: Trewendt & Granier.

———. (1923) 1936. *The Idea of the Holy: An Inquiry into the Non-rational Factor in the Idea of the Divine and its Relation to the Rational*. Translated by John W. Harvey. 6th rev. ed. London: H. Milford, Oxford University Press.

Thacker, Eugene. 2011. *In the Dust of this Planet*. Winchester: John Hunt Publishing.

———. 2015a. *Starry Speculative Corpse*. Winchester: John Hunt Publishing.

———. 2015b. *Tentacles Longer than the Night*. Winchester: John Hunt Publishing.

Williams, Alex, and Nick Srnicek. 2014. "# Accelerate: Manifesto for an Accelerationist Politics." In *# Accelerate: The Accelerationist Reader*, edited by Robin Mackay and Armen Avenassian, 347–62. Falmouth: Urbanomic.

Authors

Marie-Luise Angerer holds the Chair for Media Theory at the University of Potsdam and teaches in the curriculum "European Media Studies," a collaboration with the University of Applied Sciences Potsdam. She has been Managing Director of The Brandenburg Centre for Media Studies (ZeM) since 2015. Her main areas of research are media technological re-structurings of the social, zones of human and non-human agencies, and the notion of non-consciousness. For publications see: https://www. uni-potsdam.de/de/medienwissenschaft/professur-fuer-medientheorie-medienwissenschaft/mitarbeiter/prof-dr-marie-luise-angerer.html.

Bernd Bösel is a postdoc researcher at the University of Potsdam, with a focus on philosophy, media studies and culture theory, and has been teaching in the joint curriculum "European Media Studies," a collaboration with the University of Applied Sciences Potsdam, since 2015. Between 2016 and 2018 he coordinated the DFG-funded research network "Affect- and Psychotechnology Studies." For publications see: https://www.uni-potsdam.de/de/medienwissenschaft/ professur-fuer-medientheorie-medienwissenschaft/mitarbeiter/ dr-bernd-boesel.

Pierre Cassou-Noguès is a writer and a philosopher. The key question in his work concerns the role of fiction in the constitution of forms of life and rationality. His latest book, *Technofictions* (Cerf, 2019), is a collection of short stories that investigates the imaginary underlying several contemporary technological apparatuses. Cassou-Noguès is Professor in the philosophy department of University Paris 8-Vincennes-Saint-Denis, and co-editor of the journal *SubStance*.

Jean Clam is a philosopher, sociologist, psychologist and Research Fellow at the Centre National de la Recherche Scientifique (CNRS). He teaches at the École des Hautes Études en Sciences Sociales (EHESS-CADIS) in Paris. He has authored numerous books and articles in French, German, and English. See: www.jean-clam.org.

Mathias Fuchs is Principal Investigator for a German Research Council (DFG) funded project on gamification (2018–2021) and a Member of the Institute for the Culture and Aesthetics of Media (ICAM) at Leuphana University of Lüneburg. In 2010 he received his doctoral grade in philosophy with a thesis on the meaning of sounds ("Sinn und Sound").

He has since been Senior Lecturer and Programme Leader for the MA Creative Technology and MSc Creative Games at Salford University in the UK, Deputy Professor at the University of Potsdam, Senior Fellow at the Institute of Advanced Studies on Media Cultures of Computer Simulation (MECS), and Visiting Professor at Leuphana University of Lüneburg.

Gabriele Gramelsberger is a Professor for Philosophy of Science and Technology at the RWTH Aachen. Her research is focused on the digital transformation of science and technology. Her most recent publication is *Cultures of Prediction in Atmospheric and Climate Science* (edited with Matthias Heymann and Martin Mahony, Routledge, 2017).

Irina Kaldrack is Guest Professor for "Knowledge Cultures in the Digital Age" at Braunschweig University of Art. She holds a diploma in Mathematics and a Ph.D. in Cultural Studies. Since 2009 she has been teaching and researching in the field of Media Studies, and since 2015 in transformation design. Her work focuses on the theory and history of digital cultures, knowledge cultures and their technological conditions, algorithmic cultures, and research methods at the interrelations between artistic practices, Design and Media Studies. Recent publications include *Throwing Gestures* (with Florian Bettel and Konrad Strutz, vfmk, 2020), "Künstliche Intelligenzen" (with Christoph Ernst, Andreas Sudmann, and Jens Schröter, Schwerpunkt der *Zeitschrift für Medienwissenschaft* 21, transcript, 2019), and *There is no Software, There are Just Services* (with Martina Leeker, meson press, 2015).

Dawid Kasprowicz is a postdoc at the chair for Philosophy of Science and Technology at the RWTH University Aachen. Research interests are the philosophy of embodiment, philosophy of computational sciences, phenomenology, and human–robot interactions. Recent publication, with Lisa Schüttler and Gabriele Gramelsberger: "Computational Science Studies: A Tool-Based Methodology for Studying Code." In *Critical Issues in Science, Technology and Society Studies (Conference Proceedings STS Conference Graz)*, edited by G. Getzinger and M. Jahrbacher, 385–401. Graz: Verlag Technische Universität Graz.

Oliver Leistert is a postdoc researcher with a focus on media theory/ philosophy and epistemologies/methods of digital cultures. He is Principal Investigator for the DFG-funded project "Blockchains: Media of Sovereignty" at Leuphana University of Lüneburg. His fields of interest comprise continental philosophy, histories of control, governmentality, surveillance, political economy, and political technologies. See: https:// nomedia.noblogs.org/.

Michaela Ott is a Professor of Aesthetic Theories at the Academy of Fine Arts in Hamburg. Her research focuses on post-structuralist philosophy, aesthetics and politics, aesthetics of film, theories of space, affection and dividuation, theories of the (post)colonial and the composite-cultural, and knowledge of the arts. She is the co-editor of *Timing of Affect* (with Marie-Luise Angerer and Bernd Bösel, diaphanes, 2014) and author of *Divid-uations: Theories of Participation* (Palgrave Macmillan, 2018), *Affizierung*: *Zu einer* ästhetisch-epistemischen *Figur* (edition text + kritik, 2010), and most recently *Welches Außen des Denkens? Französische Theorie in (post)kolonialer Kritik* (Turia & Kant, 2018)

Markus Rautzenberg is Professor for Philosophy at the Folkwang University of the Arts (Essen, Germany). His main fields of research include media theory, picture theory, philosophy of the 20th century, aesthetics of digital media, and ludic epistemologies. His most recent publication is *Framing Uncertainty: Computer Game Epistemologies* (Palgrave Macmillan, 2020).

Andrew A. G. Ross is Associate Professor of Political Science at Ohio University. His main research areas are theories of emotion and affect, and the cultural politics of digital media. Recent publications include articles in *Political Psychology and International Organization*, chapters in several edited volumes, and *Mixed Emotions: Beyond Fear and Hatred in International Con-flict* (University of Chicago Press, 2014).

Paul Stenner has held a Chair in Social Psychology at the Open University in the UK since 2011. He has contributed to the development of a critical and reflexive approach to social psychology that takes process and relationality as keynotes of what is known as a transdisciplinary psychosocial approach. He is author of *Liminality and Experience: A Transdisciplinary Approach to the Psychosocial* (Palgrave, 2017) and *Psychology Without Foundations* (with Steve Brown, Sage, 2009). He has co-edited *Emotions: A Social Science Reader* (with Monica Greco, Routledge, 2008) and authored numerous articles on affectivity and liminality.

Serjoscha Wiemer is a Senior Lecturer for Digital Media/Mobile Media at the Institute for Media Studies at the Paderborn University. Together with Bernd Bösel he is spokesperson for *AG Affective Media Technologies*. In 2011 he received his doctorate with a thesis on the media theory and aesthetics of computer games at the Ruhr University Bochum. His research interests include the historicity of perception, moving image studies, affect theory, game studies, and algorithmic media. See: www.serjoscha.net.